RAVE REVIEWS FOR

Can This Partnership Be Saved?

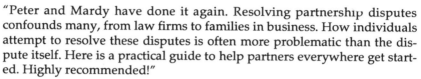

"Peter and Mardy have done it again. Resolving partnership disputes confounds many, from law firms to families in business. How individuals attempt to resolve these disputes is often more problematic than the dispute itself. Here is a practical guide to help partners everywhere get started. Highly recommended!"

—John Messervey, Director
National Family Business Council

"Grothe and Wylie make a convincing case that learning to see yourself as others see you is a key toward becoming a successful manager. Their book can help even the most experienced managers gain valuable insight into their performance and their relationships with the people they manage."

—Dean K. Webster
Former President/CEO, Vice Chairman of the Board
Blue Seal Feeds, Inc.

"With humor and wisdom culled from their years of experience, they illustrate how to prevent and cure potential disasters. Whether you are a partner, boss or employee of a family business, privately held company, government agency or a member of a Fortune 500, open to any chapter in any order and there is a gem or two to be gleaned. This is 'organizational marriage counseling' for those whose issues are simple or complex.

"It is the one book in the field I would both take to a desert island and recommend to my clients. Well written, comprehensive and fun, I plan to use it myself."

—Dorree J. Waldbaum, Ph.D., Co-Director
Institute for the Advanced Study of Psychotherapy

"I recommend that every one of our clients get this book . . .THEN USE IT! There isn't an organizational team or CEO that won't get something of great value from it. And its value extends beyond what you'll get out of the first reading. It'll be a great reference for those challenging 'people' situations yet to come. Sound and sensible advice . . .a very readable book."

—Jamie Goodwin
Goodwin Leighton Management Group

"Peter and Mardy have done exceptional work in writing this book. It is eminently readable because of their down-to-earth writing style and the very real world examples and experiences they provide. . .should be 'must reading' for anyone contemplating a business partnership. Come to think of it, it wouldn't be a bad idea for Peter and Mardy's book to be included in the required reading for MBA candidates.

"Without a moment's hesitation, I would recommend this book to anyone involved in a business relationship. Peter and Mardy's discussion on listening is, by itself, worth the price of admission."

—*William G. Harley, Executive Director*
National Utilities Contractors Association

"Reading *Partnership* was a privilege and a great learning experience. I felt Peter and Mardy were in the room, across the table from me, talking about my challenges and business relationships.

"Best of all, our conversation was comforting and non-threatening. Peter and Mardy gently reminded me of my 'responsibility' for the problems, and still seemed to understand the difficulties and frustrations of my role as an association CEO and people manager.

"And what's best is that *Partnership* is clean, simple and conversational. I recommend it highly to all who are involved in any organization where people work together—and that means it has virtually universal appeal!"

—*Gene S. Bergoffen, Executive Vice President*
National Private Truck Council

"It made me question the way we do things—and gave me lots of ideas for improvements. Intriguing and well written . . . very impressive."

—*Ken Kirk, Executive Director*
Association of Metropolitan Sewerage Agencies

"An important book for anyone involved in a small business—owner manager, employee, spouse. It's about real people involved in real situations. It's about you.

"If you read this book you will understand your business and personal relationships better. If you try just a couple of the suggestion outlined in this book, the atmosphere in your workplace and your home will be less stressful and more enjoyable. If you apply Peter and Mardy's suggestions in all your affairs, your life will be enriched.

"Practically everyone talks about the importance of empowerment and mutually rewarding partnerships today. Here's a simple, readable book that shows how to do it!"

—*James P. Norris*
Executive Vice President
Air Conditioning Contractors of America

Can This Partnership
Be Saved?

Can This Partnership Be Saved?

Improving (or Salvaging) Your Key Business Relationships

Dr. Peter Wylie
and
Dr. Mardy Grothe

UPSTART PUBLISHING COMPANY, INC.
The Small Business Publishing Company
Dover, New Hampshire

Published by Upstart Publishing Company, Inc.
A Division of Dearborn Publishing Group, Inc.
12 Portland Street
Dover, New Hampshire 03820
(800) 235-8866 or (603) 749-5071

Library of Congress Cataloging-in-Publication Data
Wylie, Peter.
    Can This Partnership Be Saved? : Improving (or Salvaging) your Key
Business Relationship / Peter Wylie and Mardy Grothe.
        p.   cm.
    ISBN: 0-936894-42-3
    1. Conflict management. 2. Partnership—Psychological aspects. 3. Family-owned business enterprises—Psychological aspects. 4. Interpersonal relations.
I. Grothe, Mardy. II. Title.
HD42.W94   1993
650.1'3—dc20   93-9713
                                                                                  CIP

Cover design by Acanthus Graphic Design, Newington, NH.

Printed in the United States of America
10 9 8 7 6 5 4 3 2 1

For a complete catalog of Upstart's small business publications, call (800) 235-8866.

Dedication

To our clients and all we've learned from them.

Table of Contents

Introduction

L et's talk about who you are and why you're reading this
book. We don't know you personally, so we can't be sure.
But we can make some educated guesses. We bet you're a
member of some kind of executive team, management committee,
or partner group. Maybe you're the head of that team, an equal
partner on that team, or report to the boss of that team. At any
rate, you belong to a group that "runs the show" in an organization or part of an organization. And why are you reading this
book? Because you're not getting along as well as you'd like with
at least one of the other members of your team. For example:

- You're a father or a son in a family business who has been
  struggling for almost a year over the critical question of "suc-
  cession." You're at odds over when the transfer of power
  should happen, how the deal should be structured, and the
  nature of Dad's involvement after it happens.

- You're one of four physicians in a group practice who've
  stopped having weekly "partner meetings" because they
  always end in a shouting match between the two most
  aggressive partners.

- You're the founder of a successful company who's been seeing more competition than cooperation on his "top team." Or
  you're a member of the founder's executive team and you're
  just as unhappy as he is.

- You're the director of a center within the federal government
  who's been trying to "manage" three division directors who
  spend more time "one-upping" each other than achieving

1

agency goals. Or you're one of those three division directors and you see the center director as more interested in political intrigue and career advancement than in running the center.

- You're the executive director of a trade association or the newly elected president of the association. The two of you have been at odds for years. Now you have to work closely together, despite your suspicion and distrust.

That's who we think *you* are. But how about us? We're a couple of psychologists who help people just like you—people at the top of organizations who are struggling in their relationships with each other. We work with our clients in much the way marriage counselors work with couples. We start off by meeting individually with each person in the group to get their perspective on things. Then we bring the group together for a couple of days. These are intense sessions where we get people to talk and listen to each other in ways they've never done before. Our job is to help them communicate effectively about the most sensitive and difficult aspects of their relationships with each other.

While what we *do* is fairly clear, we struggled with what to *call* it for years. Then something interesting started to happen. We'd be talking about our work with someone, and the person would say, "Oh, you do marriage counseling with people in organizations." After a while we began using "organizational marriage counseling" as a shorthand way to describe our work. When it came to a title for this book, it's no accident we chose one that plays off the famous question: "Can this marriage be saved?"

We *love* this work. It's challenging. It's stimulating. And it's extremely satisfying, especially when we help people who haven't been getting along arrive at new levels of understanding and heal old wounds. This work has also helped us. Watching our clients make mistakes in their relationships has taught us to be better partners and friends. After several years of talking and procrastinating, we finally got around to writing this book about our work.

We'd Like to Make Your Job
a Little Less Painful and a Lot More Satisfying

We realize that being a member of an executive team or a partner group isn't always easy. We're partners ourselves, and we know how much we've struggled with each other over the last 20 years.

Any important relationship involves struggle and pain. But we're convinced that much of the struggle and pain you experience—the kind that eats into the heart of your organization and into your life and the lives of your family and employees—is unnecessary and can either be eliminated or greatly reduced.

We don't want you to struggle any more than you absolutely have to. We don't want you to cheat yourself out of hundreds of hours of enjoyment every year because you're upset or frustrated by the people you work so closely with. We want you to enjoy each other as much as you possibly can, and we want your business relationships—as well as your business—to be more productive.

We've Got Some Things to Say That Can Help You
We're not miracle workers, but we do have a solid track record of helping people who work closely with each other talk out some pretty gut-wrenching problems. Sometimes we've helped them patch up their differences and start trusting and enjoying each other again. At other times we've helped them come to the painful conclusion that theirs is a union that shouldn't be. And then we've helped them get a "divorce"—one that doesn't involve a protracted legal battle where all the organization's resources pour out to contentious attorneys.

Along the way we've collected lots of knowledge—and a little wisdom—that we can pass on to you through this book. Chances are, though, you're not going to accept all the advice we have to offer here. In fact, your reactions will probably break down into three basic categories:

1. **"I'm sorry, but I don't buy it."** A lot of what we say you simply won't be able to go along with. It'll run too much against your grain.

2. **"This is interesting; I've never quite looked at things that way."** Some of what we say will pique your interest and curiosity. It'll stimulate your thinking. It'll get you to step back and look at yourself—and the people you may be struggling with—in a different light.

3. **"This and a couple of other ideas were worth the price of admission."** Some of what we say—at least we hope—will

have a profound effect on you. It'll not only get you to change your thinking, but it'll also get you to change your behavior. It's that kind of advice that will make the book worthwhile.

If You're Struggling with Some Other People in Your Group, this Book May Be the Only "Counseling" Help You'll Ever Receive
One of the things our work has taught us is that you probably won't seek the kind of "organizational marriage counseling" we offer—even if your current struggle could lead to serious personal and organizational consequences. For several reasons:

There aren't many people around who do this kind of work. The field is very small. It isn't even a "field," in the usual sense of that term. Chances are, you wouldn't even know about this kind of work if you weren't reading this book.

The thought of bringing in *anybody* to help you sit down and talk to someone you're struggling with is probably not very appealing. There are at least two reasons for this. One, it's difficult for people in *any* important relationship to confront conflicts in their relationships. It's something most of us would just rather not do. Two, there's always the fear that sitting down and talking about difficult issues could make things worse, not better. And who in their right mind wants to pay a healthy sum to outsiders to have that happen?

So you probably *won't* bring in a counselor or consultant to help you iron out your differences. That doesn't mean you won't make good use of a book like this. We've found that people in your situation are often hungry for books, tapes, articles, and anything else that might help them understand their situation better and deal with it more effectively. But before you delve into the book to decide for yourself whether it'll be useful to you, here are some suggestions on how to get the most out of your reading:

Browse through the book looking for interesting things. Don't spend too much time on any one section. But if something catches your eye—some idea or concept or technique—go ahead and spend a little extra time with it.

Read the book actively, with an eye to trying things on for size. Do the exercises we suggest. *Think* about the points we make. Let the book sink in and get under your skin. Put as many of the concepts and ideas and skills to use as you can.

After you've absorbed the material, give the book to at least one of your team members to read. We'll be talking about how to involve the person you may be struggling with—as well as other team members—in the book. We want to stress how important it is to share these ideas with them. If you don't, you'll be a little like the wife or husband who goes into marriage counseling without the other spouse. It might do a lot for you, but it won't do much for the relationship.

But we're getting ahead of ourselves here. Right now, don't worry about changing anything. Right now, we want you to focus on why you're struggling with one or more of the folks you work so closely with, whether it's your partner, a family member, someone who reports to you, or your boss. That's all we'll be talking about for the next five chapters. In Chapter 2, we'll assert that a certain amount of struggle is inevitable whenever two or more people join together to work toward a common goal. In Chapter 3, we'll argue that, given the importance of these relationships to you, you may not be treating them as if they were all that important. In Chapter 4, we'll make another observation you may not want to hear: You're a bigger part of any problems you're having with your team members than you think you are. In Chapter 5, we'll flatly assert that a lot of the stress and frustration you're experiencing stems directly from your tendency to avoid sitting down and talking things out forthrightly and effectively. In Chapter 6, we'll wrap up our discussion of why you're struggling by talking about some important "relationship skills" you're missing.

After Chapter 6, we'll start talking about what you can do to resolve some of the problems you're having and achieve a less frustrating and more satisfying relationship with the person (or people) you've been having problems with.

Now let's move to Chapter 1 where we'll take an even closer look at your situation.

Let's Talk About
Your Situation

Pretty soon we're going to be talking about why you and your team members don't get along as well as you'd like and what you can do to change that. But before that, we want to tell you what we think we know about you. In this chapter we'll talk about four topics:

- The organization you work for

- The position of power you have relative to the other members of your executive team

- What you're looking for

- What the answer is

Your Organization

Chances are you work for one of the following kinds of organizations:

- A privately held company (not family owned)

- A family business

- A professional partnership

- A publicly traded company

- A government agency

- A nonprofit organization

A Privately Held Company (Not Family Owned)

Although most of the privately held companies in this country are family owned, not all of them are. In a family business the company is primarily owned by the members of one family, and it's apparent to anyone who works in the business that, if possible, ownership will forever stay "in the family." In the kind of privately held company we're talking about, the business is usually owned by a couple of partners who are not related, or, more likely, it's owned by a number of investors. These investors are hoping for one of two things: to sell the company to a larger organization or to "take it public" (sell shares in the stock market). Both of these outcomes usually (not always) lead to a "healthy" return on their investment.

A Family Business

It's frequently estimated that over 90 percent of the businesses in this country are family owned. Maybe you work for one of them. If you do, you're probably either the founder of the company or closely related to the founder. Maybe you're the son or daughter of the founder, the spouse of the founder, the brother-in-law or sister-in-law of the founder. Whoever you are, you're familiar with the joys as well as the frustrations of trying to juggle business and family affairs at the same time.

A Professional Partnership

If you're a member of a professional partnership, chances are you work for an accounting firm, a law firm, a medical practice, an architectural firm, a management consulting firm, or an engineering firm. You probably spent a lot of years in school before joining the firm. And unless you were one of the founders, you probably spent a number of years working your butt off at the "associate" level before you were let into the partnership "club."

A Publicly Traded Company

Even though privately held companies (family owned and not family owned) far outnumber publicly traded companies in the United States, publicly traded companies are the ones we hear more about because they're the biggies. And the ones we hear the most about are the "Fortune 500" types with annual sales in the billions—the GM's, the IBM's, the GE's and so on.

If you work for a publicly traded company, you could be well below the top level of management and still be a member of an important executive team. Maybe you're the general manager of one of the many hotels owned by ITT. Maybe you're in charge of a flour mill owned by Archer Daniels Midland. Or maybe you're the president of a company that's a wholly owned subsidiary of Procter and Gamble. Given the tremendous number of mergers and acquisitions since the late 70's, the possibilities are endless.

A Government Agency

Maybe you work for the federal government; maybe you work for the state or for a county government, or for some large municipality like New York or Chicago or Atlanta. You may be an appointed official or you may be protected by civil service regulations. But, for our purposes, who you work for and whether you're protected isn't all that important. What's important is that you're a high-level government employee who's a member of some executive team. (The problems government executive team members have in getting along with each other are very similar to the problems their private sector counterparts experience.)

A Nonprofit Organization

There are thousands and thousands of nonprofit organizations in this country. Most of them have only a few staff members and meager budgets. But some are not so small. The AFL-CIO, the American Trucking Associations, Printing Industries of America, the United Way, the Boy Scouts of America, the University of Michigan, and the American Cancer Society are just a few examples. These organizations are not set up to make profits for owners and stockholders, but from our standpoint, they don't look or operate much differently from their profit-making counterparts—especially when it comes to the problem of people who work together trying to get along with each other. All of these large nonprofit organizations have some kind of executive team. Maybe you're a member of one of those teams.

Your Power Position

As in all cases where two or more people are gathered together for some common purpose, power is a very important factor on an executive team. Take your situation. There are probably three power positions on your team:

- The one-down position
- The equal position
- The one-up position

The One-Down Position
Chances are this is the position you're in. You're a member of the team, but you're not the boss. Here are a couple of examples:

Bill Faulkner.[1] Bill is a member of what's called the Senior Executive Service in the federal government in the Washington, D.C. area. Bill's former boss, Ed Cravis, recently retired and has been replaced by Lois Danforth. Bill had an excellent relationship with Ed. He admired and respected him and was saddened when Ed unexpectedly decided to retire to take a job in the private sector.

Bill was wary when Lois was chosen as Ed's replacement because he'd worked closely with her several years earlier before she took a position in another office. Back then, Lois was just a colleague, not a boss, and Bill questioned her ability to manage people. Now Ed is gone and Lois has been Bill's boss for about three months. And Bill is *not* happy with the way Lois is running the show. Both Bill and several other members of Lois's staff told us:

> "Lois is difficult to work for. She's very driven. She came in here right after Ed left, and the place has been a madhouse ever since."
>
> "She's got us running in all different directions. One day she makes some report or study a top-priority item. Two weeks later, after a bunch of us have devoted mega hours to *that* top priority, she's completely forgotten

---

[1]This isn't his real name. Here, and throughout the book, we'll use fictitious names—along with some other "made-up" details—to describe our clients. While our clients may recognize themselves in these pages, we don't want anyone else to. But you can be sure each case illustration is based on real people and real experiences, "doctored" slightly to protect their confidentiality.

about it, and now there's some new top-priority item she wants finished yesterday. She's driving us all crazy."

"I don't trust her. She'll tell you one thing when she's alone with you, almost like it's a big secret just between you and her. Then she'll go to somebody else on the staff and tell that person just the opposite of what she told you. What kind of effect do you think that has on our morale?"

Karen Watson. Karen is in her early 40's and the vice-president of a second-generation family business in the Midwest that does a lot of subcontracting to automobile manufacturers. Karen's father started the business in 1951 and eventually passed it on to her older brother, Tommy, about 15 years ago. At that time, Karen was working as a secretary for the company. Although Karen's father never once considered her a candidate for ownership and management of the company, Tommy saw that she had the intelligence and drive to be a strong contributor to the company's growth. Karen now owns 15 percent of the company's stock; Tommy owns the rest. Karen told us:

> "Tommy is rough to work for. Technically, we're business partners because I own a portion of the stock. But I don't feel like a partner. Not at all. Ask anybody in this place. They'll tell you. He makes all the big decisions, and a lot of the little ones, too. I hate to say it, but he's a tyrant just the way the old man was. And the funny thing is, he doesn't see that. He and Dad used to have wars over that whole issue. And before Dad died Tommy swore to me that if he ever got to run this place he'd never act like the bully Dad was. Funny . . ."

Maybe your situation is similar to Bill's or Karen's; maybe it's different. But if you're in the one-down position on an executive team, we'll bet you have a couple of things in common with both of them:

1. The boss of your executive team may be the biggest people problem on the team.

2. Your boss is in the best position to make things better on your team but may be the least motivated to do so.

Your boss may be the biggest people problem on your team. There are at least a couple of reasons for this. One is that most bosses are lousy people managers. In fact, we feel so strongly about this issue we wrote a whole book on it (*Problem Bosses: Who They Are and How to Deal with Them*, Fawcett, $5.95). But it's true. Most bosses simply don't know how to effectively manage the people who report to them. Of course, a lot of bosses think they're good people managers. For example, Bill Faulkner (the fellow we just mentioned above) had this to say about Lois Danforth:

> "It's kind of amazing. Lois actually believes she's a good boss. She's extremely bright. She has a master's in public administration. And she spent six weeks up at that Harvard Business School summer program for working executives. If any of us were to tell her we didn't think she knew the first thing about managing a group of professionals who are just as bright as she is, her teeth would fall out."

Why are most bosses such lousy people managers? If you want a detailed explanation, take a look at our *Problem Bosses* book. For now, you might want to mull these over:

Many bosses have never read a book on how to manage. (Sadly, given the enormous problem with illiteracy in this country, there are some bosses who couldn't read a management book if they *wanted* to.)

Many bosses have had no formal training of any kind on how to be a boss, not even attendance at a two-hour seminar.

Most bosses become bosses for some reason other than a demonstrated capacity to manage people. Take Karen Watson's brother, Tommy, in the example we used a little earlier. Tommy didn't become head of the company because he'd proven he knew how to manage people. He became the boss because he was the first-born son of the founder. That's how it usually works in family businesses. But the most typical reason employees get promoted is that they did a good job in the position they got promoted *from*. Salespeople become sales managers because they sell a lot of product, not because they've shown an ability to motivate a sales force. Police officers get promoted to sergeant or lieutenant, not because of outstanding leadership qualities, but because they had a good arrest record and scored higher than their colleagues on some paper-and-pencil test unrelated to the job of managing people in a stressful occupation.

The only models most bosses have had for managing people were their own bosses. We don't know about you, but neither of us ever had a boss that was a good people manager. If we'd tried to follow the examples they set, we would have been even worse bosses than we were. And we were pretty bad.

So, in all probability, your boss is not a good people manager. But that's not reason enough for him or her to be the biggest people problem on your executive team. There's another reason, and it has to do with the main theme of this part of the chapter: *power*. Your boss has power that you and the rest of your team members don't have. And that power means your boss can treat you and your team members in ways you can't treat your boss. For example:

— Your boss can ask you to do tasks you think are unreasonable or even foolish. But you can't ask your boss to do things he or she thinks are unreasonable and foolish, can you?

— Your boss can drone on and on at meetings even if it tends to put everybody else to sleep. But what happens if you drone on and on and your boss gets bored? Does your boss just sit there and endure it?

— Your boss can ask to meet you at specific times but consistently keep you waiting for 20 or 30 minutes until he or she finally gets off the phone or comes back from lunch with an old friend. But can you and your team members get away with that kind of insensitivity?

— Your boss can act moody or peevish or testy or abrupt and simply expect you to accept it because he or she is the "boss."

But what happens if you or somebody else on the team behaves that way toward your boss?

Your boss is in the best position to improve things on your team but may be the least motivated to do so. This may not make a lot of sense to you. Why would the person who has the most power to do something about it *not* be the most interested in making things better? It may be puzzling, but that's the way it is. We began to notice this after a couple of years of traveling around the country giving seminars and doing workshops. After each of these sessions, people would come up to ask questions and make comments. Every now and then somebody would pull us aside and say, "I have a very sensitive problem I'd like to talk to you about." At an early morning breakfast or over a drink late at night in a secluded corner of a bar, the person would open up to us about a painful and frustrating problem with someone they worked with. Whether these people were from a government agency or a professional partnership or a family business or a nonprofit organization didn't seem to matter. What they all shared was a strong desire for us to listen to what they had to say and to hear our ideas on how the problem might get fixed. What they also had in common was that they were usually *not* the most powerful person on their executive team. The person talking to us was typically someone like Bill Faulkner rather than his boss, Lois Danforth. Or someone like Karen Watson, who owned 15 percent of the stock in her family's business, rather than her brother, Tommy, who owned the remaining 85 percent.

At first, we were puzzled by this pattern. But after years of similar experience, we've come to a couple of conclusions. One is that whatever the relationship, whether it's between a husband and a wife, a parent and a child, or a couple of people who work together, *the folks with the least power are the most interested in getting help to improve the relationship.* For example, think of some of the married couples you know whose relationships are troubled. In each of those cases one of the partners is likely to be in more pain—sometimes a lot more pain—than the other partner. Which of these partners is more interested in getting help from a marriage counselor? Is it the overbearing and controlling husband who seems pretty much unaware of the effect his tyrannical style has on his wife? Or is it his wife who's so frustrated and depressed that she's thinking seriously about a divorce in spite of the financial and emotional hardships that would cause?

The second conclusion we came to is that most bosses have their attention focused upward and outward, not downward toward their employees. Think about your own boss. Chances are your boss is a much more significant figure in your life—at least your professional life—than you are in your boss's life. Because your boss has power and influence that affects the quality and security of your career as well as your job, you automatically spend a lot of time thinking about (possibly *agonizing* about) your boss. You may even have dreams or nightmares about your boss. The same thing holds true for the other members of your executive team.

But even though you and your team members spend a lot of time thinking about and being distracted by your boss, your boss probably spends a lot less time thinking about and being distracted by *you*. Again, your boss's attention is focused upward and outward. It's unfortunate, but your boss is much more concerned about his or her boss than about you and the other members of your executive team. Bill Faulkner may be very concerned about Lois Danforth. But Lois is much less concerned about Bill Faulkner than she is about the head of her agency, congressional committees she might have to testify before, and other outside forces that might affect *her* position and *her* career. Bill Faulkner and the other members of the executive team that report to Lois are much further down her list of priorities. The same holds true for Tommy Watson. Karen Watson may be *very* concerned about Tommy and the effect he has on her personal and professional life. But, sadly, Tommy isn't all that concerned about Karen. He's more concerned about expanding the business he inherited from his father, keeping important customers satisfied, and finding new markets for the company's products.

The Equal Position

Earlier we said you're probably in the one-down position on your executive team. There's usually one dominant member, the boss, and then there's everybody else. But not always. Even though it's unlikely, you may be in the equal position when it comes to power on your executive team. If you are, this probably means you're in a partnership where you and your partner or partners own equal shares in your organization. Two examples:

The orthopedics. Betty Bradford, Tony Lorenzo, and Cheryl Rogers are equal partners in a private practice in the western suburbs of Boston, Massachusetts. All three of them were in the same residency program in the late 70's in Louisville, Kentucky. For several years after they'd completed their formal medical training they went their separate ways. But in the early 80's the three of them came up with enough cash to buy out two doctors who were ready to retire.

All three are capable physicians but have very different personalities. Betty is a natural leader and entrepreneur whose energy and long hours of work have caused the practice to expand dramatically in the last five years. Cheryl has a strong personality and frequently clashes with Betty over how big the practice should get and how profits should be spent. Tony is more passive than either Betty or Cheryl. He's a good listener and often finds himself being complained to about Betty by Cheryl and vice versa. He feels so caught in the middle between his two dominant partners that he's begun to think about returning to academic medicine.

What's clear is that *none* of the three partners are happy. They're making a lot of money. They like the technical side of their work as well as dealing with patients. They all have excellent reputations within the field of orthopedic surgery. But because their working relationships are so strained, they're not getting anywhere near the satisfaction nor the enjoyment out of their work that they expected when they bought into the practice.

One option each of them has considered is selling his or her shares to the other two and leaving the practice. But Tony explained why none of them wanted to do that:

> "All three of us have invested a tremendous amount in this practice. Not just money, but a big piece of ourselves. It would be very hard to give all that up to go someplace else and start over again. And on the financial side, since the practice is worth so much more now than when we started, it would be tough for the other two partners to come up with enough cash to buy the third partner out."

The Van Dorn brothers. Rick and Gerry Van Dorn are both in their mid-30's. They are equal partners in a casualty insurance company in Minneapolis. They inherited the business from their father who died suddenly at 55 from a heart attack. The two brothers have been very close all their lives. During their youth they played on the same football and hockey teams. When they went out with girls in high school, it was almost always as a foursome. According to their mom, Greta, the two boys even studied together. She told us:

> "Of course, they're still very close. But it's nowhere like it used to be between the two of them. Ricky is a year and a half older than Gerry and up until they became equal partners in the business, Ricky was always the dominant one. And Gerry accepted that. He would always defer to his 'older' brother."

A sad smile drifted across Greta's face before she went on:

> "But when their father died six years ago, Gerry began to change. He started to assert himself. He started to stand up to Ricky and challenge him when they disagreed. Well, Ricky doesn't like to be challenged. He likes to be in control. And now there's always a lot of tension between the two of them. I see it when I drop in at the office. I get these nervous looks from the secretaries and the agents who work for them. And I especially notice it when we get together as a family. There's just a lot of strain. It's not good."

Over the years we've worked with a number of executive teams where each member is more or less an equal partner and enjoys an equal position. We've noticed at least two things that distinguish these kinds of teams from those where there's a boss with more power than anybody else:

1. You have much more freedom to be and act yourself.

2. If you're going to lead a team like this, you have your work cut out for you.

You have much more freedom to be and act yourself. Being in the equal position on an executive team is more like being married than it is like being in a traditional boss-employee relationship. Husbands and wives, once they get beyond the honeymoon stage, feel more and more freedom to be and act themselves. If you're married, you know what we're talking about. If you're not, ask any of your friends who've been married more than five years. They'll say things like:

> "Oh yeah! George was actually kind of a gentleman when we were dating. But six months after we were married, more and more of the real George emerged. I love the guy, but he's got some personal habits that I'd be too embarrassed to describe."

> "It took over two years of being married to her to realize what an incredible temper Sally has. She doesn't fly off the handle easily, but when she does, I don't want to be in the same county with her, much less the same house."

We see a lot of similarities between husbands and wives and equal partners on an executive team. Probably because they know they can't be fired (unless they do something egregious), partners do things we don't usually see in more traditional executive teams. If you're an equal partner, maybe you've seen some of your partners:

— Engage in vicious shouting matches at partner meetings (or even in public places) over what, at least on the surface, seem to be pretty trivial issues.

— Simply disappear for two or three days without letting anybody in the office know where they've gone.

— Turn in expense accounts for trips and entertainment that even the most liberal-minded auditor would question.

— Hire consultants to come into your organization to perform services that, in your view, are unnecessary.

— Openly carry on romantic affairs with employees in the organization who are not members of the executive team (and who automatically become privy to information they have no business having).

On executive teams where each of the members is more or less in the equal power position, being a leader is a difficult role. These "lead partner" roles are most likely to appear in professional partnerships like law firms, medical practices, architectural firms, and accounting firms. The team member who takes on the leadership role in firms like these is frequently called the "managing partner." Sometimes this role rotates through the executive team. That is, one partner will serve a two-year "term" and then the role will be passed to a different partner for another two-year term, and so on. In other organizations a partner who prefers management and administration to the technical work that the firm does often takes over the leadership role on a more or less permanent basis. If you've ever been in this kind of role, whether it was called a managing partner or something else, you know how challenging it can be:

> **You don't have the power of a traditional boss.** You can't fire people on your executive team. If you want to lead the team in a certain direction, you can't use fear tactics, intimidation, or any of the other typical tricks in the bag of tyrannical bosses. You have to rely on something else. Maybe it's your charisma. Maybe it's your power of persuasion. Or maybe it's just a quiet sense of competence that has caused your team members to have trust and confidence in you over the years.

> **You may have more than your share of prima donnas and other kinds of difficult people to deal with.** Individuals on executive teams in professional partnerships—whether they're lawyers or doctors or accountants or architects or engineers or whatever—are highly educated and intelligent folks. Many of them are independent and bristle at even the hint of an authoritarian management style from a leader. Others are arrogant and pompous. And some, in spite of their technical

competence and brilliance, have the emotional maturity of 13-year-olds. These are not easy people to manage and lead.

If you lack openness, honesty, and caring for your team members, it will eventually come back to haunt you. If you're the head of an executive team where you have a lot more power than the other members, you can rule with relative impunity. Bosses with lots of power can escape the consequences of being devious, reckless, self-centered, and uncaring for years, sometimes decades. But that's not true for teams where every member is more or less in the equal power position. If you're a leader on this kind of team, you can't get away with making unilateral, selfish decisions indefinitely. Eventually, your fellow team members will either throw you out or take you off your throne. At this writing, we're sadly watching a capable and charismatic physician being drummed out of a practice he's been in for over 20 years because he ignored this fact.

The One-Up Position

Being in the one-up position doesn't automatically mean you're the boss on your executive team. It simply means you have considerably more power than most of the other members of the team. Some examples:

Mannie Riordan. Mannie is the president of the Fitness Emporium, a chain of 150 stores located in large, suburban shopping centers. Their market is 18 to 35-year-old runners, cyclists, cross-country skiers, swimmers, and triathletes. Prior to being hired as CEO of the Fitness Emporium, Mannie was the head of two other major retail chains with a national reputation. Mannie is now wealthy enough that he doesn't have to work, so it wasn't particularly easy for the venture capitalists and other investors who made up the board of the company to lure him away from his comfortable previous position.

Mannie has now been running the Fitness Emporium for a little over nine months. He seems to like his new job, but it's clear everything is far from perfect. He says:

"This company has tremendous potential. I think we'll be going public within the next two years, and all of us who own stock in this place should end up doing very well. My biggest frustration right now is the team of managers I have working for me. They're all younger than I am, and they bring a lot of energy and creativity to their jobs. But they're also inexperienced, and they don't have any idea of how much further we have to go before we can even *think* about making an attractive public offering."

Joe Angelino. Joe will turn 60 at the end of this year. He was raised in western New York State and went to MIT on a scholarship where he graduated with a BS in mechanical engineering in the early 50's. Right after college he married his high-school sweetheart, Mildred, and went to work for GE where he remained for 12 years. When he and Mildred reached their middle 30's, they decided to take a big risk. With three small children and not a whole lot of money in the bank, they took a second mortgage on their home and bought a small valve-manufacturing company just south of Rochester, New York.

Joe and Mildred's risk paid off. The company now has annual sales just short of ten million dollars, and that figure could easily double in the next five years. When we asked Joe about his executive team, he smiled and said:

"My executive team? Right now it's my three sons. Within the next six months, it'll probably be my three sons and my daughter. I guess there's no getting around it, we're a pretty typical family business."

Mildred chimed in:

"*Very* typical! They're all great kids, but they're all so different from each other. And the most frustrating thing for me [as she shot Joe a menacing look] is that Carlie, our daughter, has much better business sense than any of the three boys. But it's only been within the last month that she and I have been able to convince

'His Excellency' here to let her come in full-time and really help out."

Jake Bradstreet. Jake is not the boss of his executive team. The boss of the team is Carl Bledsoe. Carl is the president and CEO of Bledsoe Mills, a wheat-milling company started by his grandfather at the end of the nineteenth century. Carl is approaching 65 and wants to retire. About 18 months ago he sold his third-generation family business to a large agricultural conglomerate and now has well over 30 million dollars in the bank. Jake Bradstreet (about ten years younger than Carl) is executive vice-president and his clear choice for successor. There are eight other members on the company's executive team, all of them at least ten years younger than Jake. Although Jake hasn't yet been named president, none of the other younger members of the executive team has any doubts about who's in charge. One of them said:

> "Jake runs the show around here. Carl still has the title of president, but half the time he's not here, and when he is here, it's pretty clear he's just coasting. Jake's the real boss. Everybody around here is clear about that."

If you're in the one-up position on your executive team, here are a few things we think we know about you:

We stand by what we said earlier: you may be the biggest people problem on your executive team, and you're in the best position to make things better, but you may be the least motivated to do so. If you disagree with us on these two points, take off your "boss" glasses and put on your "employee" glasses. If you currently have a boss, think about him or her. If you don't have a boss, think about the ones you've had. Think about all the problems and frustrations your bosses have caused you. It will be hard to recognize and admit it, but chances are you're causing your employees the same kinds of problems and frustrations. (Later on in the book we'll talk about ways you can test our assertion.)

The members of your executive team insulate you from candid feedback and important information. Employees tell bosses what bosses *want* to hear, not what they *need* to hear. There's a quote we use in our seminars from the film studio magnate Samuel Goldwyn that always gets a laugh: "I don't want a bunch of 'yes men' around me. I want people who will tell me the truth even if it costs them their jobs!" It's a funny line, but it's got a lot of truth in it, too. At one of our recent seminars, after hearing the Goldwyn quote, some guy yelled out, "Yeah! Tell your boss the truth, and the truth shall set you free!"

Employees *don't* tell their bosses what they need to hear because they know that being frank and candid with their bosses can get them in hot water or even canned. But your employees, especially the members of your executive team, have things to say that you really *do* need to hear. They know you well. They're "experts" on your behavior. They're in a position to give you frank, candid feedback on what you do well as their leader, but also on how you could be much more effective in your role as their boss and (probably) as the head of your organization. They're also privy to information you often get only when it's too late to do anything about it. They know about valuable employees your "favorite" managers have alienated, employees who are so disgruntled they're looking for other jobs. They know about important customers you may have offended who are thinking about taking a hike. In short, they know all kinds of things you need to know. The problem is, they're reluctant to tell you about these things because they're afraid of your reaction.

You have concerns and problems that the other folks on your executive team can't fully appreciate. It may be a cliche, but it's true: It is lonely at the top. If you're the head of an executive team (especially if you're also the head of your organization), the people who report to you do not have a clear understanding of the constant stress and strain you're under. If you're a Mannie Riordan, the young people who report to you don't know what it's like to manage energetic but inexperienced folks who think they're more knowledgeable and experienced than they really are. If you're like Joe Angelino, the founder of a family business, your kids—no matter how capable they are—have no idea what it took for you to build the company. And they have no idea how precarious business can be even if things are going well right now. If you're like Jake Bradstreet, the "heir apparent" for the presidency of your organization, the folks on your executive team can't know the exhilaration and anxiety you feel as you come closer to taking full control of the company. Nobody but you, or someone who's been through what you're going through, can know that feeling.

What You're Looking For

Up to this point we've talked a little about the organization you may be working in, and we've talked a lot about your power position on your executive team. Throughout the chapter we've talked about people whose names are fictional but whose professional lives are based on many of the clients we've worked with over the last 12 years. Our bet is that you're not a whole lot different. What they wanted when we worked with them is probably what you want now and gets to the heart of why you're reading this book. What they were looking for then and what you're probably looking for now are two things: 1) a *reduced* level of frustration and stress, and 2) an *increased* level of enjoyment and satisfaction.

Remember Bill Faulkner, the high-level civil servant whose boss, Ed Cravis, was replaced by Lois Danforth? Those were the two things Bill wanted. He said:

> "When Ed was running this place, things were far from perfect. Our jobs are very demanding here. We get a lot of scrutiny from Congress, the press, and industry. But I gotta say, when Ed was running the show, the work was actually kind of fun. We had a sense of camaraderie here. Like we were all pulling on the same oar, trying to do an important job. And Ed had a marvelous sense of humor that weaved its way down to the lowest level employee in the organization."

Bill just stopped talking for about 30 seconds. Then, half frowning and half smiling, he went on:

> "But all that changed when Ed left and Lois replaced him. Lois is not a team player the way Ed was. She's self-centered, tense, highly ambitious, and has no sense of humor. I don't look forward to coming to work in the morning anymore. I don't sleep anywhere near as well as I used to. I want to have fun again. But I just don't know if that's gonna be possible as long as Lois is running the show here."

Remember Betty Bradford, Tony Lorenzo, and Cheryl Rogers—the three orthopedic surgeons in private practice with one another? Whenever we talked with them, it sure sounded like what they wanted most was less stress and frustration and more enjoyment and satisfaction. Perhaps Betty Bradford put it best:

> "You know, I've been busting my ass since I was 12 years old. That was the age when I decided I wanted to be a doctor, and I knew I had to buckle down in my studies if I was gonna make that dream a reality. So I ground it out through junior high school, through high school, through college, through medical school, through four years of residency, and I ground it out to help build this place to what it is today. But am I really happy in my work?"

She paused a long time before continuing:

> "I love medicine. I love our patients. I love seeing the practice grow. But Cheryl and I have so much trouble getting along that I have a knot in my stomach from the time I walk in here in the morning until I go home at night. That stinks. I don't want that. And I'm sure Cheryl feels the same way. We haven't invested all this energy and time and money in our careers to walk around this place with knots in our stomachs. By this time, it seems to me, we ought to be having a little fun."

And, finally, remember Joe and Mildred Angelino, the couple who decided to give up corporate security to start their own business? What they wanted didn't really sound much different from what Bill Faulkner and the orthopedic surgeons wanted. One day when Joe was not around, Mildred told us:

> "It's hard to believe, but I've known Joe for over 45 years. In some ways he still seems like the shy high-school freshman who had so much trouble working up the gumption to ask me out on our first date. But here he is almost 60 years old, and I often wonder when he's finally going to be able to reap his harvest. He's built a

successful company. He's well-respected in the community and in our industry. But he's so distracted about whether the kids will be ready to take over the company that he doesn't seem to be able to relax and enjoy all he's achieved. When you get to be our age, you never know how much time you have left. But I want it to be the best time it can possibly be."

So What's the Answer?

So what *is* the answer? When it comes to your executive team, what do you have to do to lower your stress and frustration? And what will it take to increase your satisfaction and enjoyment? If you're like us, if you're like our clients, and if you're like the vast majority of people we've encountered in our lives, the answer is clear: "If I could only get that other person (or those other people) to change, everything would be all right." That's what Bill Faulkner wants. He wants his boss Lois Danforth to act a little less like herself and a little more like Ed Cravis, his former boss. That's what Joe Angelino wants. He wants his kids to start acting less like spoiled brats and more as if they really understand and appreciate the responsibility of running the business they'll soon be taking over. And, frankly, that's what the two of us want when we run into disagreements and rough spots in *our* partnership. In fact, it was just one of those disagreements years ago that caused us to write an article called "Why Can't My Partner Be More Like Me?"

Of course, it's not that simple. If life on your executive team is ever to become more satisfying and less frustrating for you, other people on the team may have to make some changes. But the person who may have to do the most changing is *you*. It may not seem right. It may not seem fair. It may seem like a downright injustice. But if the quality of your work life is going to improve significantly, you're going to have to do some things differently. You're going to have to look at things about yourself that aren't so pleasant to look at. You're going to have to listen to some honest and candid feedback that will be hard to stomach. It will probably hurt. And you're going to have to change some deeply ingrained habits that aren't about to give way without a fight.

2

Struggle Is Inevitable

Why are you struggling? Why are you having a tough time with one or more individuals on your executive team? Unfortunately, whenever people pursue a common goal, struggle is simply a fact of life. It may not be open warfare and it may not lead to disastrous results, but conflict, misunderstanding, divisiveness and suspicion are inevitable. Eventually these struggles lead to frustration and dissatisfaction, which often brings out the worst in people.

If you're like a lot of our clients, you probably don't see interpersonal struggle with your colleagues as something that "goes with the territory." In fact, there's a good chance your attitude toward it is one of impatience, annoyance, or frustration:

> "I've provided each of my kids with a good job and a good future in this business. You'd think they'd appreciate that, wouldn't you? Well, maybe, but I hear a hell of a lot more complaints than compliments."

> "Once, just once, I'd like to have a partners' meeting where egos, personalities, and petty jealousies get put aside and we just talk about work—you know, what we're getting paid for by our clients."

> "I didn't go to school from age 5 until age 30 to end up working for some intellectual lightweight who's more interested in the timeliness of my weekly reports than in the quality of my thinking."

If we've learned anything in our work and personal lives over the past 20 years, it's that no human relationship—no matter how good, no matter how satisfying—is immune from struggle. And we'd like you to be open to the idea that some of the dissatisfaction and frustration you may be feeling with your team members comes from this simple fact. To illustrate this notion, we'll walk you through four kinds of problems we've frequently seen in our work: 1) the formation of divided camps in business partnerships; 2) getting rid of business partners who aren't working out; 3) poor communication between bosses and valued employees; and 4) bosses who've lost the confidence of team members. There's nothing unusual or atypical about these problems. Almost all partnerships or executive teams face them at one time or another.

Divided Camps

It's very easy for divided camps to get formed in partnerships such as law firms, accounting firms, engineering or architectural firms, medical groups and the like. Here's what we've observed time and time again. Two or more camps start forming because of deepening resentment over some emotionally loaded issue. Some examples:

Equity of contribution versus equity of remuneration. Several years back we worked with an architectural firm that had a group of six senior partners, three under 40 and three over 50. All six partners received equal pay, but it was clear that the "junior" group was billing many more hours every week than the "senior" group. The younger partners were starting to resent the fact that their older colleagues were making roughly the same money while putting in about 30 percent less time. The older partners had a different view. One told us:

> "What those younger guys forget is that all three of us, when we were that age in the firm, paid our dues, too. We were putting in just as much time and working just as hard as they are now. But they don't know that because they weren't around. They were drinking beer in their fraternity houses."

Turf building. In many partnerships, it's not unusual for one sub-group of partners to work exclusively with one client or set of clients. While this is usually a wise division of labor, it sometimes causes problems. In the mid-80's we worked with a large group of pathologists who had big contracts with various hospitals in a major metropolitan area. But a schism began to form when some of the partners became annoyed at one strong-willed partner and his "loyal" associates who were treating the hospital they worked in as their own private client.

Outside glamour versus inside drudgery. In many partnerships, some partners are more drawn to the task of bringing work into the firm and other partners are more drawn to actually *doing* the work. While this natural division of talent and preference often works well, it can sometimes cause resentment and a breakdown in unity. The "outside" partners—the ones largely responsible for bringing work into the firm—tend to say:

> "Look, they don't have any idea how hard it is to close a deal. Beyond that, most of them don't have the people skills you need to make a potential client feel comfortable and trusting enough to finally decide to give us their business instead of some other firm out there—one that could probably do just as good a job as we can."

The "inside" partners—the ones largely responsible for doing the work once it's brought into the firm—tend to say:

> "We know that getting contracts isn't the easiest thing in the world. But getting the work done can be a hell of a lot more demanding and a hell of a lot less glamorous. It's one thing to travel around the country to nail down a design job. But it's a whole different ball game when you have to crank out that design while you're dealing with bad weather, strikes, and politicians who don't know their ass from a hole in the ground."

Direction the firm should be taking. About ten years ago we worked with a construction firm owned by four partners. The most senior partner in the firm (a man in his early 60's who had founded the company) owned 40 percent of the stock and his three other partners (all much younger) owned the remaining 60 percent. Jack, the founder, was very interested in having the outfit do international work, especially in third world countries where he saw the potential for unlimited work and big profits. The three younger partners felt that chasing international jobs was far too risky and that Jack was wasting precious dollars with his frequent "marketing" trips to Africa and the Far East. Each time Jack would go off on one of these trips, the other three would spend hours and hours complaining about Jack's wild-goose chases and how there was more than enough domestic work to keep the company busy.

Getting Rid of a Partner

Sometimes the natural struggle of trying to get along with a partner becomes too much for the other partners in a firm. So they decide to get rid of the partner. But that's often only the beginning of the struggle. Why? Because firing a partner is not like firing an employee. Firing a partner is more like trying to fire a spouse. It can be difficult and messy:

Partners don't accept being fired the way employees do. Most employees (except government employees) accept it when you tell them they've been fired. They don't like it. They may resist it by trying to negotiate a generous severance package. They may even try to fight it legally. But for the most part, employees accept the fact that they've been canned and go on about the business of finding another job. Partners are different. Partners don't see themselves as employees; they see themselves as owners of their firms. They are likely to respond: "Wait just a minute! I have a piece of the action here. You can't just shove me out the door. We're going to have to talk about this, and talk about it a lot!"

The financial cost of removing a partner from your team is usually much higher then the cost of firing an employee. If you fire an employee, you may have to come up with some severance pay; you may have to pay some unemployment insurance benefits; and you may even have to pay some settlement costs if the employee chooses to fight you legally. But with partners, it's different. As we said earlier, partners own stock in your organization, stock that has some monetary value attached to it. And here's the rub. When you decide to get rid of partners, they're very likely to claim their stock is worth considerably more than you and your other partners would like to pay for it. On top of that, the more the "outgoing" partners feel you're treating them badly or unfairly, the more they'll ask to be paid for their stock.

The ugly possibility of a legal battle is always there. We don't have any hard data to back up this perception, but we estimate that at least one out of every ten professional partnerships in this country could tell you a "horror story" about a painful, disruptive, and financially draining legal battle when they tried to get rid of partners who didn't want to go easily. This is not a problem business partners are eager to talk about. But it's a problem that's much more widespread than most people in the general business community would like to believe.

Poor Communication Between Bosses and Valued Employees

If there's any one factor that contributes to struggle in human relationships, it's poor communication. And over the years we've known a lot of bosses who've had at least one employee on their teams they valued a great deal but who they were having a lot of trouble communicating with. Unfortunately, too many of these valued employees either get fired by their dissatisfied bosses, or they get so fed up and frustrated they quit. Some examples:

Unpleasant arguments that don't get resolved. Maybe you have a situation with a team member that's similar to the one Tom Orford has with Kathy Flaherty. Tom is a senior level office director in the Department of Defense, and Kathy is Tom's deputy. Tom and Kathy share a lot of characteristics. Both are highly intelligent PhD's in the hard sciences. Both are ambitious and have risen to high levels of responsibility at a relatively young age. And most importantly, both are strong-willed and argumentative. When they first started working together three years ago, their frequent arguments over policy decisions were spirited but good-natured. In the last 15 months or so, however, that's changed. Now their arguments have a nasty, rancorous tone. And unlike several years ago, their arguments don't get resolved. Each walks away from the argument shaking his or her head and muttering about how stubborn and rigid the other is.

Lackluster involvement in staff meetings. Maybe you have someone on your team who used to be an active, positive contributor in your staff meetings. The type of person who always tried to "loosen things up" with a few jokes or some teasing. Someone who could listen well while others on the team offered their opinions, and then summarize what had been said and suggest good ways to reach a consensus. Or maybe it was someone who always encouraged reluctant staff members to advance new ideas. But now you notice the person is pretty passive during staff meetings and just seems to be going through the motions.

Refusal to talk about "what's wrong." Imagine you're the CEO of a successful company and your senior vice-president for marketing, Jim Conway, has been a part of your team for five years. You've seen a lot of people come and go in the sales and marketing field over the span of your 30-year career. In your opinion, Jim is about as good as they get. He's energetic and enthusiastic. He's extremely persuasive. He's charming. He's honest and his conceptual skills are first rate. In short, any CEO would love to have this guy in charge of marketing. However, in the last six months something has been eating at Jim. He seems distracted and irritable and generally uncommunicative. You've tried to draw him out and to get him to talk about what's bothering him. But your attempts have been completely unsuccessful. Jim continues to stonewall you. Whenever you mention the problem, he gives you a sort of phony smile and a curious look and says something like: "I'm fine. I didn't realize I was coming across that way. Really, I'm fine."

More than a few "unpleasant surprises." Maybe you've got someone working for you who you value a great deal but who—in spite of your best efforts at clear communication—has recently developed a pattern of hitting you with the unexpected. For example:

— You thought your company's annual strategic planning session was firmly scheduled for December 6 and 7. However, when you happened to mention the dates of the meeting just before Thanksgiving, he said: "Tom, I can't make that meeting. Sally and I have had a two-week vacation scheduled for that period for over six months. And our airline tickets are nonrefundable."

— One day you amble into the office of your head of manufacturing and casually ask about the October 1 delivery date for a huge order for a valued customer. Your manufacturing guy says, "Bob, I thought you knew. We've backed that off until November 15." More than a little shocked you try to regain your composure as you think, "Why the hell didn't somebody tell me about this?"

— On a Friday afternoon your VP for human resources catches up with you in the hall and says, "I think we've got a real winner lined up for that PR position. We're going to make her an offer this afternoon." Before you can respond, he trots off to a meeting. You just stand there shaking your head. You thought you had a clear understanding that you'd meet all the job candidates before any offers were made.

Bosses Who've Lost the Confidence Of Their Team (But Don't Know It)

Here's a particular kind of situation we encounter frequently in our work. You have your own executive team in an organization, but yours is not the highest level team in the place. The problem is that more than a few of the people on your team—people who report directly to you—are dissatisfied (maybe very dissatisfied) with the way you're managing them. They've tried to send signals that they're not happy with the way you're running the show, but you don't get the message. More and more frustrated, some of them risk going over your head and complaining about you to your boss. Now your boss is beginning to send signals that you have problems with your team, and you're *still* not getting the message.

Sound hard to believe? Unfortunately, this sort of thing happens often in organizations. About a year ago we were called in to a large mining company in the Southwest to deal with this kind of problem. Four months earlier, Tim Long, head of operations for the company, and Harold Thornton, Tim's director of sales, had both seen us put on a seminar at the annual convention of their industry's trade association. At a cocktail party after the seminar we met Tim and Harold and chatted with them for a while. They both seemed to have a comfortable relationship with each other, and neither one brought up any "people problems" back at their company.

We were a little surprised when we got a call from Tim several months later in which he expressed deep concern about Harold's situation:

> "If I just look at the bottom line, I'd have to say Harold is doing pretty well. In spite of a recession he and his sales team just finished up an excellent year. But I'm hearing more and more discontentment from some of the people on Harold's team. And these comments are coming from some of his top performers. They're telling me some pretty negative things. Harold runs disorganized sales meetings. He's embarrassed some of them on sales calls when he's offered customers half-baked advice on how to run their business. And when they go to trade shows with him, they say he spends more time in his hotel room watching movies than he does at our sales exhibits and receptions for customers."

Tim asked us if we could come and do some team-building work with Harold and his sales people. We began with two days of interviews, where we talked to Harold and each of the eight people on his team for an hour and a half each. At the end of the second day we met again with Harold and were very frank with him:

> "Harold, you have some major problems on your sales team. Morale is very low, and your people have some serious complaints—many of which sound pretty legitimate to us—about the way you're managing them."

Harold was shocked. He said he knew there were some problems, but he thought, overall, things were going pretty well—especially if you looked at the good sales performance he and his team had just turned in. We made it clear to Harold that he'd get some valuable feedback in the upcoming team-building session, and that he was going to have to make some important changes in how he dealt with his people. If he didn't, there was a good chance he'd lose his job.

Well, we did our best, but it didn't work. The team-building session was tough but seemed very productive. Harold *did* get a lot of candid feedback, and he also showed a willingness to change. At the end of the session, he identified a number of specific things he was going to work on in the next month to improve his performance. All of us left the session feeling cautiously optimistic; we scheduled a follow-up session for a month later. In three weeks, Tim called us to say he'd fired Harold:

> "I think Harold really did want to change. But we brought you guys in too late in the game. Harold did things differently the first week or so, but then he quickly slipped back into his old ways. A week ago I just had to make the hard decision to let him go. Hopefully, all of us, including Harold, have learned something positive from all this."

You may be saying, "Look, Harold had to be pretty dense not to pick up on those cues that something was wrong. A guy that thick probably shouldn't even be running an executive team." If that's what you're thinking, it's hard for us to argue with you. But the fact is there are a lot of Harolds out there heading up executive teams. And for the most part, these are not intellectually dull people. (Harold had a master's degree in biochemistry from a prestigious university.) But they are people largely insensitive to the impact of their behavior on others. Should individuals so interpersonally clumsy be running executive teams? No, they shouldn't. But the reality is that many of them are. Maybe you're one of them. Or maybe you're working for one right now.

Early in the chapter we said that some of the dissatisfaction and frustration you may be feeling with your team members comes from the fact that a certain amount of interpersonal struggle is inevitable. All we've tried to do here is illustrate some common ways these interpersonal struggles are played out. However, simply knowing that struggle is inevitable and accepting that fact are two different things. Accepting that any relationship—even a real good one—will always involve some struggle doesn't come easily. The two of us are a good example. We've been best friends for over 20 years and our partnership is very strong, probably as strong as a business partnership can get. However, when we begin to struggle with each other—and we do—there's a natural tendency for each of us to think:

> "You know, this is a bunch of crap! If you weren't so stubborn and pigheaded or wrapped up in your own view of things, we wouldn't be having this problem. Why the hell can't you see things from my point of view?"

But once the storm has passed and we're able to look more placidly and objectively at whatever our problem is, we know we'll always have disagreements with each other. Why? Because we have different personalities, different life histories, different priorities, and different ways of looking at the same situation. Plus, we know we'll occasionally do something thoughtless, insensitive, or selfish that will hurt the other guy's feelings or upset him in some other way. Why? Because we're human. That's just the way it is.

And that's the way it is with you and your group. You're a collection of very different people who simply can't be expected to always see things in exactly the same way. That, plus the fact that you all have very human flaws, makes a certain amount of conflict and struggle a certainty. In the next chapter, we'll talk about one of these flaws: the tendency to treat the important relationships you have with other people as if they were not really that important.

3

You Aren't Relationship-Oriented Enough

When people ask us what we do for a living, we often reply, "We're in the relationship business." That answer usually draws a puzzled look. But that is what we do. We help people who are struggling in important relationships sit down and work on those relationships in a way they wouldn't if we weren't there. The fact that we do this work with people on executive teams is incidental. We could just as easily do it with husbands and wives, parents and children, cabinet members, or baseball teams. It wouldn't make much difference.

Since relationships are our life's work, we pay a lot of attention to them. We look at them in much the way art experts notice things in people's homes and in museums that the rest of us would never see. One of the things we've clearly noticed is that people who run organizations don't pay much attention to the tremendously important role relationships play in the success and satisfaction of the people who work in those organizations.

In this chapter we'll be talking about the *relationships* you have with all of the members of your executive team. We'll be making two major points:

1) Being on an executive team automatically means you're involved in some very important relationships.

2) But the chances are you don't treat those relationships as if they were really important.

Being on an Executive Team Means Being in an Important Set of Relationships

Being on an executive team means being in an important set of relationships for at least two reasons. One is that you share lots of important experiences with your team members. The second is that the quality of these relationships has tremendous *impact* on the quality of all your lives.

You and Your Team Members Share Lots of Important Experiences
Being a member of an executive team means a lot of things, but one thing it *certainly* means is sharing important experiences with each other. There are a lot of ways to categorize these experiences, but three stick out for us:

- Wrestling with major problems together

- Traveling together

- Playing together

Wrestling with major problems together. There isn't an executive team anywhere in the world that doesn't have to deal with problems. Some of them are just small and annoying, like flies buzzing around a horse's rump. But some are tough, demanding, time consuming, and energy draining. For these problems to get solved (or at least to put a dent in them) means having to work closely with at least one member of your executive team.

Take Bill Forsythe and John Stanley. Bill is the head of a high-level office within the Department of Labor in Washington, D.C., and John is his deputy. Three years ago Bill and John started the necessary but painful process of trying to fire Ron Waters, a GS-14 who reported to John. Bill and John were fed up. For years they had suspected that Ron was passing on highly confidential information to outside contractors, but they could never get any concrete evidence. Finally, however, they built a paper trail that showed Ron was leaking important information that would give certain contractors a clear advantage in bidding on some kinds of work. The effort to establish this paper trail was exhausting for John. He told us:

"Trying to fire Ron was one of the hardest jobs I've ever done. Bill and I put in mega hours doing all the documentation, which, by the way, ended up being a foot-and-a-half high stack of paper. Our family lives suffered because of all the late nights and weekends we had to spend on this crap, and a lot of the important work we were trying to do in the office had to be put on the back burner."

But the biggest frustration for Bill and John was that, in spite of all their hard work, Ron didn't get fired. Throwing his hands up and rolling his eyes, Bill said:

"Unbelievable! We did *everything* by the numbers. I mean right down the line we did it by the book. And you know what happens? Ron appeals his case three different times, and each time his appeal fails. Then he appeals one more time, and the whole thing gets overturned for some stupid technicality. I felt like retiring right there on the spot."

Another poignant example of executive team members wrestling with a tough problem is Jim Stuart and Frank and Tony Santini. As sometimes happens in privately owned businesses, Jim and the two Santini brothers became partners in an unusual way. Santini Construction had been started by Albert Santini, Frank and Tony's father, right after World War II. In the mid-60's, Jim Stuart, then in his early 30's, joined the company as a structural engineer and project manager. Frank and Tony were still in high school.

Over the next 12 years an unusual story unfolded. Albert's first wife—Frank and Tony's mother—died, and Albert eventually married Sharon, an attractive and aggressive woman at least 20 years younger than he. Then tragedy struck. Albert discovered he had a brain tumor, underwent an operation, and lapsed into a deep coma. Albert's will provided for the settling of his estate in the event of his death, but not in the event of his incapacitation. It was then that things began to get messy. By this time Jim had become a stock-owning partner in the company. Frank and Tony were now in their mid-20's, and both of them owned a small share of the company. But the legal waters regarding complete ownership of the company were muddy. Jim, Frank, and Tony claimed the company now rightfully belonged to them. Sharon had different ideas. Jim told us:

> "Sharon is a strong and tenacious woman. She wanted the business, and she was gonna fight for it. She hired her lawyer, the boys and I hired our lawyer, and the damn battle raged on for over three years. And, as you might predict, the only ones to really make out on the deal were the attorneys. I never want to go through something like that again."

You travel together. If you're a member of an executive team, your job may not require a lot of travel but it probably requires some. And chances are, when you do travel, you do it with at least one other team member, if not several. We think traveling together as executive team members is an important experience. Why?

Because if you've traveled together with some of your team members even a tenth as much as we have, you've:

— Spent lots of hours sitting in airports and on planes talking about things that can range from the very personal to the very mundane.

— Met any number of unusual characters along the way, from the Hare Krishnas who accost you in airports to New York cabbies who entertain (or bore) you with their opinions of who's going to win the presidential election or the Super Bowl.

— Heard more creative lies and excuses than you'd care to remember about why your flight was canceled, your room reservation was never received, or the nonsmoking car you rented smells like a cigar.

— Been driven to three different hotels before you found the right one by a taxi driver who wouldn't admit he didn't know the city.

You play together. Over the years you've probably done a fair amount of playing with some of your executive team members. Maybe you bowl together. Maybe you play softball with some of them. Maybe you play basketball or tennis with some of them. Maybe you play in bridge tournaments with some of them. Maybe you've competed in a triathalon or a marathon with some of them. Or maybe you've just clowned around at office parties and other social functions with some of them.

These kinds of play activities may not seem like they're important experiences, but we think they are. On the one hand, they're an opportunity to relax with people you work with, to let your hair down and have fun. But beyond fun and relaxation, these activities give you and your team members a chance to see a side of each other you might never see if all you did was work together. For example, years ago the two of us were invited to dinner at the home of a client who was the head of a medium-sized manufacturing firm. Before going to his home, we'd always seen him as a serious, reserved, and humorless guy. But our impression changed that night. We'd just finished a cocktail and were sitting down in the dining room with Warren, his mischievous wife, Polly, and his 15-year-old son, Danny. Right after we sat down Polly and Danny said, "Daddy, do your Donald Duck impression for these guys." A little surprised, we just sat and waited. Sure enough, Warren did a 30 second Donald Duck impression that was near perfect. We laughed so hard we were ready for stomach surgery.

Another way playing with your team members causes you to see sides of each other you wouldn't normally see is through competitive activities. Over the years we've played a lot of tennis and volleyball with our clients. Besides being fun, these games have given us a chance to see interesting sides of our clients' personalities emerge. We get a good sense of how competitive they are. We get an inkling of how important winning, versus just having fun, is to them. And we get a good chance to see how they behave when things aren't going their way.

These three kinds of experiences—wrestling with major problems together, traveling together, and playing together—are important ingredients in the building of your relationships with your team members. Just as they have with us, these experiences bond you together. They give you a shared history. And sometimes they're the foundation from which long-lasting friendships are built.

**Your Relationships With Your Executive Team Members
Have a Tremendous Impact on the Quality of Your Life**
The experiences you have with your team members are certainly strong evidence you have important relationships with them. But maybe the strongest evidence of all is the powerful impact these relationships can have on the quality of your life. We see proof of this all the time. These relationships profoundly affect:

- Your financial well-being

- Your enjoyment of your work

- Your health

- Your family relationships

- Your view of yourself

Your financial well-being. Depending on the kind of organization you work for, the members of your executive team can have a huge effect on your annual income, and even on your overall financial well-being. If you work for a government agency, obviously this is going to be less of a factor than if you work for a small, privately held company where you and two other partners each own one-third of the stock. But even if you work for a large organization, the skills, the efforts, the personalities, and the attitudes of your team members can have a big effect not only on *your* financial well-being but that of the entire organization.

Here's a good example. Tom and Harry Dolman are brothers and run a manufacturing firm in New England that does about ten million dollars worth of annual sales. Tom is 55 and Harry is 40. Tom is so much older than Harry that he's been more like an uncle than a brother to him. In the late 60's, when their father died from cirrhosis of the liver, the business was barely limping along. Tom immediately took the reins and slowly turned the place around. In 1971 Harry came back from Vietnam and went to work for his brother. At that time Tom owned the entire company, but over the years he's been giving Harry stock so that the split is now 60/40.

The relationship between Tom and Harry was never terrific, but it's been especially strained over the last five years. Tom is a dominant and independent person who clearly inherited his father's charismatic personality, but also his tendency to be a heavy drinker. One afternoon we had a chance to interview Thelma Waters, a delightful woman in her mid-60's who'd been the company's office manager for over 30 years. She said:

> "It's not that Harry doesn't have a strong personality, because he does. It's just that Tommy has dominated him for as long as I can remember. And Tommy is not one to be questioned. If he wants to do something, he does it. And he doesn't ask for input from anybody, including his brother."

Several months later we had a conference call with both Harry and Thelma where an unusual story poured out. Recently, while Tom was overseas working on some mysterious business venture, Harry and Thelma got together and looked at Tom's files. They quickly discovered that over $500,000 earmarked for an employees' pension fund was missing. At the time of this writing the whereabouts of that money is still unknown. Tom has been prohibited by a court order from coming onto company property. And Harry has convinced the county prosecutor to hold off convening a grand jury in hopes he can find the missing funds on his own.

Your enjoyment of your work. If you're a member of an executive team, your job is probably demanding. You have a lot of responsibility. You're faced with challenging problems all the time. And there are always little crises and annoyances that creep into your day and disrupt your carefully laid plans. The quality of relationships you have with your executive team members can determine whether this challenging job of yours is fun, or a downright pain. Carline Fiera is an excellent example of this. Remember Bill Faulkner, the high-level civil servant from Chapter 1? Carline used to work with Bill on the same executive team. Both Bill and Carline had had an excellent working relationship with Ed Cravis before he unexpectedly decided to retire. When Lois Danforth replaced Ed Cravis, Carline immediately saw the handwriting on the wall:

> "After Lois had been on the job only a week, I knew I was going to have big problems with her. After two months, I knew I had to get out of there. I wasn't sleeping

well at night, and I began to hate the idea of going to work in the morning."

Frustrated and determined, Carline began a dogged search for another position within her agency. It didn't take long. Within a month, Lurleen Brown, a deputy secretary, asked Carline to come on as her head of operations. Carline's whole outlook on her work has changed dramatically:

> "What a difference! It's really ironic because I have a lot more responsibility and potential for stress in this job. This is a demanding position. But I absolutely love it. And it all boils down to the fact that Lurleen is an excellent boss, and Lois was a terrible one. And I'd say the biggest difference between the two of them is caring. Lurleen genuinely cares about how much I'm enjoying my job. Lois was so wrapped up in her own agenda that I don't think my enjoyment of my work ever crossed her mind."

Your health. Over the last 15 years there has been a big emphasis on the importance of leading a healthy life style. Books, newsletters, newspapers, radio and television programs frequently touch on the themes of eating right, getting enough exercise, not smoking, not abusing alcohol, and getting sufficient rest and relaxation. The two of us have taken all of this advice to heart. We don't lead spartan existences, but we try to do the basics. We work out. Our eating habits (except when we're on the road) are pretty good. Neither of us smokes. And we don't drink very much.

Some of our clients are as health-oriented as we are. They not only heed the advice on diet and exercise, smoking and consumption of alcohol, but they also have a healthy "glow" about them. Unfortunately, a lot of our clients have not gotten on this health bandwagon. Many of them never exercise. Some of them are way overweight. A surprising number of them still smoke. And more than a few abuse alcohol. We don't have hard, scientific data to back it up, but we strongly believe there's a correlation between the health of these clients and the quality of the relationships they have with their executive team members. Bad relationships, whether the context is a marriage or an executive team, can have poisonous effects on people. At the least, these bad relationships can cause people to look haggard and burned out. At the most they can make a strong contribution to life-threatening events like heart attacks and strokes.

Your family relationships. One of the most rewarding parts of our work is that we often get to meet the family members of our clients. Sometimes we get to meet them because we're working with a family business and these people are part of the executive team. But we often get to meet them (especially spouses) because we're interested in the perspective they can give us on our clients.

We've learned a tremendous amount from these family members. The children, the husbands and wives, and the parents of our clients have told us things about them we never would have learned otherwise. And one of the most important things we've learned from them is how they can be the unintended victims of poor executive team relationships among our clients. If you're struggling with somebody on your executive team, whether it's your boss or an equal partner or a troublesome employee, we know there's a damn good chance somebody in your immediate family is feeling the fallout of that poor relationship. Maybe it's because you're spending a lot of additional time at work trying to correct problems that result from that poor relationship. Or maybe you're too tired to spend the "quality time" you normally do with your spouse and kids.

Perhaps the most poignant example we've seen of how poor executive team relationships can affect family members occurred about ten years ago. In this case the executive team was simply a father and son who owned a small construction company in the Southwest. Dad was about 60, and his son was a little over 30. Neither of them called us in to help. Mom did. In a telephone conversation where her voice cracked with emotion, she said:

> "The two of them have always had a rocky relationship ever since Elroy, Jr. [the son] was in high school. Now it's more than rocky, it's downright awful. And it's affecting everybody in the family. But I think the person it's affecting the most is Josh, our grandson. About three months ago my husband said he didn't want to see Elroy and his wife anymore. It just made him too

uncomfortable. Now we don't see Josh anymore, either. He and I were very close. I miss him terribly, and I'm sure he misses me."

Your view of yourself. For the better part of this century, psychologists, psychiatrists, and other experts in the social sciences have been writing about the important effects that the relationship between parents and children eventually has on how children see themselves when they grow up. Simplified to its essence, the message goes like this: "Kids who have reasonably healthy relationships with their parents grow up to feel pretty good about themselves; kids who have unhealthy relationships with their parents often grow up to have poor self-concepts."

We agree. For example, we occasionally run into people who are quite average when it comes to intelligence or special skills or achievements. Yet these folks seem very comfortable and accepting of who they are as people. Unfortunately, we run into a lot more people who, in spite of considerable talent and achievement, *don't* have a very positive view of themselves. If we have a chance to find out about the family background of a person from the former group, we invariably learn he or she grew up in a loving, warm, supportive relationship with her parents. Conversely, if we have a chance to find out about the family background of a person from the much larger, latter group, we usually learn his or her parents were *not* consistently warm, loving, and supportive. In fact, they were often harsh and critical, if not abusive. Or they were distant and remote, if not neglectful.

Our work with executive teams and business partners has convinced us it's not only the relationships children have with their parents that have a major effect on how they see themselves as adults. We strongly believe the kinds of relationships people have as adults also has a lot to do with how they see themselves. We've met scores of women over the years, for example, who are married to insensitive, harsh, and verbally abusive husbands. And there's no doubt whatsoever that at least part of the reason these women feel so down on themselves stems directly from their lousy marriages. Another area where we see the powerful effect of adult relationships on how people view themselves is on executive teams. If you're on a team where your colleagues, for the most part, are caring and supportive of you, your view of yourself (at least as a professional person) is going to be different and more positive than if you work with colleagues who frequently criticize and tear each other down.

For example, we're currently working with two very different executive teams in the Northeast. One team runs the show of a medium-sized manufacturing firm whose members are mostly below the age of 40. At a team-building session we did with them several months ago, one of the young sales managers, Arlen, got a lot of feedback on how much he needed to work on his people skills. Arlen took this feedback to heart and has been working hard to be a better listener and, in general, to be more sensitive and understanding in his role as manager, colleague, and employee. All of Arlen's team members have noticed how hard he's been trying to change, and each has made a point to be supportive of these changes. All of them have gone to Arlen individually and said they appreciate how hard he's trying and to keep up the good work. And they've all told us how much more confident, self-assured, and composed Arlen seems to be, especially in situations where he normally would've acted like a bull in a china shop.

The other executive team is quite different from Arlen's. It's a group of medical doctors all above the age of 50. Each owns an equal share of the practice. But for the past five years they've designated Harry Cardozo as their managing partner. Harry was born in Argentina in 1937. When he was barely 10 years old, he and his family emigrated to the United States to escape the Peron regime. An extremely bright and motivated youngster, Harry charged through his academic career and graduated from medical school at the unusually young age of 23.

In addition to being a superbly talented physician, Harry is a good businessman, especially when it comes to marketing. He's been able to secure millions of dollars worth of contracts that none of his partners would have had the charisma and savvy to obtain. However, Harry tends to be self-centered and insensitive to the needs of his partners. Over the last year and a half, three of his four partners have formed an alliance against him. Once cheerleaders and supporters of all Harry's business development efforts, these three partners are now his detractors. They criticize him constantly behind his back, and frequently to his face. The group's weekly partner meetings, once reasonably cordial and civil affairs, have turned into "bitch" sessions where the three partners take up most of the time expressing their dissatisfaction with Harry. Valery, the only partner in the group who is still in Harry's corner, told us:

> "I'm very upset about all of this. When I first joined the group a few years back, Harry exuded confidence and self-assurance. But all of that has changed over the last 18 months. His whole sense of who he is as a professional has been severely shaken by the other three partners. He tries to mask it, but his eyes give him away. They show the deep hurt I know he feels."

Do You Act Like Your Relationships With Your Team Members Are Important?

Up to this point in the chapter we've argued that, if you're a member of an executive team, you're automatically involved in an important set of relationships. Now we want you to wrestle with a tough question: Are you acting like these relationships are important? If you're like the great majority of executive team members we've known over the last 12 years, an honest answer has to be, "No." Especially for any relationship with a team member where the two of you are not getting along.

But maybe we're wrong. Maybe you do act like these relationships are important. To help you decide, we'll take you through a list of six questions. After you read the questions and what we have to say about them, write down the names of everyone on your executive team. Then read through the questions again and try to answer them for each of your team members.

1. Do you show a genuine interest in what they want from their jobs and careers?

2. Do you show a genuine interest in the things that mean the most to them in their personal lives?

3. Are you "there" for them in times of crisis and during important life transitions?

4. Do you "check in" with them every now and then?

5. Do you offer to help them when they clearly need it?

6. Do you share as much of yourself with them as you can?

Do You Show a Genuine Interest in
What They Want from Their Jobs and Careers?

This is an especially important question if you're in the one-up position on your executive team. If you're the boss of the team (or have more power than most other members of the team), paying close attention to what your people want and need in their jobs and careers is a critical part of your job.

Unfortunately, very few bosses do this. Very few bosses take the time to find out what their employees are really looking for in their jobs and careers. And even fewer bosses make a genuine attempt to provide them with what they're looking for. Think about each of the members of your team. Have any valued employees left the organization recently or announced they are about to? Are people with a lot of talent and potential performing at a level far below where you think they should? If the answer to either question is yes, chances are you've failed to pay attention to something those individuals want or need in their job or career.

Several years ago, we were working with a consulting engineering firm in the Midwest. The president of the firm, Josh Thornton, was a bright and personable fellow in his early 50's. But Josh had a smug, "know-it-all" air about him that concerned us. We'd been working with the firm for about six months when one morning we walked into Josh's office to learn that Tray Browning had tendered his resignation. Tray was about ten years younger than Josh and one of the brightest members of Josh's executive team. In the 12 years he'd been at the firm, Tray had brought in five or six big clients who accounted for at least one-quarter of the firm's revenues. Josh was shocked: "I had no idea Tray was looking at other opportunities. I thought he was really happy and looking forward to a long future here."

For the rest of that morning and part of the afternoon we were busy doing a seminar with all the managers in the company. But late in the afternoon we got back together with Josh who was still shaking his head over what had happened with Tray. A young manager happened to be walking by Josh's office, and Josh called out to him to join us. As the young chap was sitting down, Josh said, "Jimmy, did you have any idea Tray was unhappy and wanted to leave?" Jimmy just grinned for several seconds and replied,

"You're kidding?" Josh said, "No. I'd like to know." Then Jimmy took a deep breath and said:

> "Geez, Josh, I thought you knew. He's been unhappy for at least 18 months that I know of. Probably longer. I thought you knew he wanted to set up his own division within the firm and that the two of you had been talking about that."

Tray's leaving was very painful for Josh. Tray not only walked away from the firm with some valuable clients, but he also took a number of key employees with him. It took Josh and his weakened firm a long time to bounce back from the loss of business and to replace the people who'd left. But the upside for Josh was that he learned an important lesson about being a boss and about maintaining good relationships with his team members. If you don't pay attention to their wants and needs in a job and a career, the consequences can be devastating.

**Do You Show a Genuine Interest in the
Things that Mean the Most to Them in Their Personal Lives?**
All the people on your executive team have personal lives that are very important to them. Most of them have spouses or romantic partners. Some of them have children. Some of them have parents or grandparents who are still alive. And all of them have passions, things in their lives about which they're keenly interested and probably daydream about. Sometimes these passions are their mates. Sometimes these passions are their kids. And sometimes these passions are simply leisure-time activities they adore, like playing golf or tennis, bird watching, playing in bridge tournaments, or whatever.

Even though we've been working with executive teams for quite a while, we're still surprised at what little interest many of our clients show in the personal lives, especially the passions, of their other team members. How about you? How much do you know about the family members of the people on your executive team? Do you know the names of their spouses? Do you know the names of their kids? Do you have any idea how their kids are doing in school or in their jobs or in their careers? What do you know about the leisure-time activities of your team members?

And how much interest do you show in all of these things? Do you ask questions that get them talking about their personal lives? And when they start talking, do you show more than a perfunctory interest in what they have to say?

Sadly, most of our clients can't answer yes to these questions. Now, you may be saying to yourself, "Well, this is very personal. I'm not sure I agree that people who have professional relationships really need to be talking about this kind of stuff." If that's how you feel, we'll try to convince you otherwise as you read through the book. But what's especially unsettling to us is that even members of family executive teams often don't show much interest in each other's personal lives. For the last seven years we've been working with a family business on the West Coast. The executive team consists of a father who's in his late 60's and two sons and a daughter, all in their 30's. During the time we've been working with them, Dad's wife—the mother of the three kids—has died and Dad has remarried. A couple of years ago the relationships between Dad and each of the kids were strained. As we thought, a big part of the reason for that strain had to do with the lack of interest Dad was showing in the personal lives of his kids, and vice versa. These are the kinds of things Dad was saying:

> "When Jane and I got married two years ago, it changed my life. It was no secret to the kids that my first wife and I were not happy and that we probably should've gotten divorced long ago. But what hurts, and it hurts a lot, is that none of the kids has made an effort to get to know Jane or to try to welcome her into the family. And it also hurts that they haven't been able to share in my happiness with Jane. I know they miss their mother terribly, but in missing her they seem to have forgotten about me."

And these were the kinds of things the three kids were saying:

> "We know Dad wants us to try to accept Jane and welcome her into the family. But that's hard to do when you see another woman move into the house you grew up in and completely redecorate it. But if Dad thinks we're ignoring Jane, he doesn't have any idea how it hurts us

the way he ignores our own children. Half the time he doesn't even seem to remember their names. He doesn't remember their birthdays. And he certainly doesn't show any interest in spending time with them."

Are You "There" For Them in Times of Crisis and During Important Life Transitions?

From time to time, all of us confront crises and make important transitions in our lives. People we love die. We get married. We get divorced. We, or people we care about, go into the hospital for serious operations. We get fired from jobs. We get hired into new jobs that take us from a region we grew up in to a part of the country we're totally unfamiliar with. And on and on. Life just wouldn't be life without these crises and transitions.

Right now, as you're reading this book, at least one of your executive team members is going through a significant life crisis or transition. Maybe you aren't even aware of it. In the last five years all of your team members, including you, have had to undergo one of these crises or transitions. If you were around during that period, what kind of support did you offer? Maybe you're an exception, but if you're like many of the people we've worked with over the years, you probably weren't "there" for them when they needed you. Take the small software house in the mid-Atlantic region that we worked with two years ago. Art Folger, now in his 40's, started the business in the late 70's. Art was an extremely talented systems analyst who got tired of working for one of the large computer firms and decided to go off on his own. By the mid-80's, Art had developed a number of profitable software packages for the mushrooming PC market. Art knew his strength lay in the software development arena and not in people management and business administration. Over the years he had taken on a number of investors who served as his board of directors and who offered lots of advice on business matters. At some point in the late 80's, Art's board told him he was an excellent software developer but his lack of managerial and administrative skills was hurting the business. They strongly suggested a competent CEO be found to run the company and that Art step out of his managerial role to spend all his time designing and developing software.

Within six months Sam Chavez was hired away from one of the big computer outfits to run the company. Soon after Sam's arrival, both he and the board told Art it would be much better for the company if Art stayed at home to do his creative work and came into the office as little as possible. Intellectually, Art knew this was the right decision. He knew if he continued coming into the office on a regular basis, Sam would have a tougher time running the company than if he stayed home and did what he did best.

We were brought in to help out after Sam had been on the job for about two years. It seemed Art was having a lot of trouble staying out of the office. When he did come in, he tended to make a nuisance of himself. He would second-guess all of Sam's decisions, and, if Sam was taking a route he didn't like, he'd walk around the office complaining to employees about the "big mistake" Sam had just made.

Many times when we work with troubled executive teams and partnerships, one of the team members is labeled the "bad guy." In this case, Art was clearly the bad guy. He had reneged on his agreement to stay out of the office and leave the day-to-day running of the business to Sam. Both Sam and several of the vice-presidents he'd recently hired were asking us, "Can't he see he's fouling things up by offering his unwanted advice and complaining we don't do things his way?" From Sam's point of view and that of his vice-presidents, it was a reasonable question. But what Sam and his vice-presidents couldn't see was that Art, in surrendering the helm of the business he'd built, was going through a terribly difficult transition. It was only when Sam saw that Art's situation was like a mother putting her child up for adoption (even if she knew adoption was the best thing), that Sam understood and sympathized with Art's situation.

Do You "Check In" with Them Every Now and Then?

Crises and major transitions work their way into all our lives, but they're not an everyday occurrence. Much more frequently, however, we have something on our mind that worries us or concerns us or distracts us. Maybe it's an unexpectedly large September statement from American Express. Maybe it's the right front fender of the Toyota our 16-year-old son dented but didn't tell us about until a week later. Maybe it's a 3-year-old who's just come down with strep throat. Or maybe it's the "wonderful" news that our health insurance premium will go up 30 percent come the first of the year.

These are life's small to medium-sized pains in the butt. When they happen, they don't have a devastating effect, but they preoccupy us. One of the things that helps immeasurably when we are preoccupied like this is having someone notice and say, "You look a little distracted. What's going on?" If the person just listens for a while, something special can happen. We have a chance to "vent." To get whatever is bugging us off our chests. The problem doesn't necessarily get solved, but we usually feel better, sometimes a lot better. Our burden has been lifted a little, and our psychic load seems lighter.

This is the kind of thing good friends do for each other. If you're the friend doing it, it doesn't take a lot of time and effort. But if you're the friend to whom it's being done, it's special. It seems like you've been handed a little gift just when you needed it. If you think about the good friends you've had in your life, you've probably done this kind of thing for them many times, and they for you. But what about the members of your executive team? Do you do this kind of thing for them? Do you notice when they're preoccupied or distracted by something and take the time to "check in" with them? We hope you do. But we bet you don't, or at least that you don't nearly as much as you could.

Do You Offer to Help Them When They Clearly Need It?

If your executive team is at all typical of the ones we work with, you and your team members are very busy. Maybe there are a few people on your team who don't pull their weight. But for the most part, you all work very hard. Like everything else in life, however, your work has its cycles. Sometimes you're busy, but you're not terribly busy. At other times you're stretched to the limits of your capacities, maybe a bit beyond. You've got some monster project with a deadline coming at you like a high-speed train. Or two or three problems have just cropped up that you never could have anticipated even a month ago. At times like these you—or some member of your team—need a helping hand.

The question is, are you there to offer some help? And by "help" we don't mean just being sympathetic, empathic, compassionate, and a good listener for your team member. We mean, are you there offering to pitch in and lighten the load? As busy as you are, are you willing to take on some of your team member's tasks to help him or her through this rough period? Once again, if you're like an awful lot of the executive team members we see, the answer is probably, "No." You don't offer to help out. A couple of examples:

The Investment Bankers. Several years ago we began working with an investment banking firm in Chicago that had four major partners. The firm had been up and running only five years, and it was doing extremely well when we were asked to come in. All indications were that it would continue to grow at breakneck speed. Gary Fustus was one of the four partners. He was in his late 40's and had spent the first 25 years of his professional life running companies not unlike the ones his firm was now investing in. After we'd been working with the firm a little over a year, Gary's performance started falling off. Several of the companies he'd identified as potential "winners" had turned out to be big "losers," and a couple of the other companies in his portfolio were dangerously close to going under. His three partners were so concerned that we were called in for a two-day partner "summit."

During the first day of the summit we learned a number of interesting things. One was that Gary had two "troubled" companies he was responsible for on the West Coast. He was spending a great deal of time out there trying to revitalize these organizations. In the meantime, the other companies he was in charge of were getting little of his attention. In his personal life Gary was also going through a rough time. He had a 14-year-old son who'd been thrown out of public school and was now about to get kicked out of the private school he was attending. His wife was becoming increasingly frustrated with his being away on the West Coast so much. And, to make matters worse, he was embroiled in a lawsuit with a neighbor over an accident in his swimming pool.

After we learned all this, we turned to the other three partners and said, "What have you guys been doing to help Gary out?" The uncomfortable silence and the downcast eyes told the tale. When Gary really needed their help, none of the three had gone to him and said, "Look, I know you're terribly overloaded. I'd like to help. What can I do?"

The Dermatologists. Early on in our work with executive teams we learned that what goes on in organizations is much more like what you read in novels than what you read in the business section of your newspaper or magazines like *Fortune, Business Week,* or *Inc.* A group of three dermatologists we worked with almost a decade ago is a good example. One Friday morning we were meeting in an Atlanta hotel suite with the doctors when the phone rang. It was the secretary who worked for all three of them. She asked to speak with Roger Ferragamo, a handsome chap in his mid-30's who had already established a national reputation as an expert on skin cancer. Roger wasn't on the phone more than 90 seconds before he shouted, "Oh my God!" What unfolded throughout the rest of the morning was a bit complicated, but here's the short version. Roger had been having an affair for the last five years with a young woman who was becoming increasingly frustrated at his reluctance to choose between her and his wife. Boiling over with anger at Roger, she had called his wife and disclosed everything. Shocked and enraged, Roger's wife had tried to reach him at the office. She had blurted out what she'd learned to Roger's secretary (who had been aware of the affair for a long time and was covering for him as best she could). The secretary had called Roger at the hotel suite to tell him what had happened and to warn him the boom was about to be lowered.

The next three months were tumultuous for Roger. At first, it looked like his marriage was over. But after a couple of weeks of anguish and soul-searching, he and his wife decided to make a go of it. He ended the affair, and the two of them started seeing a marriage counselor. This, of course, was a horribly stressful period for Roger. In addition to a busy professional schedule, he was facing things about himself and his marriage that were scary and threatening. But what was especially hard on him was the lack of support from his other three partners. Several months after Roger's crisis had erupted, one of them, feeling more than a little guilty, told us:

> "I'm still not exactly sure what was going on with the three of us. I guess we were just mad. For years we'd been telling him that the affair was stupid, that it was going to blow up in his face. But once he got caught and started trying to turn his life around, we should've gone

to him and asked how we could help out. How we could lighten his load. But none of us did."

Do You Share as Much of
Your Self as You Can with Team Members?

The two of us believe strongly that it's impossible to have a solid relationship with another person unless you're both willing to open up and share a bit of what psychologists call your "inner selves" with each other. And what does this mean? We think it means talking about important experiences and feelings (both positive and negative) having to do with your past, your present, and your future. Here are some examples of how people we've worked with have done this sort of thing with each other:

Out on the lake. It's May in northern New Hampshire and two partners from an architectural firm in Boston are chatting in an old rowboat as they hold fishing poles and sip beer in the fading sunlight. The conversation has slowly shifted from concerns about the business to family matters. Haltingly, and with some obvious embarrassment, one of the partners starts to open up about a 16-year-old son who has been a deep source of concern to him and his wife since the boy was 10. The other partner just listens. His colleague and friend starts to choke back tears as he describes how his youngster is about to enter a month-long rehabilitation program for cocaine addiction.

At the New Orleans convention. It's one-thirty in the afternoon and a woman of about 35 is seated on a couch in the hall of a large hotel with a man about ten years her senior. Both work for the same Chicago office. The man is listening intently while the woman talks. Sometimes the expression on her face is joyful, sometimes she seems on the verge of tears. She's telling him how proud she is to have been made a partner in the firm and how sad she is that her father (who died last year) wasn't around to see her do it. As she talks, it's more and more clear that her relationship with her father had its ups and downs. She loved him very much, and he was very proud of her, but he'd always put tremendous pressure on her to achieve. As a few tears start to flow, she whispers, "I think he would've preferred his only child to be a son."

6 P.M. in the conference room. It's a Thursday in mid-June in California. Everyone has left the office except two young managers on the executive team of a five-year-old retail clothing company that's about to go public. Both managers are blond and lean and look as if they spend most of their weekends either playing volleyball on the beach or surfing. The conversation has turned serious as one of the young fellows talks about the president of the company, an aggressive and talented woman just a few years older then they are. He says:

> "I don't know what it is about her. I've always seen myself as somebody with tremendous self-confidence. I guess some people even think I'm kinda arrogant. But I gotta tell you, this woman knows how to suck the confidence right out of me. I mean, I'll be busting my ass and thinking I'm doing a great job, and she'll walk into my office and make some cutting remark about a line of swimwear I've just bought, and whoosh, I feel like a little boy who's just been scolded by his mother."

Friday afternoon over lunch. It's two-thirty in Dallas in a large restaurant. Most of the other patrons have either headed back to the office or gotten a jump on the weekend. But at a table in a quiet corner two men in their late 40's are speaking softly. One is the president of a small publishing company and the other is his executive vice-president. The president looks tired but relieved. He's talking about how hard the last 18 months have been on him as he's scoured the country for funding for what has been a very profitable business but one with huge cash-flow problems. He says:

> "Jack, I know you're as happy as I am that we've finally sold the company. I think the deal we made is fantastic, and it's going to allow us to do things we never dreamed of even two years ago. But this past year and a half has been incredibly stressful on me and Jane. I was so focused on the business that I almost completely forgot about her, and I came very close to losing her. Maybe the biggest lesson I've learned from the sale of the company has nothing to do with business. It has to do with teaching me what's really important in my life."

Are you able to "open up" with at least one or two of your executive team members the way these people have? Unfortunately, too many of the folks we work with have trouble doing this. We hope you're an exception. But if you're not, if this sort of thing is hard for you, we'll offer some advice later on that should make it a little easier.

Why *Aren't* You More Relationship-Oriented?

After working with executive teams for a number of years, we came up with the term "relationship orientation." Relationship orientation simply means the extent to which relationships with other human beings are important (or not so important) to a person. The big point we've been making in this chapter, of course, is that you're probably not as relationship-oriented as you could be with the members of your executive team. *You* have to decide if we're right. Maybe you're a very relationship-oriented person and the problems you have with one or more of your team members are much more the result of *their* lack of relationship orientation than yours.

But let's say we're right. Let's say, after reading this far in the chapter, you've decided you don't treat your relationships with your team members as if they really are important. In this last section, we'll offer some thoughts on why you aren't more relationship-oriented than you are—at least with the folks who are such a big part of your business and professional life.

The Issue of Gender

Each year the two of us do a lot of speaking at the annual meetings of trade and professional associations that represent all different kinds of organizations—printers, metalworking companies, engineering firms, medical practices, high-level civil servants, and on and on. And when we look out at our audiences we see men. Even though career opportunities for women have opened up considerably in the last 20 years, it's still primarily a man's world when it comes to the people who are on the executive teams of America's organizations. We'd like to see this situation change just as fast as it possibly can. But it's a fact, nonetheless.

Here's another fact. Men in our society tend *not* to be relationship-oriented. It's the women in our society who are. To prove our point, try a little experiment. The next time you walk into a super-market, take a look at the covers of the magazines addressed to women—*Cosmopolitan*, *Mademoiselle*, *Working Woman*, *Ladies Home Journal*, etc. Try to find *one* issue of these magazines that doesn't have an article on how to improve or resolve problems in a rela-tionship. (It can be any kind of a relationship—between spouses, a parent and child, lovers, friends, a boss and employee, whatever.)

Now take a look at the men's magazines. You won't find many articles on relationships in *Car and Driver*. Or *Field and Stream*. Or *Guns and Ammo*. And you probably won't find many (if any) in the more sophisticated men's magazines, whether it's *Playboy*, *Gentlemen's Quarterly*, or *Esquire*. And you won't find them in the business magazines either, whether it's *Forbes*, *Inc.*, or *Fortune*.

As our society continues rapidly changing, this pattern will alter. There are already encouraging signs. Gradually, more and more women are entering the higher levels of management in organizations. And that's having a positive effect on the men. We've noticed, for example, that some of our male clients are much less embarrassed than they would have been ten years ago by their own tears, or those of the women they work with.

But the patterns of 5,000 years of Western Civilization won't reverse themselves overnight. Again, most members of executive teams are men. And most of those men are trained to be perfor-mance-oriented. They've been taught that it's how good they are at *doing* things—not how well they link up with other people—that really matters. And this overemphasis on success and under-emphasis on relationships shows up in the struggles they go through with their executive team members.

The American Business Climate

One reason you're not as relationship-oriented as you could be with your executive team members may be that you're a male. But another reason, regardless of your gender, has to do with the cul-ture of organizations in this country. The two of us have been part of this culture all our adult lives. We've observed it at close range. We've written about it. And we've read an enormous amount about it. Without the slightest doubt we can say that culture emphasizes success and achievement far more than it does the car-ing and humane treatment of people.

There are lots and lots of ways this organizational/cultural emphasis gets conveyed. Two good examples are how the performance of CEOs is measured and how being a "good" partner gets defined in a professional partnership.

If you have any doubts about how the performance of CEOs (especially in publicly traded companies or wholly owned subsidiaries) is measured, let us clear it up for you. They get measured by the bottom line. If their companies make or exceed their financial and profit goals, these CEOs get to keep their jobs and they usually get enormous bonuses. If they fail to meet these financial and profit goals, they usually get canned. It's about that simple.

We don't think there's anything particularly wrong with that kind of accountability. After all, if an organization doesn't make money, it can't survive very long. What *does* bother us, however, is the fact that these CEOs, as long as they're making money for their companies, can get away with treating the people who work in their organizations very poorly. Take Jack Welch, the chairman and chief executive officer of GE. Mr. Welch has made a lot of changes recently in the way he deals with people. But when he became president of this huge organization over ten years ago, it's not at all an exaggeration to say he was very hard on people. In fact, he quickly earned the nickname "Neutron Jack" for his wholesale firings and layoffs. More than one employee was quoted as saying, "Yeah, Jack walks into a building. When he walks out, the building is still standing, but the people are all gone." Another example of Mr. Welch's sensitivity to people during his early years as CEO of GE came in the form of a response to a reporter's questions about the stress of taking on such a big job at such a young age. Mr. Welch said, "I don't get ulcers, I give them."

Although Mr. Welch's reputation for dealing callously and uncaringly with his people was widespread, we have never heard of one instance where he was taken to task by either his board of directors or his stockholders for this kind of treatment. But we have read many accounts of how both the board and the stockholders were delighted with how Mr. Welch was able to keep GE profitable, especially at a time when other large manufacturers were feeling the severe crunch of foreign competition.

The unfortunate message that the example of Jack Welch sends to high-level managers is that relationships with the people you work with are relatively unimportant. In fact, you can behave very badly in those relationships as long as you "get the job done."

Several years ago on a drive between Hartford and Boston, we were wrestling with what being a "good" partner means in professional partnerships. We didn't agree on every measuring stick, but we did agree on the most important one: how much a partner is bringing into the firm. That one seems to overshadow all the rest.

And it's understandable. We know from our own practice that bringing in new clients and keeping old ones happy is absolutely essential to the survival of our partnership. But we also know that placing such heavy emphasis on bringing in business can cause serious problems among partners. It wouldn't be so bad if the only message being sent was that bringing in big bucks is more important than being a good team player. Unfortunately, however, there is usually a corollary message: As long as you're bringing in those big bucks, you can flaunt the rules of team play with near impunity.

Several years ago we worked with an engineering firm in the Midwest where one of the partners, Mike Hugo, was heeding this message. Mike was a physically imposing guy—about six feet four inches tall and 260 pounds. Very few of the ten partners in the firm liked Mike. One of them told us:

> "Mike's a classic bully. He's always intimidating people by standing up at meetings and pointing his finger and booming away with his foghorn delivery. If he doesn't agree with you, he'll interrupt and tell you you're full of shit. He's totally closed to any suggestions from us on how he could soften his style. He does what he damn well pleases."

When we asked why the other partners were willing to put up with that kind of behavior from Mike, he said:

> "I'll tell you why. Because Mike's got a big contract through one of his buddies in the construction business that accounts for at least 35 percent of our income. We're all afraid to buck Mike for fear he'd quit and take all that business with him. Because he's a bully, I don't

think he would. But none of us seems to have the guts to call his bluff.

This has been the first of five chapters where we offer reasons why your relationships with your executive team members may be more of a struggle and less satisfying than you'd like them to be. We've tried to make two major points. The first is that because you're a member of an executive team, you're automatically involved in some very important relationships. The second is that you're probably not treating those relationships as if they were important. In the next chapter we'll be talking about a tendency that all of us involved in important relationships have—to put the blame and responsibility for problems on the other person.

4

You Don't See How Big a Part of the Problem You Are

T he clients we work with vary a lot. They come from different ethnic backgrounds. They're located in different regions of the country. Some are highly educated. Some have barely made it through the eighth grade. Some are enormously wealthy. And some are stretched so thin they're on the verge of losing their homes as well as their businesses.

In spite of their many differences, however, these folks have a lot in common. And the thing they have most in common is what we'll be talking about in this chapter. It's their tendency to put all the blame and responsibility on other executive team members for the relationship problems they're having with those team members. We call this tendency "externalizing." We've never met anybody (including ourselves) who doesn't externalize when he or she is having a significant relationship problem with another human being. In the rest of this chapter we'll be concentrating on what it is you do when you externalize with your team members, why you do it, and why we think it's destructive. And it *is* destructive. Little you do gets more in the way of having good relationships with your team members than the tendency to externalize.

What Do You Do When You Externalize?

If you're like a lot of people we encounter, your reaction to the way we've defined externalizing may be a bit ho-hum: "Yeah, I guess you're right. I do that now and then. I guess we all do." That's the problem with abstract definitions. They aren't very interesting, and they don't bring concepts alive. To make the notion of externalizing more concrete, let's go back to two of the three power positions you may occupy on your executive team: the one-up position and the equal position.

When You're One-Up

Our work gives us an interesting look at bosses of executive teams. Here's how we usually run into them. The boss of some executive team gets in touch with us. Maybe it's the head of a family business who saw us speak at the annual trade association meeting in New Orleans. Maybe it's the managing partner of a public relations firm who heard about our work through a colleague we had worked with in the past. At any rate, it's always the boss of whatever executive team we work with that makes the final decision to bring us into the organization. By this point, we've talked to the boss several times by phone and probably at least once face to face. But so far we haven't talked to any of the other members of the executive team—the people who report to the boss. And what's fascinating is the one-sided picture we get from the boss about his or her team, *until* we talk to the other members.

Tom Rowan is an excellent example of all this. Tom got in touch with us because a member of his board of directors (also one of our clients) suggested we might be able to help out. Tom is in his early 40's and has a remarkable track record as a CEO for someone so young. When he called us in, he had just taken over the presidency of a fairly new retail company headquartered in Atlanta. The first stage of our work with Tom and his team involved individual interviews with him and each person who reported directly to him, including his secretary. Our first interview was with Tom over an early morning breakfast in our Atlanta hotel. We spent the next two days interviewing his team and then briefly checked in with him at the end of the second day just before heading back to the airport.

It was a fascinating experience. Our impression of Tom at the end of the second day was very different from the one we'd formed during our breakfast meeting. At breakfast, Tom looked and sounded the part of a highly successful young executive. He was tall, good-looking, and oozed the sort of leadership qualities you see in the photographs of CEOs in *Fortune* magazine. Tom told us his first six months on the job had been a real challenge. All of his staff, with the exception of his secretary, were about five years younger than he was and "energetic but inexperienced." He spent two hours telling us some of the things they did well and a lot of the things they *didn't* do so well. One of them was brilliant but had a drug and alcohol problem that kept him out of work a lot. One was a very competent financial manager but had no sense of vision for the company. One was a very creative marketing expert, but her fragile ego made her difficult to work with. And one showed a lot of potential as a merchandising manager but had the smugness and arrogance of many professionals under 30 who think they know more than they do. All of them, according to Tom, were reluctant to speak up and offer their opinions at staff meetings.

As our breakfast meeting was breaking up, Tom excused himself for a few moments to make a phone call. As soon as he was out of earshot, we both smiled. One of us said, "Sounds like a tough group." The other said, "Could be. Lets see what they have to say." And for the next day and a half we did. Here are some excerpts from those interviews:

> "Tom's a very bright and talented executive. But ever since he got here, he's been spending a lot of time raising money for a new expansion for the company. A lot of the time he's just not around when we need him."

> "Tom can be very intimidating. I don't know, maybe he told you he gets frustrated when we don't speak up at staff meetings. Well, did he also tell you he usually cuts us off when we do speak up and then tells us what *he* thinks?"

> "I've heard Tom talk a lot about how important it is for people like us, people who are in the highest levels of management in a company, to have vision, to have a sense of where the company is headed. I can't argue with that. But I'll tell you, I have no idea what Tom's sense of vision for the company is because he hasn't communicated that to us."

"It's a subtle thing, but sometimes I question how much respect Tom has for us as an executive team. Maybe he does respect us and just doesn't know how to show it. But all the talking he does about the 'stars' he had working for him in his last job doesn't help much. When he does that, he sounds like a lacrosse coach I had in college who would talk about all the talent he had to work with at a larger school where he used to coach."

These are just four examples of the many shortcomings the members of Tom's team identified in him as their leader. Tom never mentioned any of them to us over breakfast. Like all bosses, Tom could see the weaknesses and flaws in the people who reported to him. But what he couldn't do was see his own flaws and weaknesses and what a major role they were playing in the problems and frustration he was having with his team.

How about you? If you're the head of your executive team, you're probably pretty clear about how the people who report to you cause problems. But how clear are you about the problems you cause *them*? Lets say you're the founder of a family business. You're over 60 now, and plan to retire within the next several years. You have three kids working in the business. You'd like to hand them the reins and spend more time in that condo you and the wife bought about ten years ago. But you're afraid if you do the kids may run the business into the ground and destroy your retirement nest egg. You're very sure about what the kids' shortcomings are and how those shortcomings could eventually destroy something it took you decades to build. But how hard have you looked at your own shortcomings, both as a father and as a boss, as reasons why the kids may not be ready to take over the business? We bet you haven't looked very hard. We'd even bet you don't know what some of those shortcomings are.

When You're in the Equal Position
On most executive teams one or two people are in the dominant power position and everyone else pretty much takes their lead from them. On some teams, however, the power is shared more or less equally among the team members. This almost always occurs in partnerships (usually professional partnerships like law firms, medical practices, accounting firms, etc.) where each of the partners

owns roughly an equal share of the organization, and no one partner has a disproportionate amount of power over the others.

In these kinds of partnerships we certainly see the kind of externalizing we talked about in the previous section—where individual partners tend to see the shortcomings of fellow partners but not their own shortcomings. However, these equal partnerships are different from more typical executive teams where there's a clearly identified boss and then there's everybody else. On these more typical teams much of the externalizing goes on between the boss and each of the team members, and vice versa. In equal partnerships the power barriers aren't there. The externalizing in these partnerships seems more personal, more intimate. In particular, we've noticed three tendencies among equal partners when it comes to externalizing:

- Overvaluing your contribution to the partnership and undervaluing the contributions of your fellow partners.

- Criticizing your fellow partners for being different from you rather than appreciating and building on those differences.

- Clearly seeing your partners' sins against you but not your sins against your partners.

Overvaluing your contribution and undervaluing your partners' contributions. This is a common tendency among business partners who are struggling to get along. For each of them to think that what they're doing is more important, more critical and more valuable than whatever their fellow partners are doing, especially the ones they're struggling with. A classic example of this was a three-partner accounting firm we worked with in the late 80's. Up until her late 30's, Sally Conroy had dutifully worked for one of the old "Big Eight" accounting firms. If she had stayed on, she definitely would have been made a partner, but, as she put it, "I would have been so bored, moss would have grown over me." So, just shy of 40, she started her own business with Harold Wilkins, another accountant she'd known for almost 20 years.

Sally and Harold had decided to concentrate on a clientele of extremely wealthy individuals who have diverse incomes and need highly specialized tax advice. Sally had been able to attract several clients like this when she was working for her former firm, and she was convinced she could do the same thing when she went off on her own. She was right. Within a year of setting up the new practice, Sally and Harold had attracted enough customers to make their new venture look like it had more than a running chance at long-term survival. However, Sally and Harold were smart enough to know their strengths lay in the area of bringing in clients, not technical competence. They both understood tax law and tried to keep up with the many annual changes, but they knew they needed a "superstar" if they were going to keep their current clients and get new ones.

That superstar was Bud Thurston. Bud and Sally had become friends in New York about 15 years ago when they started out as "grunt" accountants in two different firms. Over these years Bud had developed a reputation as a "brainy" technical type who probably knew as much about tax law as anyone in the business. At first, it looked as though things were going to work out fine. Sally and Harold were the lively extroverts, good at going out and bringing in high-priced clients, and Bud was a genius at finding ways to keep the clients' money out of the hands of the tax collectors. But after Bud had been on board about six months, the relationship between him and Sally started to slide downhill. Sally noticed that Bud, normally quiet and shy, was becoming even more so. There had always been a warm side to Bud that seemed like it was cooling off rapidly. After talking it over with Harold, Sally took Bud out to lunch and, after a few unsuccessful attempts to loosen him up, bluntly asked what was bothering him. Much later on, Sally told us:

> "I had never seen Bud act like that before. He was so furious I thought he was going to tip the table over right in the middle of the restaurant. He proceeded to tell me how, if it weren't for him, the firm would have gone under. That bringing in the clients—what Harold and I were doing—was the easy part. What he was doing—figuring out how to save them all that money—was the hard part. And he thought the way we had figured out the stock ownership of the firm was grossly unfair to him."

Sally just shook her head and didn't say anything for about a minute and a half. After a long sigh she went on:

"At first I was shocked, and then I felt this rage starting to build up inside me. But I knew that the two of us getting furious at each other in the restaurant would be a disaster. So I just listened until he finally wound down, and then I said we should talk about it later. But we had that lunch over two months ago, and I'm still upset. What I wanted to say to Bud, and I still do, is that, yes, his knowledge and expertise is incredibly important to the firm. But what he seems to have conveniently forgotten is that there would not be a firm if Harold and I hadn't taken all the risks to start this business. Bud didn't take those risks. He moved from one job with a guaranteed salary to another job with a guaranteed salary. It's inconceivable to me that he doesn't understand that."

We eventually got Sally, Bud, and Harold together and made them pay attention to some rules of "good talking" and "good listening" that we'll discuss later in the book. It wasn't easy, but once they were able to communicate effectively, they started respecting and understanding the important contributions each of them was making to the firm.

Criticizing your partners' differences rather than appreciating them. As we mentioned earlier, about a decade ago we wrote an article called, "Why Can't My Partner Be More Like Me?" Whenever we mention that article to people who share equal ownership in a business partnership (or to husbands and wives), we get knowing laughs and smiles. The message both types of partners— business and marital—too frequently send to each other is this: "My style, my approach, my way of doing things is the best. If only you could do things my way, we'd be so much better off."

We could use any number of former clients as an example of this phenomenon. But it might be more interesting and helpful to you if we used ourselves. Especially since we've been as guilty of this tendency as our clients. Because we've been working together since our graduate-school days 20 years ago, our pool of examples for this type of externalizing runs deep. But one example seems to stick out above the others—maybe because it caused us so much pain and frustration for so long. It's our collaborative writing.

The trouble began somewhere in the late '70s after we had gotten a contract to write our *Problem Employees* book. We'd collaborated on writing projects before, but this was our first book, and we were taking it very seriously. Things seemed to go well in the beginning when we were drawing each other out on chapter topics in front of a tape recorder. We've always enjoyed that part of our writing. We can range far and wide with our ideas, but we don't have to worry about pleasing an editor or an audience. But when each of us went off on his own to compose chapters based on the tapes, we noticed striking differences in our styles. When we got together to discuss what we'd written, the conversations would go like this:

> **Peter:** Your stuff is frustrating to read. It's way too wordy and you introduce too many ideas too fast and without enough transition and development. And you don't use headings very often, so it's hard to see where you're going. I don't have the patience to wade through stuff like that.

> **Mardy:** Well, I think what you wrote lacks flair and passion and enthusiasm. Maybe I go on and on too much, but you don't go on and on enough. You mention a great idea, but then you don't explore it! Maybe what I write doesn't conform to all the rules of good English, but at least it sounds real.

> **Peter:** Maybe, but at least I don't repeat things ad nauseam the way you do. So many times you develop an idea with a good example and then, a few paragraphs later, I see the same point with another example, sometimes longer and more involved than the first one. Then I'm saying to myself, "What the hell is going on here? I thought we just covered that!"

> **Mardy:** Yeah, well I'll tell you what I think. I think you're more concerned with how things get said than the ideas themselves. Hey, what's more important here? The form or the substance? I know what I'm gonna vote for!

It was about 14 years ago when we had our first conversation like that. From our work and from just maturing as people, we've learned a tremendous amount about how to be better partners to each other. More and more, we've learned to value and take advantage of our differences, rather than see them as liabilities in each other. But there's still a little voice in both of us (especially when we disagree about something) saying: "Why can't you be more like me?"

Seeing your partners' sins against you but not your sins against your partners. We said earlier that the relationships between equal partners are often more personal and intimate than those on more typical executive teams. One of the ways this personal, intimate side shows up is in how partners view "wounds" they inflict on each other. What happens goes something like this: Partner A does something that bothers, upsets, or frustrates Partner B. Partner A is completely unaware he's done anything "wrong." In the meantime, Partner B has done something to upset or hurt or injure Partner A. And he's just as unaware of what he did to Partner A as Partner A was unaware of what he did to Partner B. At some point Partner A and Partner B get together to talk about the "problem." Partner A tells Partner B the hurtful thing Partner B did to him. Partner B then has several reactions. He's surprised Partner A could have taken whatever he did so "personally." He ducks any real responsibility for what he did by saying he didn't intend to hurt Partner A and that Partner A misunderstood his motives. Then he brings up something Partner A did to him that he finds just as hurtful as what Partner A accused him of doing. Partner A then responds in similar fashion, and on and on it goes.

An example. Not long ago we worked with a couple of partners, Barbara Barker and Louise Hellman, who run a successful, high-volume dermatology practice in Michigan. Barbara, the founder, is a very capable physician, but she's even more talented as a leader and an entrepreneur. Several years ago, Barbara brought Louise into the practice and soon made her an equal partner. Once we were brought in to help them work out their differences, it didn't take long to learn how each felt she'd been wounded by the other. This is a condensed version of what Barbara told us:

"Louise is a very talented doctor. There is *no* question in my mind about that. But she has a volatile temper, especially when she's under stress. And when she blows, she can say *very* hurtful things to me, to members of our staff, and even to our patients. I can't tell you the number of hours I've spent mopping up the tears Louise has caused around this place."

When we talked to Louise, she never once mentioned her bad temper. But she did have some very specific things to say about Barbara:

"I'm supposed to be an equal partner in this practice. And on paper I am. But I don't feel like an equal partner. Barbara has lots of ideas about where she wants to take the practice. But it's pretty obvious she doesn't want my involvement in those kinds of decisions. And I actually think she's sneaky about it. She'll spend maybe three or four weeks thinking out very carefully where she wants to go with an expansion or marketing idea. And then all of a sudden, at a partners meeting, she'll ask me what I think we should do. Well, obviously I haven't had a chance to think about it so I don't have a whole lot to say. And then all of a sudden she's pulling out all these charts and graphs, and I'm sitting there thinking I'm a fool if I believe this woman sees me as an equal partner in spirit."

We eventually got the two of them together to talk. When Barbara confronted Louise about her temper, Louise was genuinely surprised her outbursts had been so hurtful to Barbara and some of the staff and patients. She tried to understand what it was like to be on the receiving end of her outbursts, but her responses showed she really wasn't getting the message:

"I guess I do have a pretty bad temper, and when I get angry I guess I can say things I really don't mean. But you all need to understand that's just my way and all I'm doing is blowing off steam."

In the same vein, Barbara tried to understand the detrimental effect she had on Louise when she'd go off on her own to think and plan for a decision that had long-range implications for the practice. Like Louise, Barbara's responses showed she was having a tough time seeing things from her partner's perspective:

> "Well, I don't mean to keep Louise out of the decision and planning loop. But she doesn't seem interested in talking about the future of the practice, long-range projects, and that sort of thing. A couple of times I've tried to get her to sit down and do that with me, but she always has some excuse about why now is not a good time. It's hard to feel sorry for her about being left out of decisions and planning when she keeps giving out these signals that she doesn't want to get involved in it."

Why Do You Externalize?

So, externalizing is a very common tendency among members of executive teams. Our clients do it. We do it with each other in our own partnership. And you and your team members do it with each other. But why? Why are we so prone to do something that doesn't do any apparent good and has the potential for doing so much harm? In this section we'll talk about four reasons why people externalize. As you read through the reasons, try them on for size; see how well they fit you and your situation. We bet you'll come up with some other explanations for why all of us in significant relationships (not just with executive team members) are more likely to point the finger of blame at the other person rather than at ourselves.

It's Hard for Us to Put Ourselves in Each Other's Shoes

We live in a world where blaming and finger pointing are what people in conflict do. The history of civilization indicates people have never been good at putting themselves in each other's shoes. All the armed conflict we've ever had in the world can be at least partly attributed to the fact that one group failed to see things from the perspective of another. Imagine, for example, how the massive carnage of our own Civil War might have been avoided if the North had tried to see the tremendous economic and social threat the abolition of slavery posed to the South. And if the South had tried to see how abhorrent slavery and the prospect of severing the Union was to the North. Or more recently, think of the last 45 years of struggle between the State of Israel and its Arab neighbors. Imagine how different things might have been had the Arabs tried to understand the tremendous importance to the Israelis of that tiny strip of land on the edge of the Mediterranean. Or had the Israelis tried to sense the rage of millions of Palestinians at having been forced into squalor and treated like pariahs by their occupiers.

History seems pretty clear. Whenever two or more people or groups of people disagree about something, the natural tendency is not to try to see things from the other person's point of view. The natural tendency is to assume the other person is all wet, off base, and doesn't know what the hell he or she is talking about.

It's Easier to See Another Person's Faults and Shortcomings than It Is to See Your Own

Part of the reason we all externalize so much has to do with the anatomy of our senses, especially our vision. Physically we're built to see the rest of the world, not ourselves. Except for a few moments in the morning when we shave or put on our makeup, we're observing other people, not ourselves. If we spend a lot of time around those people (as we do with executive team members and spouses and children), we get to observe them in all kinds of situations. We see them do some things well, and some things not so well. We gather a lot of data on them, and eventually we become experts on them as people.

However, we don't get the same opportunity to observe and become experts on ourselves. We can make assumptions about how we'd look if we had a chance to get out of our bodies and see ourselves the way others do, but that's all we can do—assume. But those assumptions can be way off base. If you've ever been videotaped in some sort of casual, unrehearsed situation, you probably remember how different you looked and sounded from the way you *thought* you were coming across. Over 20 years later, the two of us can clearly recall our shock and surprise when we saw ourselves on tape for the first time in a project we were running in graduate school. Unfortunately, we can't go through our days being videotaped, and we can't sit down at six in the evening to review those tapes. If we could, we'd all spend much less time putting so much blame on people we're having relationship problems with.

It's Painful to Look at Your Own Faults;
It's Not So Painful to Look at Someone Else's
For thousands of years philosophers, theologians, and other observers of the human condition have been talking about how hard it is for people to see and admit to their flaws and weaknesses. Playwrights and novelists down through the centuries have been doing the same thing. Most of the Greek dramas written before the birth of Christ are a good example of this. These stories are often centered around the agonizing pain experienced by the protagonist when he or she ultimately comes to terms with a "tragic flaw." These same thinkers have also pointed out how relatively painless (even enjoyable) it is to look at the flaws and faults of others. (If that weren't the case, tabloid publications like the *National Enquirer* wouldn't have the astronomical circulation figures they do.)

For the last 18 months we've been experimenting with an instrument that has reminded us of the pain involved in looking at our own flaws and the relative lack of pain in looking at the flaws of other people. We call it the *Executive Team Profile*. This is not a complicated tool. It consists of 25 statements that can be answered "yes" or "no." Here are a few examples:

- is a good team player

- is a good listener

- will admit mistakes and apologize when wrong

- is level headed, even under stress

- has good "people" skills

We ask each member of the team to fill out the *Executive Team Profile* on every other member of the team. We also ask employees who are not on the team (but who are well acquainted with its members) to fill out the instrument for each team member. We're the only ones who know how a particular employee or team member rated another team member. In the course of our work with the team, we sit down with each member individually and go over the number of people who checked either "yes" or "no" about him or her for each of the 25 statements.

For some people, the results are a shock. For example, not long ago we worked with a group of 11 people. That meant each team member was being rated on each of the 25 items by ten other people. One of the individuals on the team, a hard-working chap in his late 30's, got ten "no's" in response to the statement, "has good people skills." It's not an exaggeration to say he was devastated. He'd operated for years assuming he had reasonably good people skills and this news pulled the emotional rug out from under him. (Happily, he took this information to heart and started working hard to change the way he dealt with people, not only at work, but at home as well.)

Even though "bad marks" on the *Executive Team Profile* can cause the individual who gets them pain and consternation, those marks don't have that kind of effect on the other team members. In the case we just cited, some of the team members of this young manager heard about his concern over his ratings. They said things like: "Hey, I'm glad this happened. I don't like to see the guy in pain, but maybe this got his attention and maybe he'll change."

We Gravitate to People Who Reinforce
Rather than Challenge Our Externalizing
The fourth and maybe the biggest reason people externalize is that all of us gravitate to people who reinforce rather than challenge our externalizing. For example, forget about executive teams for a moment; think about the romantic side of your life. Let's say you're a man and you're involved in an intimate relationship with a woman. Maybe you're married, maybe you're living together, or maybe you're just dating. And let's say you're having trouble in your relationship with this woman. If you're like most people, you're going to see the woman, not yourself, as the big reason for the problems. Now, who do you go to to release pent up feelings and to vent your frustration over the problems you're having? Is the person you seek out someone who's going to challenge your one-sided view of the problem and make suggestions for how you need to change? Or is that person someone who will largely sympathize with you? Someone who will say things like:

"Tom, I don't know how you put up with her. I don't think she really appreciates how difficult a person she is and how lucky she is to have you. Most guys would have taken a hike a long time ago. I'm surprised you've stuck it out this long."

What you probably wouldn't do is go to someone who might say:

"I hear what you're saying, Tom. And I can sympathize with you. But how about looking at things from her perspective. I know you pretty well, and I know you're not the easiest person to get along with. I'll be frank with you. She's a big part of the problem, but so are you."

Even though it would be helpful to talk to someone like this, you don't want to. You want to talk to someone who is sympathetic to your point of view and who'll agree with you. People on executive teams are the same way. In the early 80's, we began working with a company in the Midwest where this sort of externalizing among team members had become a major problem. It was an envelope manufacturing company that had been a family business for three generations. Chuck Taylor, the operating superintendent of the company, had been working there for 35 years. He came on board about the same time as the company president, Harry Gold, the grandson of the founder.

Harry and Chuck had never gotten along well, but Harry's father had always liked Chuck and made sure Chuck continued to get raises and promotions in spite of Harry's objections. Once Harry's father retired, everyone thought Harry might get rid of Chuck. Harry didn't do that; he wasn't good at firing people. But as time passed, Harry found Chuck an easy target for a lot of the company's problems. Plus, Harry had two or three vice-presidents who were very sympathetic to his view of Chuck. We weren't fully aware of how bad this problem had gotten until one day we called the company trying to reach Harry. His secretary, a no-nonsense, candid young woman who had read our *Problem Employees* book, said:

"I'm sorry [chuckling a bit], Harry and his vice-presidents are in his office . . . ah . . . what's the term you use in your book? Externalizing, yeah, that's what they're doing. They're all in there externalizing about Chuck. It goes on at least once every two weeks around here."

What Harry was doing with his vice-presidents is all too common—members of an executive team getting together and complaining about another team member. They can spend hours and hours talking to each other about what a problem a particular team member is and never bring up how they might be contributing to the problem. All they do is solidify the misconception that the "problem" team member is completely at fault and they're blameless.

Why Is Externalizing Bad?

Externalizing is a very understandable human tendency. All of us do it. But more and more we've come to see how unproductive and destructive it can be. There are at least three reasons for this:

- When you externalize, you deny reality.

- Rather than bringing you together, externalizing pushes you and your team members apart.

- Externalizing prevents you from growing after a failed relationship.

When You Externalize, You Deny Reality

Let's say you're having a relationship problem with one of your team members or with your spouse or with a child. And let's say you're putting the lion's share of the blame for that problem on the other person's shoulders. You're denying reality. It may seem like the other person is completely at fault and that you're just a victim. But there's another side of the story. There's another perspective that probably has as much merit, as much validity as your perspective.

An excellent example of this happened about ten years ago. The wife of the founder of a family business in a southern state had read an article about our work in *Inc.* magazine titled "Sparring

Partners." She was so concerned about the problems her son and husband were having that she insisted they give us a call. They did, and within ten days we were headed south.

This was an unusual way for us to get hired by an organization. Normally we meet at least one of the principals ahead of time. Since that wasn't possible, we were looking forward to meeting Dad and Son face to face. We met Dad first in a hotel suite near the company's offices and interviewed him for nearly three hours. During that time he took his son apart in convincing fashion. He talked about what a defective business partner his son had been and how ungrateful the young man had been to the father who was going to hand him a profitable business. Dad's descriptions were compelling. Every time he'd make a criticism, he'd back it up with specific examples. At no time during the three hours did Dad mention anything he might be doing to contribute to the problems with his son.

Just before noon we sent Dad on his way; we were to meet with his son at one-thirty. Over lunch we began to wonder about the son. Maybe he was as bad as his father was making him out to be. After all, sometimes kids in family businesses who have everything handed to them can be troublesome and ungrateful. We decided to wait and see.

At one-thirty in walks the son. He was a tall, pleasant-looking fellow in his early 30's with a friendly, easygoing way about him. He didn't look at all like the bizarre individual his father had been describing a few hours earlier. Just as we did with Dad, we listened to the son for about three hours. And we got an earful. We heard how cantankerous and rigid and overbearing a boss and business partner Dad was. But the son didn't limit his critique of his father to their ten-year business partnership. He took us back almost 20 years to tell us what a strict and demanding parent Dad had been through the son's stormy adolescent years.

The next morning we met for an hour each with three different women: Mom (wife of the founder and mother of the son), Daughter-in-law (wife of the son), and the office manager who'd worked for both the father and the son for the last five years. An interesting morning to say the least. After listening to the mom and daughter-in-law, we came up with what we now call the "Tammy Wynette, Stand By Your Man" syndrome. Because that's what both of them did. It was clear Mom dearly loved her son, but she was basically on Dad's side. Dad was the good guy; the son was the problem. And the daughter-in-law did much the same thing in reverse. Dad was the impossible one; the son, her husband, had the patience of Job to put up with such a difficult business partner for so long. In fact, she made only one really negative comment about her husband:

> "I knew my father-in-law was a difficult person the very first time I met him. And I can remember when my husband said he was thinking about going into business with his father. I told him that was one of the stupidest ideas I'd ever heard of. But do you think he'd listen to me? No!"

Finally, we got to meet the office manager who had worked for both Dad and Son for years. That was enlightening. Unlike Dad, the son, the mom, and the daughter-in-law, this young woman had no axe to grind. She told us where both men were strong, where both men were weak, and where both had glaring flaws. Listening to her, we could see how distorted and lopsided the stories were that we'd gotten from the two of them. After we thanked her for her time and candor, she left with a big grin and a, "Good luck with those guys!" For a minute or so after she left, we were shaking our heads and chuckling. Then one of us said:

> "You know what? I feel a little like a detective who's been called in right after an armed robbery. I've talked to four eyewitnesses who've given me four very different accounts of what happened. And then, almost magically, someone hands me a videotape where I can replay what happened from a bunch of different angles the way they do with sports on TV. And finally I see the truth."

Ever since that experience we've always tried to interview a few of the employees who work for our clients, but who aren't directly involved in the turmoil. Each time we do, we realize what a valuable perspective they have on our clients' problems. And we realize how all of us (not just our clients) distort reality when we externalize.

Externalizing Consumes
Colossal Amounts of Unproductive Time
As consultants we've spent hundreds and hundreds of hours listening to our clients externalize about each other. As individuals outside of our professional roles, we've spent thousands and thousands of hours listening to acquaintances and friends and family members externalize about people they were struggling with. Long ago it became clear to us that executive team members (and other people in important relationships) waste a lot of time talking to anyone who will listen about what a "bad" guy the other person is. But as much time as people waste in verbally externalizing, we're convinced they waste much more time mentally externalizing. For example:

— It's eight o'clock in the evening in a large office building. Victor Spellman has reread the same page of a tax law book for the tenth time. He can't concentrate because he's busy upsetting himself about a partner in his accounting firm who's spending too much time with a new girlfriend and far too little time on the tax returns of important clients as April 15th rapidly approaches.

— Andy McMahon tosses and turns from one a.m. until four a.m. as he frets over how rigid and authoritarian his new boss, the senior vice-president for marketing is.

— Seventy-year-old Carl Hansen is lying on a beach and gazing out at the turquoise blue of the Caribbean. But he's not enjoying the tranquility of this special part of the world. For the ten-thousandth time he's reminding himself how insensitive and selfish his oldest son was when he finally came to his father and told him he could no longer work in the family business.

— Sheila Prescott is riding in a chairlift somewhere in Colorado on a February morning. The man seated next to her points out the awesome beauty of the snow-covered Rockies as she nods her head. But her mind is 2,000 miles to the east thinking about that "rotten" undersecretary who once again embarrassed her in a staff meeting three days ago.

Externalizing Prevents You
from Growing After a Failed Relationship

One of the many unfortunate aspects of externalizing is that it doesn't cease with the end of a relationship. If anything, externalizing seems to kick into high gear once an important relationship has failed. Divorces are a good example. If you haven't been through one yourself, certainly you know people who have. Remember the bitterness and resentment you or your friends felt after the split-up? Sadly, sometimes that bitterness and resentment lasts for years, even decades.

Divorced people are not the only ones to carry their externalizing on into the future after the breakup of a relationship. We see it all the time in our work. But rather than hear our examples, think about some of the famous people who've left executive teams and who've externalized in writing about former colleagues and team members. Have you read Lee Iacocca's autobiography? He certainly has a lot of interesting and persuasive things to say about how difficult and unreasonable a boss Henry Ford was. And a lot of them sound exactly like the kinds of externalizing we've heard from our clients over the years. For example, here are some direct quotes from his extremely interesting book[1]:

- "It was the superficial things that counted for Henry. He was a sucker for appearances. If a guy wore the right clothes and used the right words, Henry was impressed. But without the right veneer, forget it."

- "When it came to the board (of directors of the company), he more than most CEO's, believed in the mushroom treatment—throw manure on them and keep them in the dark."

- "The way I saw it, Henry was always a playboy. He never worked hard. He played hard. What he cared about was wine, women, and song."

- "Liquor destroys all inhibitions and out comes the real man. So beware: this guy is mean!" [This is what Iacocca said his wife Mary told him about Ford, after observing Ford at a party. (Remember our "stand-by-your-man" illustration?)]

---

[1] From Iacocca: An Autobiography by Lee Iacocca with William Novack, NY: Bantam, 1984, pp. 103, 110, 113, 114 and 116, respectively.

- "That's when I realized I was working for a real bastard. Bigotry is bad enough . . . but Henry was more than a bigot. He was also a hypocrite."

- "It was incredible. One man with inherited wealth was making a shambles of everything, launching a company on three years of hell just because he felt like it. Guys were drinking too much. Their families were falling apart. And nobody could do a thing about it. This juggernaut was running amok."[2] [On Ford's behavior at the height of their struggle with each other.]

This is only a sampling of the negative things Iacocca had to say about Ford in his book. To our knowledge, Ford hasn't written a book where he discusses Iacocca as frankly as his former employee discusses him. We'd like to read what *he* has to say.

What about Iacocca's assessment of his own contributions to the problems he was having with Ford? We read the book carefully and about the only thing we could find was the rhetorical question, "If I was so unhappy at Ford, why didn't I just take a walk?" The answer, he says, was not complicated. He loved the work, even though he hated the guy he worked for. And the thought of giving up the money, the status, and the perks was painful:

> "I was also greedy. I enjoyed being president. I liked having the president's perks, the special parking place, the private bathroom, the white-coated waiters. I was getting soft, seduced by the good life. And I found it almost impossible to walk away from an annual income of $970,000. Although I was the number two man at the number two company, I was actually earning more than the chairman of General Motors. I wanted that $1 million a year so much that I wouldn't face reality."[3]

We don't offer this example to ridicule or disparage Iacocca. However, if we ever had any illusions that people at the very top of America's largest corporations did things more maturely than their small business counterparts—when they're struggling with a

---

[2] Ibid., p. 125.
[3] Ibid., p. 127.

colleague, this book set us straight. The captains of industry do exactly what our clients (and we) do when they describe an important relationship struggle; they externalize like crazy!

What's particularly unfortunate about all this externalizing— whether it's famous people like Iacocca doing it, or your recently divorced best friend—is that it stops these folks from growing after their failed relationships. Take yourself as an example. Imagine you were on a high-level executive team in your company and you were fired by a boss you'd never gotten along with. Or imagine that you and a former business partner had gone through an emotionally and financially expensive breakup of your firm. If you like, you can amass piles of evidence on how badly you got screwed. You can build an enormously persuasive case about what a difficult and unreasonable and rigid business partner you had for all of those years. You can feel all of the righteous indignation you want to. But that kind of thinking won't buy you much. In the long run, what will help is to examine your contribution to the demise of that relationship. You won't want to do that. But as hard as it is to do it, the payoff in terms of your personal and professional growth can be enormous.

5

You Avoid Confrontation

I n addition to externalizing, what's another big reason members of executive teams have trouble getting along with each other? They simply avoid discussing relationship problems that cry out for discussion. In fact, if executive team members didn't have this massive tendency to avoid confronting tough relationship issues, we might have to find another line of work. Usually when we get called in, it's because the members of an executive team have continuously avoided sitting down face to face with each other to talk out those problems.

In this chapter we'll describe *what* avoiding is, why all of us have a tendency to do it, and why we think it's such a destructive tendency in all important relationships.

What Is Avoiding?

We've been thinking about the tendency to avoid for a long time and our thoughts are always evolving. But as much as we've learned about it over the years, it still leaves us shaking our heads. Right now, however, we see two major kinds in the work we do with executive teams: chronic avoiding and acute avoiding. We'll look at both types in terms of the one-up position, the equal position and the one-down position.

Chronic Avoiding

Chronic avoiding is something all of us do in our important relationships—whether with our spouses, our children, our executive team members, or our good friends. It's really a form of procrastination. We know we should sit down periodically with these people and talk meaningfully about how our relationships are going and what we can do to improve them. But we don't do it. We treat these periodic relationship "get-togethers" like we do regular physical exercise or flossing our teeth. We should do 'em, but there's always some convenient excuse to put 'em off. Of course, the kind of chronic avoiding you do on an executive team depends somewhat on your power position.

When you're in the one-up position. If you're the boss of your executive team (or hold some important leadership role on that team), we think one of your most important responsibilities is sitting down regularly with each team member to have what we call a "relationship improvement session." All that means is the two of you meet regularly (probably about every three months) to discuss what you both can do to make your professional relationship as satisfying and productive as possible. Doing this kind of thing with each person who reports to you goes well beyond the concept of "people management" that appears in the thousands of books and articles written on the subject. We call it "relationship management."

If you're like most heads of executive teams, you chronically avoid this important part of your job, just like Don Garber. We've known Don almost ten years. We met him after giving a seminar when he was an up-and-coming senior vice-president in a large construction company. Don liked a lot of the things we had to say and would have hired us immediately except for one thing: his boss, Jack Sondheim. Don said:

> "Jack would never go for the kind of thing you guys do. He's a few years away from retirement, and he's just too old-fashioned and rigid to see the value of the softer things in business that you fellas think are important."

But Don made it clear to us that if he ever became president of the company he'd bring us in to work with him and his team. Well, about five years later, that happened. Don was made president of the company. Unfortunately, however, his promotion was handled very badly by Jack. Jack had put Don in a three-way contest for the presidency along with two other senior vice-presidents who were both older than Don and had been employed by the company much longer. Jack kept the three of them in suspense until one day he called them into his office as a group. With a granite expression on his face Jack said: "You know I think all three of you are very capable. But in any contest, there's only one winner and the rest are losers. Don is the winner."

A few weeks later Don told us it had been one of the worst experiences in his professional career: "It should have been a happy day for me, but it wasn't. It was a stupid and clumsy way to handle a delicate situation. I still feel terrible for those two guys."

A few months later we got Don together with the two senior vice-presidents who'd been passed over. In those meetings each of the three had a chance to talk candidly about how badly they felt the promotion process was handled. They also talked about the need to put the experience behind them and pull together as a team for the good of the company. After those meetings, we stressed to Don how critically important it was for him to meet regularly, on an individual basis, with both guys. Some of the damage that was done had been repaired, but not all of it. Those two fellows still harbored a great deal of bitterness and resentment toward Don, and he needed to spend lots of time with each of them to build and maintain healthy relationships. We warned him that things could go sour very fast if he didn't do this.

Don agreed with us and said he'd heed our advice. But he didn't. We know he wanted to, but this sort of "relationship" stuff didn't come easily to him. And like all of us, Don spent his time doing what he was comfortable at and good at: bringing in big contracts for the company.

As we predicted, the relationships between Don and his senior vice-presidents slowly deteriorated. Two guys who might have become Don's supporters became his detractors. Frustrated and disillusioned, Don eventually took a job as president of a competing company. At this writing, we're trying to convince Don not to repeat the same mistakes in his new position.

When you're in the equal position. The chronic avoiding we see on executive teams where power or ownership are equally shared is a bit different from the kind we see on teams where there's an unequal distribution of power. It reminds us of the chronic avoiding we see between husbands and wives. In fact, many articles on the subject of business partnerships have made the point that there's a lot of overlap between business partnerships and marriages. We agree. And that overlap definitely applies to chronic avoiding.

Think about your own marriage and the marriages of people you know well. How often do you sit down with your spouse and have at least an hour-long discussion about the quality of your relationship? How often do you both take the time to step back and get some perspective on your marriage—where things are going well, where things are going okay, and where things could definitely stand to improve? How about your married friends? How often do they do this sort of thing?

We wouldn't be at all surprised if your answer went something like this:

> "I'm not sure my spouse and I have ever done that . . . . And I certainly don't know any of our friends who've done it, either . . . . It's probably the kind of thing married couples should do, but I don't know many who do."

If married couples are remiss in doing this sort of periodic review of their relationships, business partners are even more so. Even though they'd get enormous benefit from it, we've never known any business partnership where the partners (without a lot of prodding from us) sit down regularly and ask each other questions like:

— How happy and satisfied are you as a member of this partnership?

— What could I and all the other partners do to make your role here more satisfying and less frustrating?

— What were some of your high hopes when you became a partner here? How have those hopes been realized? What could we all do to make some of those unrealized hopes a reality for you?

Just like husbands and wives, most business partners agree that having periodic sessions like these would be a good idea. But, just like husbands and wives, they don't do it. Why not? We'll talk about that a little bit later on.

When you're in the one down position. When it comes to power on an executive team and motivation to sit down and talk about a relationship, we've noticed an interesting phenomenon. When you have more power than the team member in question—that is, when you're the boss and your team member reports to you— your motivation to talk about your relationship with that team member is probably low. However, when you have less power than the team member in question, your motivation to sit down regularly and talk about your relationship is usually high.

What we've learned over the years is this: Even though you may never approach your boss about meeting regularly to talk about your relationship, it's something you'd probably like to do. Why? Because your boss has control over some significant parts of your job:

Your pay and perks. Bosses have lots of discretionary power over what their team members are paid, their salary increases and bonuses, and other important perks that can make a job worthwhile.

What you work on. Your boss has the power to assign you tasks and projects that are interesting and stimulating or tasks and projects that are boring and onerous.

Where you work. A good relationship with your boss can mean working in a corner office with a pleasant view versus one with no windows. It can also mean working in a geographical region you enjoy versus one you detest.

Your chances for advancement. We've seen it all our working lives, not just in our consulting work. Employees who have good working relationships with their bosses usually move up the organizational ladder faster than employees who struggle with their bosses—even if those employees who don't get along so well are more talented and hard-working than those who do.

The emotional atmosphere you work in. Even though they often don't realize it, bosses have a huge effect on the psychological tone of their relationships with their employees. If you're getting along well with your boss, life at work can be pretty pleasant. You feel relaxed when you come in in the morning. Meetings with your boss go smoothly. If the two of you disagree about something, you can iron out your differences. Maybe the two of you can even enjoy going to lunch together. But if you don't have a good relationship with your boss, even the thought of going to work can get your stomach rumbling. Spending any time at all with your boss can be a tension-filled experience. Your boss can say things that upset you for days, even weeks. Life at work can be pretty lousy.

Because bosses have so much impact on the lives of their employees, many employees would welcome the opportunity to sit down with their bosses and discuss their relationships with them. Most employees, of course, don't initiate these kinds of meetings. But they'd like the chance to do it. What's been encouraging to us lately is that some executive team members we know have overcome their chronic tendency to avoid and have gone to their bosses to propose the idea of sitting down to talk about their relationships. For example, we're currently working with a couple of trade associations headed up by male executive directors. Both of these men have a woman in the number-two spot in their associations. These women are strong, capable, and much more relationship-oriented then either of their bosses. With some prodding from us, both went to their bosses and suggested regular sit-down sessions to discuss how they can work together more productively and harmoniously. One of them said to us:

> "It was not *easy* going to Bob to propose these little heart-to-heart talks that we're now having on a regular basis. There was a big part of me that didn't want to do it. I thought Bob should be coming to me, not the other way around. But at least we're meeting regularly now and it seems to be helping."

Of course, these two women are exceptions. Unfortunately, most executive team members would never go to their bosses to propose this sort of thing.

Acute Avoiding

When you chronically avoid sitting down to talk with a team member about your relationship, you're not avoiding something that has to be done right away. Not at all. It's just something that should be done sooner rather than later. Acute avoiding is what you do when something upsetting happens between you and one of your team members. It has a much more urgent, pressing quality than chronic avoiding. The sequence goes something like this:

1. Your team member does something that causes you to have some strong negative feelings—anger, frustration, annoyance, embarrassment, humiliation, disappointment, and so on.

2. You stay pretty upset for 24 hours, maybe longer. During this time you replay whatever happened over and over. Maybe you talk out what happened with a spouse or a close friend or someone else you trust. At the end of this period you calm down; the intensity of your feelings subsides.

3. You decide not to talk to your team member about what happened. Even though part of you says talking to the person would be a good idea, you don't do it. Even though your spouse or friend or colleague may recommend it, you don't do it. You put it off, or maybe you decide not to do it at all.

4. Your feelings about what happened may subside, but they never go away completely. You may forget about them for days or weeks or even months. But then, all of a sudden, something happens to remind you of what happened, and those feelings come back.

In the past 12 years or so, we've seen hundreds of examples of acute avoiding on the part of our clients. In the rest of this section we'll talk about three that stick out in our minds, one for each of the three power positions.

The one-up position. For the last five years we've been working with a large architectural firm in the mid-Atlantic states headed up by a fellow named Stan Fromberg. Stan is in his early 50's. When he was brought in as president of the firm, he inherited a vice-president about ten years his senior named George Rudner.

The chemistry between Stan and George was never great, but the two of them seemed to get along well enough. At the least, they seemed to respect each other's technical skills and ability to bring large projects into the firm. About two years after Stan had taken over as president, he placed a call to George's office in Minneapolis. George's secretary was not in the office that morning, and no one else seemed to know where George was. Confused and annoyed, Stan called George's home and got his wife, Martha. Martha said, "You mean he didn't tell you?" Stan said, "Tell me what?" George hadn't told Stan he was about to go into the hospital for heart bypass surgery.

We talked to Stan a few days later. He said:

> "I don't know what to think. On the one hand, I feel some real compassion for the guy. Open-heart surgery is a serious thing. On the other hand, it really frosts me that he would plan to have this surgery without telling me. I still can't believe he did it."

Stan assured us that as soon as George was out of the hospital and on his feet, he'd have a long and serious talk with him. But he never did. Several months later, when we asked him why he hadn't sat down with George, he looked embarrassed:

> "I don't know what to tell you. I really wanted to talk to him about it. But his recuperation was long and painful, and the time never seemed right. And now it's months later and . . . I don't know."

The equal position. Very soon the two of us will spend a couple of days with four partners in a venture capital firm. For well over six months, three of the partners have been deeply concerned about the lagging performance of the fourth partner. A number of "deals" this fellow made went sour, and the prognosis is bleak for several others he's in charge of. The other partners have discussed this problem at length between themselves and with us. But despite our exhortations to go to their partner and get this problem out on the table, they've conjured up excuse after excuse for why "this is not a good time for a confrontation." Now that the problem has reached crisis proportions—the three are seriously considering getting rid of the fourth—we've been called in to help them talk this thing out in depth.

The one-down position. Almost ten years ago we began working with a medium-sized architectural firm in Arizona. Ernie Brine (founder of the firm and 80 percent owner) and Hank Sherman (his junior partner and 20 percent owner) were having trouble getting along. Ernie was a big, strapping fellow in his early 50's who had an expansive, outgoing personality. Hank, on the other hand, was very short and thin and a bit of an introvert. They were probably the two most unlikely partners we've ever worked with. Ernie saw Hank as a whiner and complainer who was impossible to please. Hank saw Ernie as a self-centered entrepreneur who didn't really want a partner and only offered Hank equity in the firm to keep him from going to a competitor.

When we began our work with the firm, the first person we interviewed was Billy Olson, a talented architect who had pushed Ernie and Hank hard to bring us in. Over breakfast one morning Billy said:

> "Both of these guys do things that really get in the way of their working well together as partners. For example, I don't know if you know it or not, but Hank happens to be very short. Over the last two weeks, behind his back, Ernie has begun referring to him as the "little shit." I know Hank has found out about this, and I'm sure it hurts his feelings."

When we asked Billy if Hank had confronted Ernie about this, he said, "I don't think so, but you'll have to talk to him." When we interviewed Hank, we asked him to tell us how he felt about these remarks. He said:

> "My rational, intellectual side tells me to ignore comments like that. Ernie is an unbelievably insensitive man, and I know he doesn't really mean anything harmful when he says those things. But comments like that hurt. They hurt a lot."

When we asked Hank why he hadn't confronted Ernie about making these remarks, he said, "I guess that's why you guys are here, isn't it?"

Why Do You Avoid?

This is a question we've given a lot of thought to over the years. Why do people avoid talking about relationship problems when the evidence is so overwhelming that not confronting these problems makes things worse? We see at least two reasons:

- Most of us have a strong distaste for any sort of conflict.

- We're afraid of how our team members might react if we confronted them.

A Strong Distaste for Conflict

Just as we're attracted to things and activities that give us pleasure, we're repelled by those that cause us displeasure and discomfort. And for most of us, the prospect of confronting another human being about a touchy subject is unpleasant. If we confront this person, there might be conflict, and conflict is not fun. So we scurry away like little forest creatures who sense the approach of a predator. If you're avoiding a heart-to-heart talk with one of your team members, the reason may be no more complicated than that. You sense an unpleasant situation, and you feel uncomfortable. So you put it out of your mind, and you turn your thoughts to other things. That's it.

You're Afraid of How Your Team Members Might React

We don't think avoiding is a good thing. On the other hand, given the way a lot of team members respond to criticism (real or imagined), we can understand your reluctance. Why try to talk about improving your relationship or about how something upset you if the person could react badly and make things worse between the two of you? For example, here are some typical fears we've heard from team members:

"I could get in deep trouble or fired." We see this kind of situation all the time. You're a junior member of an executive team who wants to confront somebody more senior on the team, but you know if you do confront this person, you may get your ass in a sling or even fired. The more senior person—whether it's Dad in your family business or the managing partner of your law firm—may be a domineering individual who's got the interpersonal skills of a grizzly bear. As much as you want to get some important issues out on the table, you know the chances of having a productive interaction are slim to none. So you say to yourself, "It's not worth the hassle," and you go on about your business. But your frustration and dissatisfaction keep building.

"He's going to get mad and tell me to mind my own business." In any business the line between what's personal and what's professional is never sharply defined. This is especially true on executive teams. Team members bring their personal lives to work, and sometimes this can mean a disruptive intrusion. However, you may be reluctant to confront your team member about it. On one hand, you feel the issue may be causing the organization some harm. On the other hand, you fear the team member might go ballistic or simply tell you to mind your own business.

A good example of this occurred in a rapidly growing contract research firm we worked with a few years ago. The firm was owned by three partners. One owned 70 percent of the stock and the other two, 15 percent each. The senior partner, Cal, was a bright, handsome chap in his early 30's. Cal was smooth and fast-talking. His two partners, Mike and Jim, were more serious and introverted. We learned from Mike and Jim, as well as a number of other employees, that Cal had a reputation as a philanderer and that he was carrying on affairs with several different women in the firm. Mike and Jim strongly disapproved but were reluctant to confront Cal about it. When we asked why, Jim said:

> "It won't do any good. I know exactly what he's going to say. He's going to say he's being discrete about it, which is bullshit, and then if we press the issue he's gonna get pissed off and tell us to mind our own business."

"I could alienate somebody who can make life miserable for me." Sometimes someone in the one-up position is reluctant to confront another team member for fear that person might end up causing problems. A good example was a trade association we began working with about ten years ago. The executive director, Jake, and his second in command, Vaughn, had taken over the management of the association when it was a small operation in the mid-70's. In the beginning their relationship was excellent; they were as much friends as they were colleagues. Both were energetic and hard-driving and had a clear vision of where they wanted to take the association. Within five years they had tripled the membership and increased the annual budget by 600 percent.

Somewhere along the line their relationship began to sour. Maybe it was a case of two dominant personalities not being willing to compromise and cooperate. At any rate, they started to work at cross-purposes. Jake had a loyal following on the board who didn't particularly like Vaughn, and Vaughn had his own following on the board who didn't particularly like Jake. Jake tried hard to keep the problems between them out of the limelight. Vaughn, however, was not at all reluctant to "bad mouth" Jake to outsiders, and he was especially prone to doing it at the annual convention. Since Jake was clearly the boss and had such a strong personality, we were confused as to why he hadn't confronted Vaughn about this. Jake told us:

> "Believe me, I don't like what he's doing one bit. But I know if I confront him, he's just going to squawk louder to his buddies on the board. It's gotten to the point where I'd fire him if I could. I just don't have enough documentation yet to do it. His supporters would make too big a stink if I tried to do it now. But I'm watching him very closely. The next time he really screws up, he's gone."

Why Avoiding Is So Bad

Whenever you're having problems with someone, you experience some kind of negative feeling or feelings. Sometimes these feelings can be powerful. Like the anger you might feel if your boss took all the credit for a major report you wrote. Or the resentment you'd feel when the nephew you brought into the business said you weren't a good manager. Sometimes these feelings aren't so strong. Like the annoyance you feel toward one of your colleagues who has a tendency to hog the conversation at staff meetings. And sometimes these feelings aren't sharply defined. Like the hurt and disappointment you might feel if the best friend you started your business with had begun to show a devious side of his or her personality—a side you'd never seen when you were growing up as kids together.

If you don't sit down face to face with people to talk out your problems, these negative feelings don't go away. If anything, they intensify; and they seek release. They're a lot like steam building up in a pressure cooker or a boiler. But unlike steam, they can have a harmful effect when they come out. We think of them as the psychological equivalent of a toxic spill. These spills can be harmful to lots of different people: to your team members, to you, to your family, and even to the employees who work in your organization. In the rest of the chapter we'll describe eight toxic spills we've seen when executive team members avoided confronting important issues with each other. You should recognize all of them.

- Put-downs
- Faultfinding
- Blowing up
- Arguing and bickering
- Lecturing
- Calling a team member on the carpet
- Giving your team member the cold shoulder
- Complaining to other people

Put-Downs
A put-down makes the person on the receiving end feel diminished or demeaned. We once worked with a father and son in a family business where the father had "retired" but remained an active member on the board of directors. The son told us his dad would frequently put him down at board meetings. In one meeting the son was describing a new machine the company was about to put on the market. At the end of his presentation several board members were "oohing" and "aahing" about the potential for such a product. Then the room went coldly silent when the "old man"

scoffed: "I don't know why the hell we'd even want to think about making something like that. It's a bad idea, and the goddamn thing would never sell anyway."

Was this hurtful remark just another example of a nasty father with a history of verbally abusing his son? Not at all. In fact, the father was a kindly person who rarely said anything negative to anyone. So why was he putting his son down in board meetings? For us it was clear. The father was having a host of feelings about letting his son take over the business. He felt ignored. At one time in their relationship the son would seek his dad's advice on even the most trivial matter. Now he almost never did. He also felt something precious was slipping out of his grasp. The father had spent more than 25 years building what he was now giving to his son. For him the business was almost as special as a child. Now it was changing and growing in ways he couldn't fully understand. That saddened and frightened him.

But the father wasn't talking to his son about these feelings. He was avoiding a discussion where these sensitive—even tender— emotions might emerge. To us, the father's board room put-downs were a sign of the painful feelings he was unwilling and unable to express to his son.

Faultfinding

Faultfinding is pretty common in our society. Generally, it's done by people with more power to people with less power: parents find fault with children; teachers find fault with students; bosses find fault with employees; and senior partners find fault with junior partners.

We see lots and lots of faultfinding in our work. One of the most classic examples happened recently to the head of an architectural firm we've known for a long time. Several years back, Jack and the other partners who founded the firm sold it to a larger company. The sale made Jack and his partners wealthy, but Jack was an independent cuss and never liked having to report to the parent company. And he particularly disliked reporting to Harry, the senior vice-president for operations at the parent. Jack was impatient with Harry's detailed, tight-reined approach to management.

However, in spite of his impatience with Harry, Jack has never sat down with him and talked out his feelings. But not long ago Jack *did* vent his frustrations to Charlie, the CEO at the parent company. Jack said:

"Look, I just don't like reporting to the guy. He's all wrapped up in details. He doesn't see the big picture worth a damn. Bottom line, he gets in my way. I'd appreciate it if you'd get him to back off, or find somebody else for me to report to."

Well, it seems Charlie spoke to Harry, but it didn't have the effect Jack wanted. Rather than letting up on Jack, Harry is now finding fault with almost everything Jack does. He told us:

"The guy has become a royal pain. He's asking for all kinds of detailed written reports. No matter how conscientiously I fill them out, there's always something wrong with them. I feel like I'm back in elementary school with Mrs. Thayer who had me convinced I could do nothing right."

Harry, of course, wasn't displeased with Jack's work. He was upset Jack hadn't come to him directly with his complaints. And his feelings of hurt and annoyance toward Jack were spilling out in the form of faultfinding.

Blowing Up

Blowing up is not something we've studied in depth, but we've noticed some interesting aspects to it:

Some people are predisposed to it and some aren't. We call people who blow up frequently "over-reactors." These are folks who erupt almost like a volcano when they get angry or frustrated. Their tempers seem to flare up out of nowhere, and then, almost as quickly, the storm passes and they're back to normal. Probably about 15 to 20 percent of the executive team members we encounter are over-reactors. The other 80 to 85 percent are much less likely to blow up. If they do, they don't cool down quickly like over-reactors; they stay "mad" for a while. Take the two of us. Peter is a classic over-reactor. It doesn't take much to trigger his temper—an inconsiderate motorist, a less than helpful front desk clerk, a surly waiter. Mardy, on the other hand, rarely blows up at anyone. If he does, unlike Peter, he may take several hours, or even longer, to cool down.

Fatigue, stress, and drinking are catalysts for blowing up. People are much more likely to blow up when they're tired, under a lot of stress, have been drinking alcohol, or some combination of the three. A good example of how these factors can work together happened to the two of us about 12 years ago. We were in New Orleans preparing for a seminar to be done in front of several hundred people. At that point in our partnership we were new to giving large group seminars, and the prospect of doing them still made us a bit nervous. It was about three in the morning, and the seminar was scheduled for eight-thirty. Both of us had imbibed too much at a cocktail party the evening before. Conditions were ripe for a blow up, and that's what happened. The shouting and name-calling (followed by an icy silence) lasted maybe five minutes. Then we both cracked up at the ridiculousness of the situation.

Blowing up has a frightening quality about it. When some people blow up, the effect can be comical. One of us had a boss a long time ago who was five feet six inches tall and weighed well over 250 pounds. When he got mad, his face would get red and he'd vault out of his chair waving his arms and bouncing up and down on his toes. It took Herculean restraint not to break up when those little squalls blew through the office.

But normally when someone blows up at you, you don't feel like laughing. You feel a bit frightened. Why? Because when most people blow up, they go a little crazy. It's not unusual for a person who's blowing up to:

- yell and scream,

- have his face turn crimson with a look of rage in his eyes,

- pick up a chair or phone and throw it across the room,

- say abusive and hurtful things like, "You stupid son of a bitch!" or

- announce bizarre decisions like, "I'm gonna fire all you idiots and hire people who really want to work!"

Blowing up is a scary thing to behold. When we see it, most of us want to get away from the person as quickly as possible—until he or she has had a chance to calm down and start acting like a rational human being again.

People, especially people who are overreactors, blow up for all kinds of reasons. It may simply be that they're tired or stressed out or have had too much to drink, and almost anything will set them off. On the other hand, blowing up often *does* mean an important issue (or issues) is being avoided. For years we worked on and off with two senior partners in a large law firm who had once been good friends but whose relationship had slowly disintegrated over the years. Just about everyone in the firm agreed that they had become adversaries. One of the two, Harold, was a classic overreactor. Both Harold and Jim liked to drink, and they were frequently together in public situations where alcohol was being consumed. Once, at an office Christmas party, Harold got enraged over some comment Jim had made and yelled, "That's just the kind of stupid comment I'd expect from a pompous ass like you!" Jim shook his head and tried to walk away, but Harold gave him a hard shove from behind. If a couple of burly associates hadn't intervened, the two would have come to blows.

In this situation, Harold was prone to blowing up because he was an overreactor. But here Harold was also blowing up because he and Jim had not taken the time to sit down and talk out some major issues in their partnership. Even when we finally convinced them to get together and talk with our help, they refused to go beyond the first stages of these discussions. Their relationship eventually ended when Jim forced Harold out of the firm. The bitterness between the two of them exists to this day.

Arguing and Bickering

A certain amount of arguing and bickering is part and parcel of any significant relationship, and probably even healthy for it. But the kind that's not healthy is the chronic type we sometimes see between executive team members. Chronic bickering has some distinct characteristics:

It usually occurs between pairs of team members. More than two team members can be involved in arguing and bickering, but it's usually two people who are the principal offenders. Maybe it's you and your father. Maybe it's you and your brother-in-law. Maybe it's two other people on the team. At any rate, this "terrible twosome" becomes the center of attention when all of you get together as a group.

It's constant. Chronic bickering means just that. Whenever the two team members get together to talk about anything having to do with business, you know they're going to contradict each other, or point the finger at each other, or disagree for the sake of disagreeing. You know you're going to see a lot of head shaking, a lot of eyes rolled to the ceiling, and a lot of interrupting.

It derails meetings. Both as consultants and as workers we've been in scores of meetings where two people had a habit of bickering with each other. The bickering always seemed to take the meeting off track and bog it down in side issues that had little or nothing to do with why the group was assembled in the first place.

It's frustrating, tiresome, and (often) embarrassing to those who have to put up with it. If you and one of your team members have a habit of arguing and bickering with each other, you may not be aware of the effect it has on others in the group. But if you're a witness to this bickering, you're definitely aware of its impact. You find it frustrating because it tends to push your group away from the business at hand. You find it tiresome because it seems to go on and on and on. And you probably find it embarrassing if it occurs in front of employees, or worse, in front of clients or customers.

It seems so senseless. As we said a little earlier, if you're involved in chronic bickering with a team member, it's hard to get a good perspective on the problem. You're too close to it. But if you see two *other* team members constantly arguing and bickering, it can seem downright senseless to you.

Take a company we're currently working with. The president is a fellow in his early 40's. One of his vice-presidents is a woman just a few years younger. Until recently, whenever the two of them got together, either by themselves or in a group, the arguing and bickering started up. Everybody else on the executive team saw this style of interacting as a big waste of time. Plus, they all knew these two were fighting because they were avoiding some important issues in their relationship. One young guy on the team said it pretty clearly:

> "To me it's obvious what's going on. It has to do with the whole issue of competition. Both Sam and Carla are very ambitious. They like to win, and they hate to lose. So every discussion turns into this contest of whose ideas are better, whose ideas are more creative, who has a better 'grasp' of where the industry is headed over the next five years, you know, that kind of thing. And, of course, the rest of us sit there and wonder when the hell they're gonna stop trying to one-up each other and get back to solving the problem at hand."

Then he leaned back with a sad grin and said:

> "But I think the biggest part of the problem between them may not have all that much to do with competition. I think what's going on right beneath the surface— and you can almost see it in Carla's eyes when she looks at Sam—is that Sam can be a little nasty without meaning to. I think the guy has hurt Carla's feelings with some of his 'cutesy' little comments about how she dresses or does her hair. Insensitive stuff like that. And I think half the reason she argues and debates so much is that's her way of getting back at him. They need to sit down and work some of this stuff out. It'd sure make life easier for the rest of us."

Lecturing

Lecturing is the tendency lots of people have to talk down to someone who has behaved in a way they don't like. When people lecture us, they generally tell us what we did wrong, why we shouldn't have done it, and what we should do differently in the future. And they usually talk to us in a condescending, patronizing tone.

When we were kids, all of us got lectured a lot. Remember what it was like? Maybe you laughed too loud in the hall on your way to recess. Maybe you came home with booze on your breath after the junior prom. Maybe you wore a miniskirt that was too short and too tight. Or maybe you were just watching television rather than doing your homework. Whatever it was, the attending adult (your dad, your mom, your teacher, whoever) got upset about it and then you heard something like this:

> "Terry, what's it gonna take to get through to you? How many times do I have to say it? I don't want you to ___. It's dangerous. You could get hurt, or even killed. This has gotta stop. Do you need to be grounded for me to be any clearer about what I'm telling you here?"

It would be nice if, once you grew up, you didn't ever have to be subjected to lectures again. But, unfortunately it doesn't work that way. A good example is how employees get lectured by their bosses. As we've said, most executive teams have a pecking order. And team members in the one-up position definitely tend to lecture team members in the one-down position.

One extremely common lecturing pattern we've seen is what fathers do with their kids in family businesses. Here's Dad, who founded the place, and now he's taken on three partners—his two sons and his daughter. These three kids really are partners. They own stock in the company (about ten percent each), and they'll get the whole shooting match when Dad eventually retires or dies. But in Dad's eyes the kids are still just that: kids. When they were little and they did things he didn't like, he lectured them. He does the same thing today, even though all three "kids" are over 30.

A few years back we worked with a family business where Art, the founder, had died. The way Art left things, his wife, Ruth (about 55), was the principal owner, but his son Ray (about 35) was supposed to run the business. One day we mentioned the concept of lecturing to Ray and how common it was for parents to do it with their adult children. Ray leaped out of his chair and began pacing back and forth:

> "That's all my mother does. She doesn't approve of the way I run things around here and all she does is lecture me about it. I swear to you, when she does it, I feel like that little 10-year-old kid who used to track mud onto her kitchen floor about 25 years ago."

If you find yourself lecturing a team member or being lectured by a team member, there's a good chance one or both of you is avoiding an issue in your relationship that should be discussed effectively.

Calling a Team Member on the Carpet

The only people today who call employees on the carpet are bosses from the "old school" who have an authoritarian view of how people should be managed. Maybe you're one of those kinds of bosses. Here's what happens. One of the people who reports to you "screws up." Maybe someone is slow to respond to a request from one of your valuable customers, and that customer calls you up saying, "Who the hell is this guy, anyway, Jack? When you were dealing with me directly, I never had to wait this long to get a question answered!" Maybe someone mishandles the firing of an employee who has just filed a wrongful discharge suit against both you and the company. Or maybe someone botches an audio-visual presentation designed to snare a potential client you've been after for years.

Whatever the screw-up, you're upset. So you call the offending employee "on the carpet" and chew him or her out. Now, you could argue that you're at least not avoiding the problem here. And that's true. But when you call someone on the carpet, your behavior is not fueled by a rational, well-thought-out desire to deal with a performance problem. Your confrontation with the employee is fueled by strong negative emotion.

A good example of this occurred about three years ago with one of our clients, Doug Gleason. Doug was the president of an East Coast subsidiary of a multi-national company located on the West Coast. For the first two years in his job, Doug had been working for the crusty but kindly founder of the parent company. When this fellow retired, Larry Peters took over the helm. In the beginning, Doug and Larry seemed to get along reasonably well, at least on the surface. But after just a few months in his new job, Larry discovered that Doug was having some major financial problems with one of his large projects in the Middle East. When Larry learned that the "problem" might mean the loss of a hefty sum, he hit the ceiling and immediately arranged for a three-way conference call with Doug and the comptroller of the parent company. Doug told us:

"I haven't been talked to as abusively by a boss since I was a kid working construction 35 years ago. It was bad enough to be told that I was doing a lousy job as CEO of the subsidiary, but to be told that with another guy on the line was extremely embarrassing. And I was very direct with Larry. I told him I didn't deserve to be talked to that way, and when he kept going with his tirade, I hung up on him."

Several days after the abortive conference call, Larry phoned to offer what Doug termed a "half-assed apology." For a few months there was an uneasy peace between the two of them, but their relationship continued to disintegrate until they parted company about a year later.

We think this is a typical example of what happens when you call one of your executive team members on the carpet. Even though it may seem justified, it doesn't usually work. It's a one-way interaction where a more powerful person sends an intimidating message to a less powerful person: "I'm the boss and you better not repeat the same mistake again." It's a clumsy way to try to improve someone's performance, and it almost guarantees a deterioration in the quality of your relationship with that person.

Giving Your Team Member the Cold Shoulder

Giving someone you work with the cold shoulder is the organizational equivalent of the "silent treatment" husbands and wives give each other. If you've ever been married, you know what that is. It goes like this. You and your spouse have a heated argument over something, but the argument doesn't get resolved. You break off the discussion and an icy wall forms between the two of you. After a while, one of you approaches the other to make up. But your spouse is still upset and gives you the silent treatment. Sooner or later the silence is broken, a few tears are shed, and the argument is gone like a cool breeze.

Something similar happens on executive teams. However, it's a little different and that's why we prefer to call it "giving the cold shoulder." In most marriages extended silence is unusual. Sooner or later the passion and caring that originally brought the pair together pierces the silence. But the silent treatment on executive teams can go on for quite a while—weeks, months, or even years.

An icy coolness prevails and at least one of the team members (if not both) tries to:

Avoid the other team member as much as possible. If you're about to go into the office kitchen to get a cup of coffee, you first peek in to make sure your colleague is not there before you hastily fill your cup and scurry back to your office. You try to time your arrival and departure from work so they don't coincide with the comings and goings of the other person. If the two of you ever have to travel to the same location, you ask your secretary to get you on a different plane and to put you up in a different hotel.

Say as little as possible to the other team member. You realize there has to be some communication between the two of you, but you keep it to a bare minimum. Maybe a curt "hello" or nod if you happen to get stuck in the elevator together. Maybe a perfunctory "excuse me" if you have to pass each other in a narrow passageway. That's about it. If you have to convey any significant information, you try to do it via memos or intermediaries who are not particularly thrilled about being put in the "messenger" role.

Ignore the team member when he or she is speaking. If you're sitting in a staff meeting and the person you're struggling with is talking animatedly to the group, the expression on your face sends a host of simultaneous messages: "I'm bored." "I think this is stupid." "I couldn't care less about what this person is saying."

This "cold shouldering" is particularly apparent in informal situations. Let's say it's the office Christmas party. Everybody is standing around holding a drink, and the mood is jovial. Your "unfavorite" team member is telling a joke and everybody is cracking up until they see your granite face. Then the laughter trails off pretty quickly.

We said earlier that giving a team member the cold shoulder usually results from avoiding an effective confrontation with that person. But what are the negative effects of cold shouldering? There are several:

It eliminates all but the most formal of interactions between you and the team member. When you give one of your team members the cold shoulder (or vice versa), your organization loses. It loses your joint creativity, your joint energy, and your joint enthusiasm. In short, it loses anything positive the two of you could do together that neither of you can do alone. Maybe it's a marketing concept both of you come up with that allows your firm to grow enormously. Or maybe it's just the two of you having fun together that lightens the mood of your office and makes it a happier place to work. Whatever that joint product might be, the organization doesn't get the benefit of it as long as the struggle continues.

If it's done by a boss to an employee, it can make the employee's life miserable. Within the last six months we've worked with two different organizations where the head of an executive team has given the cold shoulder to one of the employees on his team. In both instances the bosses were males (one in his early 50's, the other in his early 60's) who were having problems with younger female employees. Both women had done something to gain the disfavor of their bosses. (In our opinion they were just being a bit more assertive than these two fellows were used to, especially from women.) Rather than sit down and talk candidly with their employees about their feelings, these two guys pulled into their shells of resentment and simply avoided them. We had a chance to interview the women in some detail. Both were in a lot of pain. One said:

> "It's awful. For a week he wouldn't even look at me. Finally, I started giving him as cheery a hello in the morning as I could, and he would barely grunt back at me. I have no idea what he's thinking, whether he plans to fire me, or just not give me a raise, or what. It's an absolutely rotten situation."

The other said:

> "What happened was he embarrassed me at a staff meeting. So I went into his office, asked if I could close the door, and gave him some frank feedback on how I felt about what he did. I normally believe in being assertive. But if I had to do it over again with Jack, I wouldn't. He just turned red in the face, nodded, and waited for me to walk out of his office. Then he didn't

speak to me for a month. And it was the worst month of my professional career."

It sets everybody else on edge when the two team members come into contact with one another. Recently we've been working with a couple of doctors who are partners in a large, bustling dermatology practice. When we interviewed them, they made it clear they weren't getting along well and that there was a lot of tension between them. But it wasn't until we interviewed two nurses in the practice that we discovered how bad the tension was and what a powerful effect it was having on the staff. After taking a deep breath and rolling her eyes to the ceiling, one of the nurses said:

> "I guess I've just been realizing how bad the situation is between them. The two of them are very angry at each other, but it's all contained, it's all held in. They're very cold to each other, and they don't say anything more to each other than they absolutely have to. In staff meetings, the tension is palpable. Everybody has these strained looks on their faces. And we're all delighted when the meeting is over and they go their separate ways."

Complaining to Other People

Since we're a culture of complainers, it should come as no surprise that executive team members frequently complain about fellow team members. We see it all the time. We do it, too. As good a relationship as the two of us have, we complain to our wives about each other every now and then. And years ago, when we first started working together on the management team of a government-funded project, we spent hours complaining to each other about the "problem" boss we worked for (and the "problem" employees who worked for us).

So, complaining to somebody else about another person *is* a common tendency. But we don't think complaining is necessarily bad. Complaining is only "good" or "bad" depending on how you do it.

Good complaining. Now and then all of us need to "vent" our frustrations and other negative feelings. If we don't, those feelings can cause us all kinds of emotional and physical problems. Imagine, for example, the following scenario. You're in business with your younger brother. It's Friday morning and he's left a note on your desk saying he's gone fishing in northern Michigan and will be back Tuesday morning. And you are *hot*. You go home to have lunch with your husband, it all comes pouring out:

> "That little jerk! If I had him in front of me right now, I'd wring his neck. He doesn't even have the decency, he doesn't even have the consideration to talk to me directly and let me know he wants to go away on a fishing weekend, an *extended* one I might add, when we're as busy as we have been in six months. I *cannot* believe it. I love him dearly, but that little twerp can be so irresponsible! He's 31-years-old, but at times he acts like he's still back in junior high."

Your husband just listens. Occasionally he smiles, maybe he shakes his head a little bit, but he just listens. Finally, you wind down. He waits for about 30 seconds and then says, "So, what do you want to do about it?" You just shake your head and don't say anything for a while. Then, resigned you look your husband in the eye and say, "I guess I've got to have a talk with him, huh? A *long* talk." Your husband nods his head and says, "Uh-huh." You say, "Well, what do you think I should do?" He says:

> "I definitely think you need to have a talk with him. And I think you need to get some things straightened out. But if you go in there and read him the riot act, I don't think it'll go very well. You're a strong person, and when you come on that way with me after I've done something to upset you, it doesn't work well with me, either."

So you say, "Okay, fine. What *should* I do?" He slowly nods his head and replies:

> "First of all, I think you need to calm down a bit. You can't have a productive conversation with anybody when you're all pissed off. But more importantly, I think

it needs to be a two-way conversation. As much as he does things to annoy you, I know you do stuff that bothers him, too. So you've gotta give him a chance to say his piece. I've been pushing you to have that kind of conversation with him for a long time."

Now, if you do what your husband suggests, that's "good" complaining. You've vented some strong feelings to somebody you trust completely and whose judgment and opinion you respect. That person has listened patiently and offered a helpful perspective on the situation. And you "hear" the advice you're getting.

That's good complaining. You get frustrating and annoying feelings off your chest. You get some candid feedback from a patient listener about what you should do about the problem. And you agree to follow the advice.

Bad complaining. We think there are at least three kinds of bad complaining. One kind is where you go to a person who simply agrees with your negative, one-sided view of the other person. It goes like this. Let's say you're a very neat person. You clean off the top of your desk at the end of every workday. You neatly print out a "to do" list every morning before you start working. As you complete each task on the list, you cross it off using a ruler and a red felt-tipped pen. You're organized. Some might say a bit compulsive. But you are proud of your orderly monk habits. However, you work closely with Harold, who is *not* a neat person and who has sloppy work habits. Normally, this wouldn't bother you so much. But right now you're working closely with him on an important proposal. He's out for the morning, and you've just walked into his office looking for an important file. The place looks like it's been stirred with a stick. There aren't stacks of papers on Harold's desk, there are *mounds* of papers shaped like those African anthills you see on PBS nature films. You're aghast. You immediately go down the hall to Francine's office and ask if you can sit down for a minute. She says, "Sure. What's up?" You say:

"I want to kill Harold! I just went into his office looking for an important file we need for the proposal that has to go out the day after tomorrow. I mean, the place looks like a recycling dump for paper products. He has been so incredibly frustrating to work with!"

As you talk, Francine rolls her eyes and continuously nods her head in agreement. Finally, she interrupts and says:

"I know. I know. He is impossible. I had to work with him on a similar project last year when you were on leave. The guy is a total slob. I told Charlie and Al, if they want me to keep working here, they better not ever assign me to work with Harold again. It was *too* frustrating."

After you hear Francine sympathize and agree with you about Harold, you feel pretty good. Your view of Harold as the "problem" and yourself as the "victim" gets confirmed. Unfortunately, however, even though Francine may be helping you *feel* better, she's not helping you solve your problem with Harold. And that's the trouble with complaining to someone who agrees and sympathizes with you. They just reinforce your natural tendency to externalize. Even though it wouldn't be a pleasant experience, you'd probably be better off complaining to someone like Jody whose work habits are similar to Harold's. Jody's not going to agree with you, or even sympathize with you. Jody's going to say something like:

"You're right, Terry, Harold is not neat. He's even sloppier than I am. But he is a *producer*. He gets things done. You, on the other hand, spend so much time cleaning your office and neatening up, I'm not sure how much real work you ever do."

Another kind of bad complaining is the kind we hear about when we talk to the spouses of our clients. Here's how it works. You've been having problems with one of the members of your executive team. Maybe it's the new division director who took over your agency 18 months ago. Maybe it's your sister who inherited her one-third of the business when your father died. Or maybe it's a valuable but difficult employee you got when you took over as CEO six months ago. Whoever the person is, you've picked out someone (probably your spouse) to complain to about that person. And you complain, and you complain, and you complain. Your spouse (or whoever) tries to be sympathetic and understanding at first. But after a while, your complaining gets tiresome—especially since you don't show much interest in doing anything about the problem. This kind of chronic complaining doesn't help you. It doesn't help the person you're complaining about. And it eats away at the quality of the relationship you have with the person you're complaining *to*.

The worst kind of bad complaining is the destructive kind. It's the kind that often gets referred to as "talking about people behind their back" or "running people down behind their back" or (sometimes) "character assassination." This kind of complaining is much more common in the work place than it should be. The reason it's so destructive is the indiscriminate way it's done. You're upset (maybe *very* upset) with a team member. But rather than complain about that team member to someone you know well and trust a great deal, you complain to anyone who will listen. That "anyone" might be a good friend of the team member you're complaining about. That person could be an employee of the person you're complaining about. That person could be a fellow employee of the person you're complaining about. That person could be a blabbermouth with a voracious appetite for office gossip. The point is, you've chosen the wrong person to complain to, for a number of reasons:

There's a good chance what you say will get back to the person you're complaining about. And there's also a good chance that what you say will get back in a distorted form, making it sound even worse than it was. And guess what your team member's reaction is going to be to whatever it is you supposedly said? It's only going to make a shaky relationship that much worse.

You're putting the person you're complaining to in an awkward position. Let's say the person is either a friend or an employee of the team member you're complaining about. That person feels a certain degree of loyalty to your team member and is going to feel uncomfortable listening to you complain. Even though he or she might not come right out and say it, the person is going to be thinking, "Why are you telling *me* this? If you need to talk about this so much, why don't you go talk to somebody who's neutral, not somebody like me who feels caught in the middle of things?"

The person you're complaining to will end up thinking less of you. When you indiscriminately complain like this to someone, their respect and trust for you automatically goes down. People in the work place just don't think well of those (especially high-level managers) who go around carelessly and indiscriminately complaining about someone they work with. They also don't trust people like that. They start thinking, "If he's saying those things about Jack behind his back, what's he saying about me when *my* back is turned?"

You're making the place you work more stressful. When you indiscriminately go around complaining about a team member, you automatically "stir things up" for people who "don't need the aggravation." We recently worked with three business partners where one of the partners was angry and upset with the other two. But rather than share his feelings with his two partners, he chose to go around and talk to any employee whose ear he could bend. One of the young women in the office who'd been subjected to his ranting and raving told us what it was like:

> "It was terrible. I was embarrassed. I was angry at him for doing it. The guy is in his 50's. I wanted to tell him to grow up and act his age. We've got enough problems around here without having to put up with that crap."

In this chapter we've been focusing on a tendency all of us have when it comes to our important relationships. It's the tendency to avoid confronting important issues with the other person (or people) in the relationship. We do it in our role as spouses; we do it in our role as parents; we do it in our role as adult children; and we do it in our role as colleagues.

In the last part of this chapter we've focused heavily on the negative effects avoiding can have on your key business relationships. In the next chapter we'll be talking about another major reason you probably get less satisfaction and more frustration than you'd like out of being a member of your executive team: *You're missing some important skills.*

6

You're Missing Some Important Skills

I f you're at all like most of our clients, you have some extreme-ly well developed professional skills. Maybe you're a highly regarded expert in machine-tool design or software program-ming. Maybe you're a nationally recognized pathologist or oncolo-gist. Maybe you're as good as they get when it comes to suspen-sion bridge engineering or landscape architecture. Or maybe you're a whiz at taking over failing organizations and turning them into winners when most thought they were beyond sal-vaging.

On the other hand, like most of our clients, you probably have some very undeveloped skills in two areas important to the rela-tionships you have with your executive team members—good "talking" and good "listening." Before you protest, read through the rest of the chapter. Maybe we're wrong about you. In fact, we'd love to be wrong. But if we're right, there's no need to get discouraged. Just accept the fact that you're one of millions of business and professional people who need a lot of work when it comes to interpersonal skills.

In fact, the heartening thing about these "people" skills is that they're relatively easy to learn. Think of all the hours you've devoted to improving your "short" game in golf, your backhand in tennis, your bridge game, your chess moves, the Spanish you now speak fluently, or any activity where disciplined practice brought you to a level of excellence. If you devote even a fraction of that time to learning interpersonal skills, your frustration with the important people in your life will go way down, and your sat-isfaction will go way up. That we guarantee. But more about that later on in the book.

In this chapter we'll talk about some of the common mistakes our clients (and we) make in the interpersonal skills arena. We'll break these mistakes down into two broad categories: 1) not being a good talker, and 2) not being a good listener. Let's take a look at "bad talking" first.

Not Being a Good Talker

When we say "good talking" in the context of relationships, we mean something quite different from what this term normally conveys. For example, here's a list of adjectives people often use when they describe somebody who's a "good talker":

Persuasive: A lot of good talkers are persuasive. They can change people's minds and they can dramatically influence their opinions.

Succinct: Good talkers aren't long-winded, they're succinct. Instead of beating around the bush, they get to the point quickly. They don't use a lot of words, but their words speak volumes.

Witty: Good talkers are usually adept at saying something witty or humorous, especially when the situation calls for it. With a pointed anecdote or clever turn of a phrase, they put people at ease and into a receptive frame of mind.

Charismatic: Many good talkers are charismatic. Whether it's delivering a report at a Monday morning staff meeting, making a presentation at a regional sales conference, or giving a formal speech at an annual convention, they find a way to captivate their audiences. They know how to "move a crowd."

This is not what we mean by good talking. If we did, we'd have to admit that many of our clients are good talkers. Some are very charismatic. Many are extremely persuasive. A lot are quite succinct. And a number are witty enough to make a living as stand-up comics. But our focus here is on "good talking" in the *personal* arena—with spouses, romantic partners, close friends, and family members. In personal relationships, "polish" and "facility" take a back seat to genuineness and candor. In the personal sphere, it's "talking from the heart" that matters most, not charisma, succinctness, or persuasiveness.

We've noticed the same thing in our work with our clients: "Public" speaking skills aren't nearly as important as "private" speaking skills—the kind of skills that are essential when:

— Two business partners are trying to talk through a misunderstanding after weeks of giving each other the silent treatment.

— A father and daughter in a family business are trying to reconcile after a blow-up where each said hurtful things to the other.

— An executive vice-president and CEO, good friends since their college days, are trying to figure out why they aren't "clicking" together in their newly formed company.

— A brother and sister, who inherited a company from their father, are trying to talk through "touchy" subjects, like who cares more about the business, who works harder, and who's more able to lead the firm into the future.

These situations—even though they're happening in a business setting—call for a softer, more personal mode of communication. Here, "good talking" has less to do with "public speaking" skills and more to do with things like:

• Apologizing when you've screwed up.

• Expressing tender or "hard to express" feelings, especially the kind that make you feel vulnerable.

• Giving compliments and positive feedback.

• Giving constructive criticism or "needs improvement" feedback in a way the other person can hear it.

If we define "good talking" this way, most of the people we work with are not good talkers, and far too many are "bad talkers." How about you?

Apologizing

Apologizing is a fascinating topic, largely because so many people find it hard to do. And for some, cutting off a thumb would be easier than making an apology. Years ago one of us worked for a guy like this. Tom was extremely bright. He had a PhD in industrial psychology, and his massive intellect and encyclopedic knowledge would probably have qualified him for doctorates in several other fields.

But despite his intelligence, Tom had some major shortcomings when it came to dealing with people. One of the most glaring was his inability to say "I'm sorry" when it was necessary and appropriate. The typical drill went something like this. Tom would get upset—very upset—when an employee would make some kind of mistake. He'd rant and rave, fuss and fume, and then go into a stony silence for the rest of the day. The next morning he'd be especially cheery and pleasant. It was obvious to everyone in the office that Tom felt guilty about how he'd carried on the day before. It was also obvious that he wanted to say he was sorry, but just couldn't do it.

At least Tom realized he'd done something wrong (even if he couldn't express his regret). But there are lots of people who don't apologize because they think they haven't done anything to apologize *for*. Everybody else may think their behavior is unacceptable, inexcusable, or even downright reprehensible—but not them! They either explain away their behavior ("I was going through a difficult time") or minimize it ("You're just making a mountain out of a molehill"). Or they justify their actions as the necessary means to an end ("I know people are upset, but if I hadn't kicked a little ass, we'd never be where we are today"). Whatever their reasoning, these people never apologize, and everybody around them resents it.

Maybe the most famous example we've ever seen of an executive who couldn't apologize was Richard Nixon. About ten years after Watergate, Barbara Walters was interviewing the ex-president on TV. The conversation went something like this:

> **Walters:** Mr. President, it's been said that you betrayed the trust of the American people and that, even years after your resignation, they're still angry and resentful for what you did. How do you respond to that?

Nixon: I can understand how they might feel that way.

Walters: (With a look of stark amazement) That's it?

Nixon: (Nodding) Yes.

While some people never apologize, other people apologize quite easily, but don't change the behavior that necessitated the apology in the first place. Art Sedman is a good example. The founder of a family business that employs about 100 employees, Art has problems controlling his temper. Two or three times a month, he erupts and does or says things he regrets. When we began working with Art and his team, he told us he often felt guilty after a blow-up, but at least he would go up to someone the next day and say, "I'm sorry I lost my temper yesterday. I said some things in the heat of the moment I shouldn't have said, and I want you to know I didn't mean them." Having apologized, Art felt a lot better. But his operations manager had a different perspective:

> "Is Art good at apologizing? Yeah, I guess you could say that. But his apologies are meaningless. If he really meant it—you know, if he really was sorry—he wouldn't do the same thing over and over again. Hell, Art'll ream somebody out on Monday, apologize on Tuesday, and ream 'em out again on Wednesday. So, is he good at apologizing, or is he just good at offering a bunch of empty words after he screws up?"

Expressing Tender or "Hard to Express" Feelings

Many of our clients are powerful people who walk around with an air of bluster and bravado that says: "I'm in control and I'm confident I can handle any kind of situation that might arise." Often they truly feel that way, which is probably one of the reasons they frequently succeed where others have failed. But sometimes, it's an act. Sometimes, these "in charge" types are experiencing something very different on the inside from the way they appear on the outside. For example, they may be feeling:

— doubt and anxiety about their ability to keep the ship afloat during a financial crisis.

— distracted, embarrassed, and down on themselves for a screw-up they made at an important meeting last week.

— a confusing mixture of happiness and envy over a colleague's good fortune.

— overwhelmed and resentful at being given one more major assignment when another member of the team who isn't so busy could have been asked to do it.

What do many confident-appearing people do with these powerful feelings going on just below the surface of all their professional posturing? What they almost never do is *disclose* these feelings to the people they work closely with (or to anyone else, for that matter). They "stuff" these feelings; they bury them deep down inside. They make the mistake of hiding these feelings to avoid appearing weak or vulnerable.

Occasionally, we make the same mistake. One of us was painfully (but helpfully) reminded of this several years back. It was a Sunday afternoon in September in Chicago. We'd been working all weekend with a group of physicians who were trying to iron out some knotty relationship problems. Somewhere around two o'clock one of the doctors said something to Peter that Peter thought was rather critical. As it turns out, it probably wasn't, but he felt stung by the remark nonetheless. Describing the incident to Mardy several weeks later, he said:

> "I was really bothered by what George [the doctor] had said. I remember being distracted—just sort of half there—for the rest of the afternoon. Somewhere along the line I asked myself whether I should talk it over with you, or be a 'big boy' and handle this on my own. I was really starting to let it eat away at me, even to the point of questioning my professional competence."

As much as the incident was bothering Peter, he didn't bring it up to Mardy after the session was over. Early Monday morning, Peter and Mardy flew home from O'Hare. Peter described the next several days as not being a lot of fun:

"Linda [Peter's wife] kept saying I seemed distracted and distant. She kept insisting that something was bothering me and that I wasn't telling her about it. And for three days I kept telling her I was just tired from having worked so hard over the weekend. Finally—I guess it was Thursday morning—I looked in the mirror and admitted it was time to stop wrestling with this thing on my own and tell Linda about it."

So Peter did tell Linda about it. And a few days later he told Mardy about it, too. Talking to a seminar audience several weeks later, he said:

"Of course, after I opened up to Linda and Mardy, I felt much better. Both of them were patient and caring listeners, and they just let me think out loud. They let me verbalize thoughts and feelings that had been rumbling around inside me that I just wasn't getting a handle on by myself."

But the real insight for Peter was this:

"I realized how much I reacted like one of our clients when that doctor in Chicago made the threatening remark to me. I tried to deal with my feelings of inadequacy and insecurity on my own. I didn't want to admit to myself—and especially not to Linda or Mardy—that I wasn't man enough to work this thing out on my own. I chose the stoic route."

Peter *was* acting like one of our clients after that Sunday afternoon "crisis" in Chicago. In spite of all his training and his belief in the value of talking out feelings, when push came to shove, he acted like a typical American man. He clammed up and tried to handle it by himself. We thought it might be interesting to get Linda's perspective on what had happened, since she's a woman, knows Peter so well, and is very familiar with our work. She said:

"I actually think Peter is pretty good at opening up to me about things that bother him. But there's something about the professional world and positions of power and authority that cause men a lot of problems. And I don't think Peter is immune from them. In our society we have all these men walking around who are in charge of things. They have a whole lot of responsibility, and they're supposed to know what they're doing. I think it's hard for them to admit that at times they feel very power*less* when they're supposed to be so power*ful*."

And she added:

"But I think these men, Peter included, pay a high price by not being able to let down their guard and talk about these occasional feelings of inadequacy with people they trust. They experience a lot of pain, but the people around them do, too. When Peter was trying to wrestle with that Chicago problem without talking to me about it, I definitely felt shut out. And I think there are millions of women who often feel the same as I did. What women want—and the magazines and books we read are filled with advice on it—is to have the men we're involved with open up to us and talk about what's going on inside. We do that with them, and we want them to do that with us."

We want to stress that it's not just feelings of insecurity or inadequacy we're talking about here. It's any tender or "hard to express" feeling that might make you appear weak or ineffectual or that makes you feel vulnerable. Not talking about these feelings isn't going to help you very much, and it certainly won't improve the quality of your relationships with other people. In this case, no talking becomes "bad talking."

Giving Compliments and Positive Feedback

In everyday parlance people use the expression "giving compliments" or "praising" people. Psychologists and other human development folks often prefer fancier terms like "giving positive feedback" or "using positive verbal reinforcement." Whatever it's called, when you tell people they've done something well or that they have traits or qualities you admire and respect, the effect on how those people feel about themselves can be powerful. But everybody knows this, right?

Nope. For some reason, it often seems easier to find fault and criticize. If you have any doubts about this, think about your behavior in consumer situations. Even if you don't travel as much as we do, think of the hundreds of interactions you have every month with:

- waiters and waitresses
- flight attendants and airline ticket agents
- hotel desk clerks
- retail store salespeople
- receptionists
- bank tellers
- bus and taxi drivers
- U. S. Postal Service clerks
- policemen and security guards
- government workers in "service" positions (e.g., Dept. of Motor Vehicles)

If your experience has been anything like ours, you've had more than your share of negative or disappointing interactions with people in these "customer service" roles. Too often they are sullen, impatient, distracted, incompetent or impolite. If you're like a lot of seasoned travelers, you've probably ended up giving lots of "needs improvement" feedback (see next section) to the guilty parties or to their supervisors. We've certainly given our share over the years.

However, despite the lousy service you've received, we'd bet you've also gotten a lot of good service. Maybe it was a rental car clerk who went out of her way to find a map that helped you get to a difficult location. Or maybe it was a conscientious reservation agent who put in extra effort to find you the best fare for a cross country flight. Be honest. When you get this kind of special service, how often do you say something like:

"You're very good at what you do. I wish everybody I came into contact with were as nice and as helpful as you've been. Thanks. I really appreciate it."

We haven't done any scientific research, but we think most people lodge about twenty complaints for every compliment they give to people in sales and service positions. And some people never give these folks a compliment like the one above. And that's sad. Because when you do compliment people in customer contact jobs, they usually say, "Well, aren't you nice!" or "You've made my day! Thank you very much." And occasionally they'll say:

"I wish you'd tell my boss what you just told me. All he (or she) ever notices are the bad things. In fact, I can't ever remember my boss saying anything to me like you just did."

It's not just bosses who focus on the negative and fail to "accentuate the positive." Parents make the same mistake. Ask the typical teenager, "What do your parents like most about you?" and you'll often get a response like this:

"Like most? Ah, let me see. Well, I know what they *don't* like. They don't like my choice of friends, the grades I get, the way I keep my room, the music I play, the way I dress, my study habits, and how I treat my kid sister. But what do they like most? I'm not too sure they like all that much about me, to be honest."

It always saddens us when we hear a young person say something like this. What's really tragic, though, is this: teenagers who respond this way often have parents who brag to other people about the same child! Why can't these proud parents say the same positive, complimentary things directly to their children?

We see the same problem with our clients. For example, one of the items on our *Executive Team Profile* we described earlier reads, "Good at giving compliments and positive feedback." Of the 25 items on the questionnaire, this is the one where people usually get the worst ratings. What's interesting, however, is how easy it is to turn this pattern around. For example, whenever we take an executive team away for a "retreat" or "team-building" session, one of the first things we do is get them to practice giving positive feedback. We break the group up into pairs and say:

> "When you give feedback to the other person in your pair, just mention positive things—two or three characteristics you really like or admire or respect or value about the other person. And try to back up each thing with a specific example or two. Don't mention anything about how the other person can improve. That comes later on."

We let the first pair go for about 15 minutes. Then we form new pairs for another 15 minutes. We do this until each person has had a chance to get some feedback from every other member of the team.

Even though we've been through this kind of exercise scores of times, we're always a little surprised and touched at what happens. We see people who've worked together for quite a while (maybe even decades) saying positive, touching things—things they've never mentioned before! Warm smiles appear on faces that are normally sullen and taciturn. Tears well up in eyes that look as if they could never cry. Every time we do this exercise, for a brief moment, the room becomes an almost magical place.

We'll talk more about the whys and wherefores of giving positive feedback later on. For now, though, think about how "good" or "bad" you are when it comes to this important interpersonal skill. What would the people you work with (and live with) say about you? Would they say you give praise freely and generously? Or would they say you're downright Scrooge-like? Why not ask them? Go to your spouse; go to one of your kids; go to one of your team members; and go to one of your employees. To each one say something like this:

> "In a second I want to ask you a question, and I'd like you to give me a frank and candid answer. Be honest. Don't worry about hurting my feelings. Whatever you say, I won't hold it against you. Here's the question: How good would you say I am at giving compliments and positive feedback to people? "

Then listen. Don't interrupt. Don't defend yourself. Don't offer any explanations. Just listen.

Giving Constructive Criticism and "Needs Improvement" Feedback

Telling people what they're doing well is relatively easy, even though most of us don't do it often enough. The other side of the coin—telling people what they're not doing well and where they need to improve—is hard. As some wag once said, "Criticism is hard to take, especially when it comes from friends, family, co-workers, and strangers." Even when it's honest, well intended, and accurate, criticism doesn't go over well. We see this with our *Executive Team Profile* when we collate all the ratings for a group and give each member individual feedback on his or her "results." When people get "good marks," things generally go smoothly. But it's not at all unusual for people on the team—especially the boss—to get "poor marks." Their reactions to the "bad news" cover a range of emotions: shock, hurt, denial, anger, and confusion.

We recently worked with one team where the boss only got one "yes" (out of a possible thirteen) to the statements, "Is a good team player" and "Has good people skills." His reaction? He told us the *Executive Team Profile* was a "destructive instrument" and assured us his wife and the people in his men's group would rate him more accurately. This fellow, by the way, was no dummy. He had written a number of books and was widely respected in his field.

The boss on another team was so bothered by his results that he constructed a results sheet of his own (much more positive than the real one). As he handed it to us, he said: "If these people really knew me well, these are the kinds of ratings I *would* have gotten." We had to muster every ounce of professional restraint to keep from cracking up.

As bad as people are at receiving criticism, we think they're just as bad when it comes to giving it:

— Some people are so "nice" or afraid of conflict that they never give it—even when it's called for.

— Some give criticism so indirectly, abstractly, or obliquely that the other person doesn't "get the message."

— Some folks get frustrated and upset very easily. Their criticism comes out with too much anger and harshness.

— Still others give criticism in front of other people—like fellow employees or even customers. They end up humiliating the person whose performance they're trying to improve.

You may recall those examples of "bad talking" in Chapter 5 where we discussed problems that result from avoiding confrontation, such as: put-downs, faultfinding, blowing up, lecturing and calling someone on the carpet. Each of these illustrate just how poorly most of us give feedback of a negative, critical, or "needs improvement" nature. Since this is such an important topic—there are hundreds of books, articles, and tapes devoted to it—you'd think most business and professional people would know how to do it right. But they don't, not even at the very highest levels of organizations.

A good example of this comes from the book, *The Acting President* by Bob Schieffer and Gary Paul Gates. It seems that in the fall of 1981 an *Atlantic Monthly* article appeared that freely quoted David Stockman as having a dismal view of President Reagan's economic program. At the time, Stockman was the head of the Office of Management and Budget, and many of his peers in the high levels of the Reagan administration were upset at what he was quoted as saying. James Baker (White House Chief of Staff and Stockman's boss at the time) was particularly upset. According to Schieffer and Gates, Baker gave Stockman a "dressing-down that would have done credit to a Marine drill sergeant." They added:

> "Baker had ended the meeting by ordering Stockman to meet the President for lunch. The menu, explained Baker, would be 'humble pie,' and Baker said he expected to see Stockman's 'sorry ass dragging the carpet as he left the oval office.'"[1]

Did Stockman deserve to be reprimanded or chastised by Baker? Who knows? But was "a dressing-down that would have

---

[1]From *The Acting President* by Bob Schieffer and Gary Paul Gates, NY: E.P. Dutton, 1984, p. 146.

done credit to a Marine drill sergeant" appropriate? No. It was just another example of how badly the task of delivering criticism and "needs improvement" feedback is handled by people who are skilled in so many other ways. Now let's talk about the other important interpersonal skill you may be missing: listening.

Not Being a Good Listener

We think listening is an essential skill for all people to have, particularly when it comes to the important relationships in their lives. Sadly, however, the great majority of human beings who walk this planet are not good listeners—especially when they need to be. When the chips are down and it's critically important to help another person simply "think out loud," very few of us have the skills to do it.

What continues to fascinate us, however, is that most people see themselves as good listeners, even when the evidence is overwhelming that they aren't. How about you? You probably think of yourself as a reasonably good listener. But what if we asked your spouse, your children, the people you work with every day, and your closest friends? What would they tell us? Why don't you ask them? Say something like this to each one:

> "Imagine a scale from zero to ten, where zero means an absolutely terrible listener and ten means a superbly good listener. How good a listener am I? Being coldly frank, what number would you give me? And after you rate me, why don't you tell me 1) why you gave me the rating you did and 2) what I'd have to work on to get a higher rating from you."

You may be pleasantly surprised, but we doubt it. We think most people will say you need to work on your listening skills. And some may say you *really* need to work on them.

Bad Listeners

Here we'll try to bring the concept of "bad listening" alive by describing five types of poor listeners we often encounter in our work and personal lives:

- the reactive listener

- the distracted listener

- the cadaverous listener

- the impervious listener

- the nonstop talker

The Reactive Listener

Reactive listeners are very common. They tend to be energetic, "hyper" people whose minds are in high gear most of the time. When you're talking to them, their attention is focused on what they're thinking, not on what you're trying to express.

— Generally their faces, especially their eyes, show they're champing at the bit to respond to what you're saying.

— You can see they're thinking about and analyzing what you're saying, not absorbing it.

— They interrupt constantly with their reactions to what you're saying making it impossible to develop an idea or complete a line of thinking in their presence.

— Whenever you say something negative or critical, they stop listening; and are planning their rebuttal.

Barbara Gillespie, a marketing vice-president on an executive team we worked with a few years ago, is a great example of a reactive listener. Peter Drucker had folks like Barbara in mind when he said, "Strong people have strong weaknesses." She was highly intelligent, extraordinarily creative, a tireless worker, and a likable person. But most of all, she had an energy level that was off the charts. She was happiest when juggling a dozen projects at the same time. She confessed she had trouble even sitting still in staff meetings: "I often feel like my mind is exploding with ideas. Bing! Bang! Bing! It makes life exciting, but I wish I could turn it off sometimes."

Barbara wasn't the only one who wished she could turn it off. When we took her group on a two-day team-building session, every member of the team gave her the same kind of feedback:

"I know you don't mean to, but you sometimes come across as if all you really care about is what *you're* thinking or what *you're* feeling. Well, we have thoughts and feelings too, and we'd like a chance to get them out. [Lots of head nodding around the room.] Often, when I'm trying to say something that might be a little negative or critical, I look over at your face and it's clear you're not listening to me. You're thinking about how you're gonna *respond*. It's frustrating! It's discombobulating! It's insensitive! But, most of all, it's not fair, because you expect us to give you our full attention when you talk."

The Distracted Listener

Distracted listeners are very different from reactive listeners. They don't wait impatiently for you to finish so they can have the floor. And they don't interrupt you a lot to respond with their own thoughts and feelings. They may even pretend to be listening. But their minds are focused on something else. Reactive listeners, as bad as they are, at least listen a little. Distracted listeners aren't listening at all. A lot of wives complain (with great justification) that their husbands are distracted listeners. We've heard hundreds of them say something like:

> "George? He's a pretty bad listener. Sometimes he puts on a good act at listening to the things I want to tell him, but most of the time I can tell he's completely tuned out. His mind is off somewhere on a sailboat or on the golf course or on some problem at work. I don't like it, but I've pretty much accepted it. After all, he's a great husband in so many other ways."

Distracted listeners are easy to recognize. Often they have a glazed, unfocused or faraway look in their eyes. (As one of our colleagues used to say, "You know you've lost 'em when you see that bovine expression on their faces.") When you pause for a second, they frequently change the subject to something completely unrelated to what you've just said, leaving you to wonder, "Did he hear one word that came out of my mouth?" Distracted listeners will try to read the newspaper, balance their checkbook, or skim a memo while you're talking, and it's not unusual for their eyes to wander just as you're trying to say something important. Perhaps the most frustrating habit they have is continually sneaking glances at their watch when they think you're not looking.

A good example of a distracted listener is Henry Overton, a 60-something CEO we worked with a few years ago. Henry was a very successful—and very charming—guy who succeeded his father as president of his 100 year-old company (his father had succeeded his father, who founded the place). Henry was now the senior statesman and was surrounded by four family members in senior positions (a son and a daughter and two sons-in-law). We met Henry at a seminar in Palm Springs and spent several hours with him and his wife at poolside talking about his company, his top team, and his desire to build a more cooperative, less contentious group. Within several weeks, we began to meet the rest of the team. We weren't surprised when Henry's people told us he was a pretty bad listener. And Henry's specialty was distracted listening. This is a sampling of what "the kids" said about him:

> "Dad's always thinking about *something*, but you can bet it doesn't have much to do with what you're saying."

> "He actually picked up the tendency from his father, who would also drift off into his own world when he was around people."

> "At times it's so frustrating! You want to say, 'Earth to Henry! Earth to Henry!' He's off somewhere, but you don't know where."

> "Usually it doesn't bother me. But sometimes we have important things to discuss, and we need his attention."

The Cadaverous Listener
Talking about cadaverous listeners, we remember Ed Sullivan and the famous remark that comedian Don Rickles made to him one night many years ago. Sullivan was a good example of a cadaverous listener—about as "stiff" as they get. Rickles paused in the middle of his act, looked over at Sullivan, and said, "Hey, Ed! You wanna move a little so they don't throw dirt on ya!"

While reactive and distracted listeners may not be listening to you, at least they show signs of life when you're talking to them. With cadaverous listeners, you start looking at their toes for a tag. When you talk to them, they use about as much "body language" as Lot's wife or Michelangelo's David, and they maintain the same impassive look no matter what you say, whether it's serious, humorous, sensitive, or even outlandish. Their poker-faced expressions make you wonder, "What's going on behind that mask?"

Jeff Yarborough, a nationally respected biologist with the Department of Health and Human Services, is a cadaverous listener. Jeff actually thinks he's a pretty good listener. He tries to listen and even hears what people are saying when they talk to him. But the people he works with aren't so sure. One of his colleagues said:

> "Even though I know he's listening, it's hard to talk to Jeff. He just sits there motionless. He doesn't look interested or uninterested. He just kind of looks, I don't know, inanimate. If he didn't blink once in a while, I'd swear I was talking to a statue. It's unsettling."

It's easy to misinterpret cadaverous listeners like Jeff. We've made that mistake. Several years ago, we were doing a half-day seminar for 50 to 60 physicians, most of whom seemed interested in the topic. Many were taking notes, nodding appreciatively, laughing at some of the humorous anecdotes, and so on. Except for one guy sitting in the rear of the room. He didn't move a muscle the entire morning. Not a smile. Not a frown. And we were thinking:

> "This guy looks as if he wants to be anyplace else but here. He's probably only here because his firm paid his way, and he wanted to spend a few days in San Francisco."

After the session, a number of people came up to shake our hands and tell us how much they enjoyed it. As we were packing away the handouts and transparencies, the poker-faced guy from the back of the room approached. With the same impassive expression on his face, he stuck out his hand and said, "I just wanted you to know this session changed my life!" We were astonished but tried not to show it. As we listened he talked about how deeply he'd been moved by what we had said. Like the other doctors who had come up before him, he talked about using many of our concepts to improve his relationship with his wife and kids. Then he was off.

As we chatted for a few moments about that little incident, we thought:

> "We're just a couple of guys he met at a seminar who he'll probably never see again. It's really not all that serious if we misinterpret his level of interest or involvement. But what about his partners or his wife and children? What if they misinterpret him? *That's* serious!"

The Impervious Listener
The dictionary defines *impervious* as "not capable of being penetrated or passed through; impenetrable." We think it's a good word for a particular type of bad listener. You send words and messages their way, but what you say doesn't "get through." Impervious listeners are a little harder to spot than the other types we've described, but you can pick them out. They:

— seem unmoved by even the most emotional pleas or poignant remarks.

— don't change their behavior or modify their operating style, no matter how many people tell them or how much people tell them.

— seem to think their point of view is the only correct one and everyone else is out of whack, off base, or flat-out wrong.

— have a very definite idea about how things should be done and won't explore other alternatives.

— make up their minds and no amount of debate or discussion will sway them.

We've encountered so many impervious listeners in our work, it's hard to select one as an illustration. So we'll let you choose the example this time. Think of someone you know—a person you work with or someone in your personal life—who you've been trying to influence or change, but who's not "getting the message." Fix the person in your mind. Think of the frustration and impotence you feel at not being able to penetrate those rigid defenses. Think of how different it would be if the person were open and receptive to what you have to say.

Now answer this question: Is it possible that someone else would consider you an impervious listener? Maybe someone on your executive team. Or, worse, someone you live with everyday, like a spouse or a child?

The Nonstop Talker

All of us know some nonstop talkers. They're terrible listeners because they're always talking. It's hard to get a word in edgewise when you're around them. As they go on and on and on, you wonder, "Doesn't he *ever* stop?" or "Doesn't she realize she's turning everybody off with her incessant blather?" Unfortunately, many nonstop talkers are unaware of their annoying habit. We've even heard a number of them claim they were actually pretty good listeners.

You can spot nonstop talkers by their behavior, but also by the behavior of people around them. Nonstop talkers take up all the space in a conversation. They have opinions about virtually everything and they offer those opinions freely—even when it's clear people don't want to hear them. While they're talking, the people around them often have a "pained" expression on their faces, and when the nonstop talkers aren't looking, they roll their eyes at each other or make the "yap-yap" sign with their hands.

We've run into a lot of nonstop talkers in our work, but one sticks out: Jeff McCall. He was one of the first entrepreneurs we ever worked with. Like a lot of these guys, Jeff was a "good talker" in the classic sense. He was persuasive, charismatic, sometimes eloquent, and often very funny. He started off by himself to build a sales and service business; ten years later he had hundreds of employees and a dozen offices scattered across the Midwest. Like a lot of entrepreneurs, he was great at building a business, but not so hot at running it once it was built.

One of Jeff's biggest problems was the way he interacted with his top team. We observed him many times in meetings, and Jeff dominated every discussion. He consumed about 90 percent of the "air time" leaving his five or six top staff people to compete for the other ten. Jeff began to experience problems when several of his top people left the company, often for lower paying jobs with less potential. Here's what a few of them told us:

> "Jeff doesn't just like to talk, he likes to pontificate. I was willing to put up with that from my old man, but as a 35 -year-old sales executive? Nope. I decided to work for someone who wanted to listen to my opinions, not just his own."

> "Communication has to be a two-way thing if it's going to work well. With Jeff, it was one-way. He did all the talking and expected us to do exactly what he wanted, no questions asked. He was a classic example of the entrepreneur who says he wants to be a team player, but doesn't know how to do it."

> "Jeff reminded me of those movies about eighteenth century kings in Europe. He'd sit up there on his throne and issue orders, directives, pronouncements, edicts, and opinions. Often what he said made sense. But a lot of times it didn't. And whether he was right or wrong, he never said, 'That's what I think, what do you think?' If he had, I might've stayed."

Now that you've read through all five descriptions, try to decide which, if any, are like you. But don't stop there. Ask some people who know you well—and who'll be honest—if any of them fit you. After they do, ask them to talk about how your particular kind of bad listening affects them. And be prepared for some unsettling revelations.

A Personal Testimonial

So, where are we as we approach the end of this chapter? Up to this point, we've argued that you're probably not as good a talker or as good a listener as you can be when it comes to the important personal and professional relationships in your life. But what if you (and some of these other folks) really improved in these two critically important areas? What would be the result? We can't be sure, of course, but we certainly know the effect it's had on our partnership and friendship. We've both worked hard to improve in these two areas, and the impact has been enormous. So, let us both offer a brief testimonial to the power of good talking and good listening.

Mardy: Peter and I are not only business partners, we're best friends. And the reason I know we'll be business partners and best friends until one of us dies is that we've both paid the price to learn the very important communication skills of good talking and good listening. Over the years, we've learned to talk about sensitive and touchy subjects, stuff that would've been easy to avoid or pretend didn't exist. I don't know of any two people on this planet who talk and listen to each other better than the two of us. We've experienced almost all the relationship and business problems we've seen among our clients: the misunderstandings, the hurt feelings, the competitiveness, the tendency to blame the other guy when things are going bad, all of it. But one of the primary differences between us and our clients is this: We have these special skills to fall back on when we run into problems with each other. If we didn't, our friendship—not to mention our partnership—would have disintegrated long ago.

Peter: We get evidence from our clients all the time of the power of these communication skills in helping them solve major rifts in their business relationships. But what has really sold me on their power is not our clients' success with them, but how I have benefited from Mardy's ability to be a superb listener when I've needed that from him. Being by nature somewhat shy and introverted, I don't think out loud with the fluidity and facility that Mardy does. He's a natural talker. Since I'm not, being able to think out loud in his presence has been enormously helpful to me. His skills were most helpful when Mom died unexpectedly a few years back.

An hour here, a half hour there, he would just let me pour out my feelings about this very special person I loved dearly but with whom I certainly did not have a perfect relationship. By being a good listener, Mardy helped me gain a perspective on my relationship with Mom that I don't think I ever would have if he hadn't paid the price to learn how to be a quality listener. There's no way I could ever repay him for that.

OK. Enough about why you and your executive team members struggle with each other. Now let's talk about what you can do to reduce some of that struggle and start having some more fun and enjoyment with each other.

7

How Willing Are You to Try to Improve Things?

We've spent the better part of the first half of this book talking about why you and your team members have more trouble getting along with each other than you'd like. In the rest of the book we'll be taking on a more positive tone. We'll be talking about what you and your team members—but especially you—can do to make these important working relationships more satisfying and less frustrating.

But before talking about specific things you can do, we want to put your feet to the fire. We want you to ask yourself this question: "Just how willing am I to try to improve things with my team members?" To help you with your answer, we'll walk you through a series of more specific questions. For the time being don't worry a whole lot about how you'd answer any one of them. Just read through the chapter and absorb what we have to say. You may even want to put the book down and revisit these questions a week (or even a month) from now. Eventually, however, we'll want you to answer them as honestly as you can.

- Am I ready to take a lot of responsibility for whatever the "problem" is?

- Am I willing to learn some new concepts and skills?

- Am I willing to really *work* on my relationships with my team members?

A couple of additional thoughts before you take a detailed look at these questions. One, when you do get around to answering them, the more you can give a hearty "yes" to, the more likely you'll be able to make some positive changes in the way your team functions. Two, this is especially true the more power you have on your team and the more power you have in your organization. People on executive teams and in organizations usually take their lead from the people with the most power. And what's important if you're a person with a lot of power is not that you show an aptitude and natural inclination for the "relationship" approach we're recommending in this book. Not at all. (You can even be a bit clumsy.) What's important is that you *try*. What's important is that you make a sincere effort to improve the quality of your relationships with the people on your team. If you do that—especially in your role as a boss or powerful person on your team—you'll be amazed at the positive difference you can make. You'll be more productive, the people you work with will be more productive and all of you will get a lot more enjoyment out of your jobs.

Am I Ready to Take a Lot of Responsibility for Whatever the "Problem" Is?

In Chapter 2 we talked about how hard it is to see *our* contribution to relationship problems with other people and how easy it is to see *their* contribution. Well, if you're going to have much chance of improving things on your team, you'll have to take a hard look at your responsibility for the problem or problems you're having. Some examples:

The "senior" executive director. Let's say you're in your late 50's and have just taken over the helm of a small trade association after retiring from the Air Force as a Brigadier General. You've had a long and distinguished career managing operations much larger and more complicated than the organization you're now heading up. Your new staff is bright and energetic but nowhere near as experienced as the professionals you're used to supervising. In your view, these folks have a lot to learn and you're keeping a close eye on them.

After about six months on the job you sit down individually with two of your staff members and ask them to tell you "how things are going." At first they're cautious and seem to be pulling their punches, but as they warm up they also open up. These are the kinds of things they start telling you:

> "Jack, everybody here has a lot of respect for your intelligence and experience, but just because we're much younger than you are doesn't mean we don't know anything."

> "I know our lack of experience makes you a little nervous. But you have a tendency to second-guess even some of the most trivial decisions we make. You asked me to be candid here. Well, I gotta tell ya, Jack, I think I'm capable of deciding on the printer for our office stationery. When you get involved at that level of decision making, it just slows everything down."

> "Jack, you're an impressive guy. You're an excellent public speaker. You've got some real good ideas about where this place should be headed. Now, don't take this the wrong way. But a lot of us are wondering why you spend so much time around the office and get so involved in the day-to-day running of the place? Why don't you spend more time out with the members doing things that you know how to do well that the rest of us, frankly, can't do?"

Most employees would never be this candid with you. But some will. Let's say you get this kind of feedback from them. How are you going to react? Are you going to get defensive? Are you going to feel hurt and misunderstood? Or are you going to take their comments to heart? As hard as it will be to do, can you swallow the fact that much of what they're saying is accurate and that you need to be willing to change your ways a bit?

The "part-time" daughter in the business. Imagine this scenario. You're a divorced woman in her late 30's with a ten-year-old son. Your younger brother, your older sister, your father, and you each own 25 percent of the stock in the business your father started 30 years ago. The four of you go off on a weekend retreat with a psychologist who has just started to work with the company. During the retreat each of you gets some candid feedback from the other three. These are some things they told you:

> "Cheryl, we know it's hard raising a child on your own. But we don't think you're holding up your end of the log in this partnership. The three of us *act* like owners of this business, but you don't."

> "I usually get into work by seven-thirty, and a lot of times I don't leave until six or seven at night. We're lucky if you get here by ten, and you're usually out the door by four o'clock."

> "Cheryl, it's not just how much less time you put in than the rest of us. It's the *attitude* you seem to have about the business. For example, when we have the monthly owners meetings, a lot of times you don't even show up. You act more like a part-time employee than you do an owner. I mean, you're my sister and I love you dearly, but I resent your attitude."

Feedback like this is tough to listen to. It can sting; it can hurt. But the important question is, how are you going to deal with it? Are you going to have the courage and the emotional maturity to face up to what your brother and your sister and your father are saying and try to do something about it? Or are you going to build a wall of defensiveness and resentment that pushes them even further away from you?

Am I Willing to Learn Some New Concepts and Skills?

If you're going to make any real, positive difference in the relationships between you and your other team members, it'll help you a great deal to get involved in a self-improvement program. For some people self-improvement is a way of life. These folks are always on the lookout for opportunities to learn new things, to expand their horizons, and to constantly explore the richness and abundance life can offer them. If you're one of these people, you can probably even skip this question. On your own, you'll be seeking out different ways you can improve the important relationships in your life. This book will be only one more of the many steps you take in that general direction.

However, if you're not this kind of growth-oriented person, don't skip over this question. Don't skip over it because it implies you'll have to do a couple of things you're not used to doing: devote time to learning new concepts and skills, and put up with the frustration that automatically goes along with breaking old habits and forming new ones.

Let's talk about devoting time to learning. There are lots of ways to learn new concepts and skills. Reading is one way. Some people—like the two of us—are voracious readers. Some aren't. Other people prefer to get new information through audiotapes or videotapes. Some people prefer to take courses or attend seminars. And some people learn best by watching experts on something and then trying to emulate those experts. How you learn new concepts and skills to improve relationships with your team members isn't important. What's important is that you choose a method comfortable for you and that you devote regular and consistent time to that method. And it doesn't have to be a lot of time. If you spend as little as half an hour a week reading articles and books or listening to audiotapes or watching videotapes on improving your relationships, you'll learn a great deal within a year's time.

Now let's talk about the frustration that goes with learning a new skill where you have to break old habits and form new ones. If you have any doubts that learning a new skill can be frustrating, consider these examples:

Learning how to control your temper. Peter knows how frustrating this can be:

> "I definitely have a bad temper. It's something I've struggled to control all my life. But ever since Mardy and I started working in this area, I've felt I couldn't look at myself in the mirror unless I made a concerted effort to stop expressing my anger inappropriately, especially to my wife, Linda, and other family members. I haven't licked the problem yet. I'm making progress. But that progress has been tough and slow."

Getting organized. Maybe you're like Sarah Peters. She was a client of ours for years, and she's since become a good friend. Sarah is a wonderful person, but she's terribly disorganized. She's often late for appointments or cancels them at the last minute because she does a lousy job of planning her time. When she gets into her office in the morning, she jumps right into her work without a second's thought to what her priorities are. And she gets so caught up in crises that she waits forever to return phone calls from clients and good friends. Sarah's brother, who works closely with her, told us:

> "I love Sarah's energy and enthusiasm for our business. But the fact that she's so disorganized causes us a lot of pain and turmoil around here. Sarah *wants* to change; she *wants* to get her act together and lead a more orderly existence. But I see how hard it is for her. She has to force herself to write out a 'to do' list every morning when she really wants to just plunge headlong into that ocean of things to get done. She's got signs posted all over her office about returning calls. And she encourages the rest of us to tell her to slow down when she starts to get real hyper. But it's a struggle for her. A real struggle."

Being more open and aboveboard. Maybe you're like Clarence Folsworth. Clarence is on a team of vice-presidents we're working with right now. He's a guy in his late 40's with a lot of experience as a "short-term" CEO who can go into a company and turn it around in a year or two. But Clarence's colleagues have one big problem with him: his lack of openness. This is typical of the kinds of things they've told us about him:

> "The guy's loaded with ability. He's probably brilliant. But when he tells me something, I'm never sure I'm getting the full story. He's awfully good at painting a rosy picture of whatever project he's working on. But then, usually when it's too late to do anything about it, he drops the other shoe on you. You find out there's this big goddam problem he neglected to mention six months ago when we coulda done something about it."

> "Like last week when we found out the fourth quarter for one of his companies was gonna be terrible. Clarence knew that would happen way back in September. But he never mentioned anything about it to the rest of us. We thought things were going great."

We're convinced Clarence wants to be more open and above-board with the other vice-presidents in his group, but it's not easy for him. He says:

> "Those guys are right. I'm not always as straightforward as I should be. But I grew up in a family where honesty got you in trouble—like a whack in the mouth, or being locked in a closet for a few hours. I learned real quick that bending the truth and smooth talking were ways to avoid punishment. I'm trying. I really am. But those old habits don't give way easily."

There's no question that learning how to control your temper, learning how to get organized, or learning to be more open and direct are all frustrating experiences. But there's another frustrating experience you'll have to endure if you're going to improve your relationships with your team members: learning how to listen. In Chapter 9, we'll talk about what good listening means, and we'll talk about how you can start becoming a better listener. But we won't mislead you: good listening is hard. Sitting face to face with someone who's expressing strong, negative feelings about you—and that happens when you start working on a relationship with a team member—is frustrating. You'll have a powerful urge to interrupt the other person to talk about how badly and unfairly you've been misjudged. But you can't do that. You have to continue to listen, to pay attention, to stay on the other person's wavelength. That's frustrating. But, it's frustration that will pay off enormously if you can tolerate it.

Am I Willing to Really Work on My Relationships with My Team Members?

If, at some point in the near future, you can't give a definitive "yes" to this question, we don't hold out much hope things will improve between you and your team members. But what does really working on your relationships with your team members mean? At least four things:

- Making the time to meet regularly

- Actually meeting with your team members

- Talking about your relationships and each other

- Making some changes in your behavior

Making the Time to Meet Regularly
If you're like most of the people we work with, the chances are you are a very busy person. Now we come along and ask you to put even more stuff on your plate. Before you throw your hands up in exasperation, let us explain. We don't want you to work longer hours. We just want you to make meeting regularly with your team members a priority. For example, let's say you're the head of an executive team with five people reporting to you. We'd like to see you meet four times a year with each of these folks for at least an hour and a half. We'd also like to see you meet four times a year with the entire group for a half day session. And we'd like you to meet at an off-site retreat for an entire two days with your team. This comes out to a total of less than 80 hours a year. There's no question that's a significant amount of time. But it would be time extremely well spent. In the long run, spending these 80 hours with your team members will save you massive amounts of time that would have been spent solving problems that could have been avoided. But right now you have to take our word for it. And the question remains: Will you make the time to have these meetings?

Actually Meeting with Your Team Members
Even if you make a firm commitment to meet with your team members and set aside the time to do it, things will happen that get in the way:

— For well over a month you've been trying to schedule a meeting with your boss so the two of you can talk about improving your working relationship. The meeting is scheduled for two o'clock on Thursday afternoon. At noon on Thursday your biggest client calls and says, "Pat, can you break away for lunch today at one? Our president came into town unexpectedly and he'd really like to meet you."

— You're the managing partner of an engineering firm. You and the four other senior partners are headed out of town this weekend for a two-day partner retreat in West Virginia. You've never done this sort of thing before. All of you are anxious about it, but looking forward to it, too. On Thursday morning there's some bad news. The mother of one of your partners has just suffered a severe heart attack. He and his wife will be spending the weekend in Milwaukee with other family members who fear their mother is close to death.

— You just turned 40 last month. For the last nine years you've been putting your heart and soul into building a computer services company. You started reading this book because you have two vice-presidents, about five years younger than you, who are extremely talented and who you'd like to keep on your team. Your relationships with both are okay, but you sense some dissatisfaction on their part, and you're nervous another outfit will steal them away. Several weeks ago you committed to meeting with them individually just to talk about your working relationships. The problem is, last week you got a call from an investment banking firm representing a company who'd like to buy you out. For the last three days you've been scurrying around to prepare some materials for the banker. You've decided to put your meetings with your two vice-presidents "on hold."

Here's the point. There are always going to be activities and events that will compete for the time you set aside to meet with your team members. Sometimes these competing activities should win out. Maybe it is critically important to have lunch with your important client and his president. A death or serious illness in the family of one of your key partners is reason enough to cancel a weekend retreat. And maybe preparing materials for that investment banker should take precedence over your meetings with your vice-presidents. But our experience is that these meetings often don't get rescheduled. They keep getting canceled or postponed and eventually are forgotten. It'll take a lot of persistence and commitment to make sure this doesn't happen.

Talking about Your Relationships and Each Other

We want to be clear about this. The purpose of these meetings with your team members is to talk about your relationships with each other and how you can improve them. The purpose of these meetings is not to talk about business, about things like:

— How you can get more highway engineering contracts in southern California.

— The strengths and weaknesses of the three new candidates you've just interviewed for the human resources director position.

— Why the direct mail advertising campaign for your new exercise machine isn't "pulling" well.

— Whether it really is a good idea to construct a new headquarters building for the association, given that your members have been hard hit by the recession.

The purpose of these meetings is to:

— Ask questions like, "What do you think I can do to make your work here more enjoyable?"

— Tell that new associate who's been working 60 and 70 hour weeks how much you value her effort and the quality of her work.

— Really take it to heart when one of your junior team members screws up the courage to tell you you dominate staff meetings and cut off the free and open discussion of new ideas.

— Have the guts and caring to tell one of your partners you think he has a drinking problem and you'd like to help him solve it.

Talking about these kinds of things isn't easy; you'll tend to avoid it. And you have to face how hard you're willing to try to overcome this tendency.

Making Some Changes in Your Behavior

Let's say you start holding these "relationship" meetings with your team members. You're going to get some important feedback. Your team members are either going to tell you directly—or strongly imply—they'd like you to change your behavior in certain ways. Some examples:

— You and your younger brother are partners in a manufacturing firm you both inherited from your father 15 years ago. For a long time your brother has been trying to send you the message that you're too much of a "lone ranger" in the way you run the company. In your last meeting with him he made it clear he'd like you to sit down with him and go over some international projects you're working on but never talk to him about.

— You're a senior partner in an investment banking firm in Chicago. You and your three other partners have recently hired a facilitator to help the four of you get together every other week to talk about your partnership and how all of you can get along with each other more harmoniously. In the last meeting you got some frank feedback:

> "Susan, you have an uncanny gift for sniffing out good deals. When it comes to mergers and acquisitions, you're probably stronger than all the rest of us put together. But you don't keep us informed. We don't know the status of your deals until they're completed or until some crisis erupts. We almost get the sense that, at times, you're being secretive with us. We don't like that feeling. Please try to do a better job of keeping us informed."

— You're a research scientist who's been working for the Department of Health and Human Services for the last 15 years. For most of that time you've been working on highly theoretical and complicated studies that have won you an international reputation in your field. You've recently been promoted to the head of administration for your research center. You and your boss, the director of the center, don't have a real good relationship. You've been meeting regularly to try to improve the relationship. This is what your boss has been trying to say to you:

> "George, I know your heart and soul still lie in the work you were doing before you got promoted. But things have changed. We're getting tremendous pressure from the agency and from Congress to make our work here more relevant to public health concerns. I don't see you picking up that banner. I see you still very much on the side of scientists in the lab who just want to do their work unrestrained by administrators and political concerns. I don't know if you realize how serious the situation is. If we don't change, I'm afraid they might go ahead and close us down."

When you give your teammates a chance to open up like this and suggest things you could do differently, you set an expectation that you'll change your behavior in some way. And here are a few things we've learned from our clients about setting this kind of expectation:

The more power you have on your team and in your organization, the more important it is for you to try to change. We've mentioned it before, and we'll mention it again. If you have power on your executive team and in your organization, people will take their lead from you. They'll follow your example. If you try to make some positive changes in your behavior, chances are they'll try to make some positive changes of their own .

You don't have to make big changes. Changing behavior is hard for all of us. Your team members realize that. They don't expect you to change a lot. What they're looking for are some signs that you care about making their lives at work more pleasant and more fulfilling. Take the example where your younger brother has asked you to act a little less like a "lone ranger" in running the company. Let's say over the next year you simply meet with him once a month for an hour to discuss some of the international projects you're working on and to get his input on these projects. Doing something like that is not a drastic change in your behavior. But the positive effect on your brother can be enormous. Rather than feeling left out of an important component of the business, he now feels involved and valued.

If you're not going to change at all, it's better not to set the expectation in the first place. We really mean what we say here. It takes a lot of gumption to swallow your anxiety and be straight with a team member about how you'd like him or her to change. If that team member—especially if it's a boss—doesn't then make some kind of change, it can be horribly deflating. So if you're that executive director we mentioned at the beginning of the chapter and you're not willing to make at least some of the changes your staff members might suggest in that upcoming retreat, cancel the retreat. They'll be disappointed. But they won't be as disappointed as they would be if you led them to believe you were going to be more forward thinking and "out front" with your members—and then went right back to your old operating style.

At the beginning of the chapter we said we wanted to hold your feet to the fire by getting you to ask yourself the question: "Just how willing am I to try to improve things with my team members?" Even though you've read through the chapter and thought about some of the implications of this question, we doubt you're ready to answer it. In fact, we'd prefer that you didn't answer it at this point. It's too soon for that. But we would like you to keep the question in mind as you read through the rest of the book. Because in each chapter from here on, we'll be talking about a lot of things you can do to make life with your colleagues less of a struggle and more enjoyable. Each of these "things"—whether it's raising a touchy subject, paying better attention when you listen, or simply setting time aside to talk with a team member—will require effort. Effort that, right now, you may not want to expend. But at some point you'll have to decide whether you're willing to make that effort. All we can do is coax you. We *know* it's worth the effort. But now you just have to take it on faith.

8

Improving Your "Talking" Skills

In Chapter 6 we said that, if you're like most folks on executive teams, you're missing some important "people" skills you'll need if you want to improve your relationships with your team members. Then we went on to argue that—at least when it comes to relationships—you're not as good a "talker" or "listener" as you could be.

In this chapter we're going to expose you to six "talking" skills. By the end of the chapter you'll have a pretty good idea of what we mean by each skill and how you can start practicing and using each of them right away. Before we intorduce the skills, we want to take one more crack at trying to "sell" them to you. Here's the pitch:

They work. We've seen the power of these skills with our clients but especially in our relationships with our wives, with each other, and with other people in our lives about whom we care deeply.

You _can_ learn them. These skills will take some practice, some effort, and some tolerance for the kind of frustration we talked about in the last chapter. But you _can_ master them if you put your mind to it.

The more power you have, the more important it is to learn these new skills. We've made this point before, and we'll make it again before you get through the rest of the book. The more power you have on your executive team and in your organization, the more influence your day to day behavior has on the quality of life and productivity in the place where you work. If you bust your butt to learn these skills—especially the ones you're not so good at right now—you have no idea of the dramatic effect you can have on the people around you. They'll become more productive. They'll become more creative. They'll "buy in" more to what your organization is all about. But most important, their lives will become a little happier and a little less stressful.

The six "talking" skills we'll be covering in this chapter are:

- Giving feedback

- Expressing positive feelings

- Expressing negative feelings

- Raising a touchy subject

- Making an apology

- Expressing anxiety and feelings of inadequacy

Giving Feedback

The expression "giving feedback" has been kicking around organizational settings for the last 20 or 30 years. For us it means what you do when you offer your opinion/assessment/evaluation of someone else's performance—whether that performance is how the person hits a forehand in tennis, writes a final report, or gives a sales presentation. In Chapter 6, we argued that most managers are not good at offering constructive criticism (another term for giving feedback). But, whether you call it giving feedback or offering constructive criticism, it is an important skill for you to have for several reasons:

A lot of us really want it. Some people are very threatened by any feedback (no matter how tactfully delivered) that points out weaknesses or where they need to improve. Their egos, their sense of self-esteem—whatever you want to call it—are simply too fragile. But a lot of us aren't like that. We'd really value getting feedback on our performance in an area that matters to us. That area could be how we hit a tee shot in golf; it could be how we came across in that speech we gave last week at the convention; or it could be on a very broad area like how we could be a more supportive and and helpful business partner.

All of us can benefit from feedback, especially if it's given effectively. Considering the very sensitive nature of our work, we get to see our client's flaws up close and personal. And we've seen the tremendous value they've gotten from giving each other frank and helpful feedback. But sometimes (probably not often enough) we realize we're just as flawed as our clients. And we realize how much we've benefited from this sort of straightforward and well-intended feedback. Not long ago we were trying to give some examples of this in front of a large audience. Peter said:

> "I've certainly given Mardy a lot of candid feedback over the years. And I know he's taken what I've said to heart and grown from it. But I think the feedback he's grown from the most is the kind he's gotten from his two kids, Hilary and Jordan. Mardy's not only forced himself to become an excellent listener, but he's also put those skills into practice with the kids. He'd ask them to be frank with him about how he could be a better dad. And they told him. I think sometimes what they said probably hurt. But he always took it to heart, and he always tried to make some changes."

And Mardy said:

> "Peter doesn't make any secret about the fact he has a bad temper that he's struggled with all his life. But I've seen him change enormously in the last ten years in how he *controls* his temper. Ten years ago he would embarrass me at least once a month by reaming out a rental car agent or a desk clerk or a flight attendant over some trivial offense. He doesn't do that any more. And I think the reason he doesn't is that he's really gone to school on some very blunt feedback I've given him, and his wife, Linda, has given him, and even some of the feedback the guys he plays tennis and paddleball with have given him."

If you're a manager, giving feedback is an important "people development" tool. We'll make a flat assertion. If you currently supervise other people, you're not giving them enough feedback on their performance. Employees *need* feedback from their bosses. They need to know what their bosses think they're doing well. And they need to know where their bosses think they could improve. Perhaps we're wrong about you; maybe you do sit down periodically with the folks who report to you and give them precise, well-thought-out feedback on how they're doing and where they could stand to improve. But we doubt it. Just think back to all the bosses you've had in your career. Think of how much more you would have grown, especially during your 20's and early 30's, if your bosses had given you good feedback.

Now let's talk about giving feedback to one of your executive team members. (For a more detailed and focused look at how to give feedback, we suggest you read our book *Problem Employees: How to Improve Their Performance*, Dover, NH: Upstart Publishing, 1991.) Here we'll cover five principles we think it's important to keep in mind:

- Do some analysis first.

- Give feedback when your team member shows some signs of wanting it.

- Start with the positive, then move to the "needs improvement."

- Avoid emotionally loaded expressions.

- Be prepared to stop talking and start listening if receptivity drops.

Do Some Analysis First

When we say "analysis" here, we're not talking about some complicated process. We just think it's a good idea to "pre-think" what you're going to say to your team member when you do offer feedback. Let's work through an example. Imagine you and your father-in-law, Ralph, are partners in a medium-sized beer distributorship in upper New York State. You and Ralph are attending a weekend seminar in Philadelphia on the management of family owned businesses. During the Friday night orientation session the seminar leader has asked all participants to be prepared to give the family member they came to the seminar with some feedback on their managerial styles tomorrow afternoon. Later that same evening you're alone in your hotel room, not feeling the least bit tired, and Ralph has gone off to bed. Now is a good time to do some analysis.

Here's what we'd suggest. Take out a blank piece of 8 1/2 x 11 paper and draw a line down the middle. At the top left-hand side of the page write the word *Strengths*. On the right-hand side of the page write the word *Areas Needing Improvement*. Start with Ralph's strengths. Try to think of at least three areas where Ralph does a pretty good job as a manager. For example, you might decide he is a risk taker; he has an exceptionally high energy level; and he can be a very inspirational leader.

On the right-hand side of the page, under the heading *Areas Needing Improvement*, try to think of just one area where you think Ralph could improve as a manager. (We'll explain the choice of only one improvement area later on.) For example, you might simply write down the sentence, "Ralph needs to pay more attention to long-range planning."

This is a good start. You've thought of three general areas where Ralph does a pretty good job as a manager, and you've thought of one area where he could stand to improve. Now you need to get a little more specific. For example, on the left-hand side of the page you've listed Ralph's strengths as being a risk taker, as having an exceptionally high level of energy, and as being a very inspirational leader. All of that sounds nice and complimentary. But if you want Ralph to really believe your sincerity when you talk to him about his strengths, it's going to help a lot if you can come up with some examples of what you mean by each of these strengths. These are the kinds of examples you might come up with:

Ralph is a risk taker.
1. Ralph started this business in his mid-30's after leaving a secure job.
2. More than three times in the last 30 years Ralph has secured business loans with his personal property in order to help the business expand.

Ralph has an exceptionally high energy level.
3. Ralph is 62-years-old but has the stamina of someone who is 25.

4. Many times I've seen him stay out late entertaining customers and still be raring to go the next morning at eight o'clock.

Ralph can be a very inspirational reader.
5. Ralph does a great job of motivating his sales people, especially those who don't have his charisma and easy way with people.

Now let's talk about the one item you've put under the "needs improvement" side of the ledger. You've indicated that Ralph needs to pay more attention to long-range planning. But what does that mean? Let's say Ralph agrees to pay more attention to long-range planning. How are you (and how is Ralph) going to know he's actually doing this? Here's one way you might get more specific about what you have in mind:

Ralph needs to pay more attention to long-range planning.

"I'd like to have a clearer sense from Ralph of where he'd like the company to be five years from now in terms of sales, new markets, and what he sees as his and my role in the company at that time."

This isn't the most exhaustive analysis you could do in preparation for your feedback session with Ralph, but it's good enough as far as we're concerned. You've listed three areas where you think Ralph is pretty strong as a manager, and you've come up with some very credible examples of what you mean by these strengths. You've also come up with one area where you think Ralph could improve as a manager and you've been fairly specific in terms of how you think he could improve in this area. Of course, you could easily apply this same analysis format to other kinds of feedback you might give to one of your executive team members.

For example, let's say you and four other partners comprise the team that runs the show in a medium-sized consulting engineering firm. One of your partners is very excited because he's just learned the firm has been "short-listed" for a big city project your partner has been pushing for 18 months. Your partner says to you:

"Tim, Barbara, and I have been rehearsing for our interview with the planning commission on the fifteenth of this month. I think the presentation is pretty polished, but we're all a little close to it. Would you mind taking a look at this videotape we've made of ourselves and tell us what you think? That would be very helpful."

Perfect. Watch the tape. Think about it a little. Maybe watch it again. And then think about three aspects of the presentation you think are strong and one that could stand some improvement. Then, just as you did with Ralph, come up with examples of what you mean by each of the strengths of the presentation and one specific suggestion on how you think it could be improved.

Give Feedback When Your
Team Member Shows Some Signs of Wanting It

This is something very important to keep in mind when you give a team member (or anybody else) feedback. We know it from the work we've done with our clients and from all the reading we've done. But how do you tell when a team member wants feedback? Actually, that's fairly easy. When people want feedback, they usually make it pretty clear. Take the two examples we've used so far in this section. Your father-in-law, Ralph, wants some feedback on his managerial style. He's attending the seminar with you, and he's agreed to participate in the feedback session scheduled for tomorrow afternoon. And your partner in the engineering firm wants feedback. He's asked you to look at the tape of the practice presentation and offer him your reactions.

The big problem with giving feedback is not deciding when people want it. It's deciding when they *don't* want it. Here are some instances when it's very unlikely your team members will want any feedback from you:

When they're upset over a recent failure. Let's say one of your colleagues has just been called on the carpet by the "big boss." Even if you agree with some of the things your boss had to say to your peer, now is not a good time to offer any feedback. Rather than listen carefully to what you have to say, he or she is going to feel annoyed and resentful.

When they're seriously distracted by something. All of us go through periods in our lives when something important is preoccupying us. Maybe one of our kids is very sick. Maybe we've just lost a close family member. Maybe we're coming down to the last three weeks of preparation for an annual convention we're running. Or maybe we're engrossed in preparing for the bar exam or for board certification. At times like these, if a team member comes up and starts offering us feedback on our performance, we're not going to be very receptive no matter how tactful they are.

When they clearly have a need to talk about a problem. Imagine this situation. You're a few years shy of 60, and your daughter is about 30. The two of you own and operate four small gift shops in the Baltimore suburbs. It's about nine-thirty at night and you're very tired. The phone rings and it's your daughter. She starts right in:

> "Mom, I don't know what the hell to do with Jerry Stoner from Freemont. I get taken in by him every time. He's such a charming guy. The line he sells is absolutely gorgeous. But he *never* meets his delivery dates. I want to get mad at him. I want to call him at home right now. And if I do he's just going to go into his charm routine."

As you listen to your daughter, you have to exert tremendous self-control not to interrupt. *You* know what the problem is. You know the solution to the problem is just getting tough with the guy and letting him know that, even though you adore his line, you're going to drop him the next time he blows a delivery date. But as much as you want to interrupt your daughter and straighten her out, it's not the effective thing to do. The effective thing to do is let her talk. Trying to offer feedback before she winds down and gives you a sign she's interested in your opinion is a big waste of time. In fact, perhaps the best thing you could do here is let your daughter talk as long as she needs to and then say, "Honey, let's talk about it tomorrow morning before we open up." Chances are she'll be a lot more receptive to your feedback after a night's sleep.

Start with the Positive, then Move to the "Needs Improvement"
Why all this emphasis on the positive? Why do we recommend coming up with three strengths as opposed to only one area needing improvement when you give feedback? First, executive team members don't give each other anywhere near enough positive feedback. We talked about this in Chapter 5, but it bears repeating. All of us need positive feedback from the people we live and work closely with. Think about the people on your executive team, and think about the people who report to you. How often do you tell any of those folks how much you value working with them? How much you appreciate certain skills they have that you don't have? How much better a place your organization is to work because of their presence? We'd bet you don't give them that kind of feedback anywhere near as much as you could or should. The two of us—and we're supposed to be experts on this kind of stuff—don't do it with each other anywhere near as much as we could or should. Giving positive feedback is important. We all need to do more of it.

Second, it makes the "needs improvement" feedback a lot easier to take. The "needs improvement" portion of your feedback to a team member is the tough part. When someone (even someone we trust and respect) tells us we need to improve in some area, it almost always hurts at least a little, no matter how caring and well intended that person is. Any suggestion about how we can improve is going to sting a little. It just is. And it's a lot easier to hear that suggestion if we've just heard three sincere descriptions of how we're doing pretty well.

Avoid Emotionally Loaded Expressions
Emotionally loaded expressions are words and phrases that tend to hurt or annoy or anger people when you give them feedback. For example, how would you feel if one of your team members used adjectives like fussy, rigid, controlling, hot-tempered, compulsive, insecure, egocentric, self-absorbed, superficial, arrogant, overzealous, or shortsighted to describe you or your performance during a feedback session?

Occasionally, when we talk about the use of emotionally loaded expressions to an audience, we'll get a reaction like this:

> "Ah, I'm not sure I agree. I think, sometimes, using words like that can get somebody's attention. I mean, if

somebody is really pompous and arrogant, maybe telling them that flat out would be a good thing to do. Maybe it would get their attention. So it hurts a little. Sometimes it takes getting your feelings hurt to make important changes in your life."

Maybe. But we think you turn a lot more people off than you convert when you use emotionally loaded expressions. Besides, there are better ways to get your message across. A couple of examples:

Rather than Say:	It Would Be Better to Say:
"You have a tendency to be very fussy about the letters you ask other people to write for you."	"I think the people who write letters for you would appreciate your being a little bit more accepting of their writing style even if their writing isn't as concise and clear as your own."
"Too many of your decisions are impulsive and uninformed."	"When you make decisions, I think it would be better if you spent more time exploring the consequences of various options—even if that means delaying some of your decisions."

**Be Prepared to Stop Talking
and Start Listening if Receptivity Drops**
As we indicated a little earlier, the hard part of giving people feedback is not telling them the positive stuff, the things you feel they do well. All of us like to hear that sort of thing. The hard part of giving people feedback comes when you start talking about where they could improve. That's where their "receptivity" to what you're saying can drop like a stone. Let's go back to the example of you and your father-in-law, Ralph. It's now Saturday afternoon and the feedback exercise has begun. We'll eavesdrop on the two

of you as you're about to finish talking about Ralph's strengths as a manager and move to the area where he needs to improve:

> **You**: So, Ralph, to sum up I think three of your real strengths as a manager are that you're a risk taker, you've got an unbelievably high energy level, and you can be a very inspirational leader, especially with the sales people on our team who don't have your natural sort of charm and charisma.

> **Ralph**: (smiling) OK. That's nice to hear. All right, what do I need to work on?

> *(Right now, obviously, Ralph's receptivity to what you have to say is pretty high. Now let's see what happens.)*

> **You**: Well, Ralph, I do think there's one area as a manager where you could really stand to improve.

> **Ralph**: (nodding) Uh-huh.

> **You**: And it has to do with this whole issue of the future and planning for it. I'd just like to have a much clearer sense from you of where you'd like the company to be five years from now in terms of sales, new markets, and especially how you see my role in the company at that time.

> *(Ralph wrinkles his forehead and slowly starts shaking his head. Even though he hasn't said anything yet, it's clear that his receptivity is dropping. At this point you have a choice to make. You can keep talking and try to "override" Ralph's obvious skepticism with what you think is a persuasive argument, or you can simply stop talking and listen to his objections. Even though your natural tendency will be to keep talking, to press your case, we don't think that's a good idea. We think you should stop talking and listen very attentively to what Ralph has to say.)*

> **Ralph**: (with some real intensity on his face and in his voice) Look it, Billy, I know what you're saying makes a lot of sense in theory. But I've been in this business a long time. And I know how hard it is to predict trends. Five years from now? Who knows if there will even be a

market for alcoholic beverages five years from now? You see, what I'm saying is . . .

(Letting Ralph interrupt you here and go on and on about his objections may seem like a waste of time. But if you can stay with him, if you can try to really hear what he's saying and then "read it back"—we'll explain what that means in the next chapter—you'll be amazed at how Ralph's receptivity will go back up.)

Whether you're trying to give Ralph or anyone else feedback, our point here is this. It's a waste of time to talk to someone who isn't ready to listen to you. Your most eloquent, compelling argument will fall on deaf ears. So, if you see the person's receptivity go down (either through body language or a verbal interruption), stop. Let 'em talk. And listen. When they're convinced you understand their objections, they'll be a lot more amenable to what you have to say. And a lot more likely to make some of the changes you'd like them to make.

Expressing Positive
Feelings Toward a Team Member

In spite of all the problems that people on executive teams have in getting along, many of them have strong, positive feelings about each other. A few examples:

Trust. Maybe you have a chief financial officer working for you whose integrity, in your opinion, is beyond reproach. Given the power he has over the company's revenues and expenditures, he could find ways to line his own pockets that even the most sharp-eyed auditor could never uncover. But you know he wouldn't do something like that. Or maybe you have a sister you work with in whom you can confide the most personal of your concerns without the slightest worry those confidences would ever get violated.

Respect. Your boss is the president of a wholly owned subsidiary that, ever since they bought the company, has been trying to impose their way of doing things on your organization. Most recently, the parent company tried to make major cutbacks in your benefits package. You have tremendous respect for the way your boss handled the problem. He simply told them, "You do that and you can find yourself another boy." They backed down and since then they've been meddling a lot less.

Admiration. You have a woman on your team who's been working for you just a little over ten years. You recruited her right out of graduate school when she was still in her 20's. She probably has the best mix of scientific and administrative skills you've seen in the last 25 years. Three years ago her husband was killed in a tragic automobile accident. In addition to doing a superior job at work, she now has the task of raising three boisterous teenage boys on her own. Your admiration for her is enormous.

These are only a few examples of the kinds of positive feelings you may have for some of your team members. Several others might be pride, confidence, and the kind of affection we talked about in Chapter 5. But even though you may have these feelings for your team members, the chances are you rarely, if ever, express those feelings to them. Maybe you're an exception. We hope you are. But all our consulting experience tells us the great majority of executive team members simply don't share these kinds of positive feelings with each other.

Why Is It So Important to Express These Positive Feelings?
A good question. And, frankly, it's hard to give a clear answer. This is fuzzy, emotional sort of stuff that doesn't lend itself to precise description. All we can offer is some impressions:

It seems sad, almost tragic, for these feelings to go unexpressed. This is a very personal sentiment we've experienced scores and scores of times in our work. Here are these executive team members, these folks who work so closely together and have such strong, positive feelings for each other, but these feelings don't get expressed. That saddens us. It just does.

There's so much more potential for bonding and closeness when these feelings do get expressed. Earlier in the book we talked about an exercise we do in our team-building sessions where people break off in pairs to spend 15 minutes or so just giving each other positive feedback. We talked about the very powerful effect that always seems to have on team members and how, for just a little while, the room becomes almost a magical place. But beyond the specialness of these moments, we've seen old walls between team members begin to crumble. Just by exchanging feelings of respect or trust or admiration or whatever, people who've never had much of a relationship start to click together. And that's nice to watch.

It means so much to all of us to be told these feelings. If you have doubts about this, think about the last time someone you work closely with told you how much he or she admired you or trusted you or respected you or had confidence in your abilities. How did the expression of those feelings affect you on an emotional level? Your answer may be all the argument you need for the importance of shared feelings.

What Stops Us From Expressing These Feelings?

A good question. And a tough one to answer. In Chapter 5 we've touched on some of the answers people in the world of business and organizations often give to a question like this. These folks are inclined to say things like:

— "It's unprofessional to talk to colleagues this way."

— "It's very important to separate personal matters from business matters, and talking about that kind of stuff is getting way too personal for a business setting."

— "We're trying to get a job done here, not become best friends. If you need to talk about that kind of stuff, don't do it at work. Talk about it with your family or your friends or at church. Not here."

We think there are big flaws in this kind of reasoning, but these sorts of attitudes hold a lot of sway out there in organizations. Psychologists, psychiatrists, and other people in the psychotherapeutic arena would offer a different answer to this question. They'd say that what stops executive team members from expressing these kinds of feelings to each other is a fear of intimacy, a fear of getting too close. A fear that has deep roots going all the way back to our childhoods. And, while we agree, that answer seems more complicated than it needs to be. For us, a simpler and more understandable answer is that expressing these kinds of feelings makes a lot of people feel embarrassed. And since embarrassment is an emotion we'd all just as soon avoid, why do something that's going to bring it on?

A Few Suggestions

So what do you do? We're saying that expressing these kinds of positive feelings to team members is important. But you know that doing it is likely to embarrass you, or at least make you feel uneasy. Here's what we suggest:

Do it sparingly. Telling team members that you really trust them or admire them or really respect them or that you have a great deal of affection for them is not something that needs to be done frequently. In fact, if you do it too often, it can lose its potency. It can seem insincere or manipulative. So just do it once in a while.

Pick your moments and then talk from the heart. When you express positive feelings toward a team member, it's probably as important to pay attention to when and where you do it as it is to how you do it. As far as "when" and "where" are concerned, try to do it during a period of relative quiet in a private place. As far as "how" is concerned, listen to your feelings and to your heart. They'll help you say what you need to say. Imagine yourself in these two different situations:

It's about two-thirty on a beautiful Friday afternoon in late September. You and one of the other senior partners in your firm are sitting outside on the terrace of your office building overlooking the Potomac River. Neither of you is talking as you both gaze at two rowers bucking the current as they head upstream. You turn to your partner and say:

> "Trust is something I really value in people. And outside of an old friend I've had since grammar school, I don't think there is anyone in the world I trust more than you. When I found out my brother was infected with the HIV virus, I just ached for him. But because of

the stigma attached to it, I didn't know who to talk to. Except you. I knew you were a sensitive and caring person, but most of all I knew I could trust you to keep it to yourself. And I can't tell you how much that meant to me."

It's about seven-thirty in the morning and you and your boss are in your office just shooting the breeze over a cup of coffee. After he finishes cracking up over one of your corny jokes, you pause for a few seconds and say:

"Brady, I don't know if I've ever told you directly, but I've always had a hell of a lot of respect for you. And I think a good example of where that respect comes from is how you handled that offer from NASA you got about a month ago. I know that would have been an easier, better paying, and higher prestige job for you. And I know you turned it down mostly because of what the five of us have been trying to build here since the mid-80's. Most people, probably me included, would've said the heck with it and taken that job. And I just want to say I respect the hell out of you for that."

Raising a Touchy Subject

So much for expressing positive feelings toward your team members. But what about expressing negative feelings? Feelings like anger, annoyance, disappointment, and frustration to name just a few? That's what we want to talk about in this section.

To begin, lets go back to Chapter 5 for a few moments and briefly review the topic of "acute avoiding." We said acute avoiding is the kind of avoiding you do when something upsetting happens between you and one of your team members. The sequence goes something like this:

1. Your team member does something that causes you to have some strong negative feelings.

2. You stay pretty upset for 24 hours, maybe longer.

3. You decide not to talk to your team member about what happened.

4. Your feelings about what happened may subside, but they never go away completely.

Rather than follow this sequence of acute avoiding, what can you do? How can you talk to a team member about "touchy subjects" that are going to crop up in even the healthiest of business relationships? Over the years we've come up with some steps that seem to work pretty well:

1. Arrange a time and place to meet with your team member.

2. Structure the meeting.

3. Describe what your team member did that's been bothering you.

4. Describe right from the heart how it made you feel.

5. Do the best job you can of listening to your team member's response.

Let's work through these steps using an example from Chapter 5. Do you remember Ernie and Hank? These two fellows were co-owners of an architectural firm in Arizona. Ernie owned 80 percent of the stock and Hank the other 20 percent. Ernie was a great big guy with a a boisterous personality, and Hank was a technical genius who was also very short and shy. Recently Ernie had begun to refer to Hank (behind his back) as the "little shit." Hank had found about this and was very upset.

Arrange a Time and Place to Meet with Your Team Member
If Hank is going to talk to Ernie about this very touchy subject, we think he needs to arrange to do it with Ernie ahead of time. Hank might walk into Ernie's office late in the afternoon when most people have cleared out and say:

> "Ernie, there's something on my mind I'd like to talk to you about. It's probably going to take at least 45 minutes to an hour to discuss, and I was just wondering if you've got some time that you can free up to do it in the next several days."

Chances are Ernie's curiosity will be piqued and he may ask, "Well, what do you want to talk about?" This is not the time for Hank to discuss the touchy subject. So a good way for him to respond would be:

> "Ernie, I'd rather not get into it now. It's going to take some time, and I'd rather do it earlier in the day when we're both fresh. I don't care where we meet as long as we can have some quiet, uninterrupted time for about an hour."

As soon as Hank gets an agreement from Ernie about a time and place to meet, he should close off the conversation:

> "Great. Thanks a lot, Ernie. I appreciate it. I'll see you right here in your office on Wednesday morning at seven-thirty."

Structure the Meeting
Now it's seven-thirty Wednesday morning and Ernie and Hank have just walked into Ernie's office, each carrying a cup of coffee. After closing the door to the office, the two sit down and complain a little to each other about what a bad season the Cardinals are having. Then they start to get down to business.

> **Ernie**: So, pal, what's up? Why are we having this meeting?
>
> *(Here Hank will structure the meeting. He'll talk about why he wanted to meet. How he'd like the meeting to proceed. And how he thinks the two of them can get the most out of the meeting.)*
>
> **Hank**: Ernie, there's been something on my mind for a couple of weeks that I've wanted to talk to you about. It's what I would call a "touchy subject." Now, I know you're wondering what the hell I'm talking about.
>
> **Ernie**: (Smiles and nods his head vigorously.)
>
> **Hank**: Well, I'll get to that in a moment. After I talk about what I've got on my mind, I really want to hear

what you have to say. And I'll just try to be the best listener I possibly can. I think we can get the most out of this meeting if we can just be as honest as possible about how we feel and try to do as good a job of listening to each other as we can.

(Now Hank will pause to get any reactions Ernie might have before he proceeds.)

Ernie: (Still smiling and shaking his head good-naturedly.) Okay. I'm still not sure what you're talking about. But go ahead.

Describe What Your
Team Member Did that's Been Bothering You

(Here Hank will try to be as precise and objective as he can. He'll especially try to avoid the kinds of "emotionally loaded" words and expressions we talked about earlier in the chapter.)

Hank: Well, as you might have imagined, Ernie, this is hard for me to talk about. But here's what's on my mind. Several people in the office have mentioned that they've heard you refer to me more than a few times as the "little shit."

(Hank pauses here to check Ernie's reaction. If Ernie starts talking—whether it's to defend himself or to deny what Hank has said or whatever—the best thing Hank can do is stop talking and listen to whatever Ernie has to say.)

Ernie: (Obviously blushing and looking very embarrassed.) Look, man, I don't know what to say. If I did say those things—and I guess I did—it was really stupid. I certainly didn't mean anything by it, and I sure didn't think it would ever get back to you.

Hank: (Nodding and pausing to make sure Ernie is not going to add anything.) Well, Ernie, what I want to do now is just tell you how I felt and how I still feel about your saying those things about me.

(Hank will pause again here to make sure that Ernie won't interrupt him.)

Ernie: (Looking sheepish and nodding his head) OK, go ahead.

Describe Straight from the Heart How It Made You Feel

(Here Hank will talk about his feelings, about his emotions. As much as he possibly can, he'll avoid saying anything judgmental or evaluative about Ernie.)

Hank: Well, Ernie, since you're not short, it's probably hard for you to know how I felt when I heard what you were saying about me. But comments like that always cut me. They always tear away a little at me. They hurt. There's just no getting around that.

(Ernie nods and looks like he's really tuning in to what Hank is saying. It's fascinating. When you talk to another person at this deep emotional level, you usually get a very attentive listener. That's one of the nice things about talking right from the heart. You're able to connect with the other person because you've cut through the crap and are revealing yourself in an honest and unvarnished way.)

Hank: I think it hurts when anybody says those kinds of things about me, but I think it especially hurts to hear they were coming from you. We've certainly had our differences and antagonisms over the years, but we are partners, and I'd like to think we're friends, too. And when a friend says things like that about me, they hurt all that much more.

Do the Best Job You Can
of Listening to Your Team Mate's Response

(Hank has now talked specifically about what Ernie did, and he's talked candidly and poignantly about how it made him feel. Now his task is to listen intently to what Ernie has to say.)

Hank: (Leaning forward a little bit in his chair.) Ernie, I've said a lot of stuff here. And I'm sure you've got some reactions. I'll try to be the best listener I can be.

Ernie: (A mixture of embarrassment and thoughtfulness on his face.) Gee, pal, I don't quite know where to start.

Again, I want to say how sorry I am. I don't think anybody deserves to be talked about like that. I guess I just feel kind of ashamed of myself, and I wish I'd never said those things. On the other hand, maybe I've learned something from this experience. I'm just sorry I did it at your expense.

(Hank leans forward a little more and nods but doesn't say anything. Sometimes pausing and not saying anything is one of the best things you can do as a listener.)

Ernie: (After about 30 more seconds of silence.) I'll tell you this, for what it's worth, I'm never going to call you names again. Never. Not to your face, and not behind your back.

(Here Hank will use a listening skill that we'll be talking a lot about in the next chapter. It's called "reading back." It's an attempt on Hank's part to summarize the main points Ernie has been making.)

Hank: (After pausing for another 30 seconds.) Ernie, several things are coming across for me as you speak. One thing, clearly, you're feeling sorry for the things you were saying about me. (Pausing for a few seconds to check Ernie's reaction.) Another thing you were saying is that you feel ashamed of yourself for having said those things. You were also saying that, maybe you learned something from this—you're just sorry it was at my expense. And the last thing I heard was pretty clear. You're very committed to never calling me names again.

(Now that Hank has "read him back," Ernie will probably elaborate on his remarks, and Hank will stay in "listening mode" a while longer. But at some point the conversation will wind down.)

Ernie: Hank, I guess I just don't have anything else to say except that, again, I'm real sorry and it ain't going to happen again.

Hank: Well, I'm just glad we talked about this. (Getting up from his chair and extending his right hand to

Ernie.) I'm a little pooped from all this. How about if we adjourn?

Ernie: (Standing up and shaking Hank's hand and simultaneously patting him on the back.) Yeah. I think that's a good idea.

Obviously, raising touchy subjects with team members is tough. It's much easier to avoid talking about them and, of course, that's what you do most of the time. But we think taking the risk to get these touchy subjects out on the table is worth the risk. Admittedly, doing it doesn't always go smoothly. Sometimes it doesn't work at all. But talking about this kind of thing with team members can go a long way to healing wounds that might otherwise fester and poison relationships.

A Couple of Other "Talking" Skills

So far we've gone into a lot of detail about three "talking" skills we think are very important to building and maintaining solid relationships with your team members. However, there are a couple of other skills—which we won't treat in such depth—that we'd like you to think about. One is making apologies. The other is expressing feelings of insecurity or inadequacy.

Making Apologies

In Chapter 5 we said how hard it is for some people to apologize, to say they're sorry. Maybe you're one of those folks. Maybe it's almost like cutting off a thumb for you to:

—go up to someone who works for you and say:

"Pat, I'm sorry I snapped at you the other day in the hall when I found out the Hanforth report wasn't gonna go out on time. I still think we should have been able to get it out, but that's no excuse for talking to you the way I did."

—or sit down with one of the other senior partners in your engineering firm and say:

"Stan, I've been thinking about the other night when we were having a couple of beers with Murphy and Turlock. You know, they're probably the biggest clients we've got, and I think I'm always a little nervous when we're around them. I think that remark in front of them about your being 'stiff' was a little insensitive. I could tell from the expression on your face that it bothered you a bit. I'm sorry."

—or walk into your boss's office and say:

"Bob, I know and you know that I've been giving you the silent treatment over the last week ever since you told me that you had second thoughts about the decision I made on Danbert. I'm still a little annoyed that you couldn't go along with me on that one. But I think it would have been better if I could have come in and said that, rather than giving you the cold shoulder for a week. I think that was immature and unprofessional. I apologize."

Even though it would be hard to imagine yourself in any of these three situations, we want to push you a little. We think admitting mistakes and apologizing for them—especially when those mistakes may have had a hurtful effect on a team member—is worth the effort for several reasons:

People usually appreciate it a great deal. We're not sure why, but we've seen the coldest, hardest people melt in the face of a heart-felt apology. Somehow, when you apologize sincerely, with no attempt to manipulate, you touch people in a very fundamental way. And you can see the appreciation written all over their faces.

It often keeps resentments from building up. If you do something that hurts or upsets one of your team members, the chances are good the person won't confront you about it and will harbor some resentment toward you for a long time. Unless you apologize. But once you apologize, all that resentment tends to melt away. And someone who might have remained distant or even looked for a way to get back at you can now turn into an ally and even a good friend.

If you're a boss and you apologize to your employees, it can be one of the best motivators going. Think about all the bosses you've had over the years. How many of them were good at making apologies to you or other employees when those apologies were really warranted? If your bosses were like most of the ones we see out there, they were probably pretty bad at admitting mistakes and apologizing when it was appropriate. This is a fact most employees accept about their bosses, but they don't like it. But every now and then you run into a person who can apologize when he says or does something that hurts or otherwise upsets an employee. And what a remarkably positive effect someone like that can have on employees. Employees will say:

— "That's really amazing. I don't think I've ever had a boss apologize to me, no matter how obnoxious their behavior was."

— "It's so refreshing to work with someone who can apologize when he does something that's rude or thoughtless. It just means a hell of a lot to me."

— "I was simply amazed when Mason came up to me after the meeting and said he was sorry for the way he snapped at me in front of everybody. For a man of his generation to do something like that is unusual. I have a lot of respect for him."

Expressing Feelings of
Insecurity or Inadequacy to Team Members
Can you imagine yourself in either of these two situations?

Feeling over your head as a manager. Right after getting your PhD in biochemistry you went to work for a federally funded research center in one of the Western states. For the last 15 years you've been supervising a small group of scientists but have been concentrating heavily on your own research. You're now a highly respected figure in your field and are frequently invited to deliver papers at scientific conferences all over the world. The newly appointed director of the center has asked you to become the administrative chief. The position sounds attractive because you have been so unhappy with the way the previous administrator (not a scientifically trained person) seemed to categorically ignore the needs of all the researchers in the center. But you've got some reservations, too.

It's about two-thirty in the afternoon and you're sitting in the cafeteria talking quietly with the new director about some of these reservations:

> "Tom, I'm gonna be frank with you. I want to take this job. I think it's a great opportunity to do some things for the center. But I'm a little scared, too. Maybe more than a little scared. The most people I've ever supervised is five or six scientists. Now I'm gonna be responsible for over 85 people. That makes me nervous. In addition, I'm gonna have to work with systems and procedures that I'm not familiar with. I hope I can do away with some of them because I think they get in the way. But some of them I know are necessary and it's gonna be hard for me to deal with them. I guess I feel a little like the kid about to go off to the first day of kindergarten. I'm excited, but I'm a little frightened, too."

Feeling like a fifth wheel. Next month you'll turn 55. It was almost 20 years ago that you took over a small trade association in Chicago that was on the verge of bankruptcy. Getting the place up and running was a huge struggle the first five years, but after that the association and its membership began to grow steadily and without a lot of pain. A little over ten years ago you hired a woman in her mid-20's, Tory Watkins, to be your receptionist. At the time she seemed like just another new employee who would stick around for a year or two and then be gone. But things didn't work out that way. Tory turned out to be a real gem. Each year she would take on more and more responsibility. Now, a decade later, she's the number-two person in your organization.

It's a Saturday morning and you and Tory are sitting in her office chatting over a cup of coffee. The two of you have just finished editing an important report that needs to go out Monday morning. No one else is in the office. You've just broached a subject that's not easy for you to talk about:

> "This is not that easy to explain but it goes something like this. You know I spend a great deal of time on the road talking to our members and to the customers they have to deal with. But when I come back here to the office, I feel—how to put it—I just feel uncomfortable. I feel out of place. Yeah, I've got the big fancy office, but it's really you, not me, that runs the show here. And I'm tremendously proud of what you've been able to achieve, but I also feel like you've left me a little in the dust. Not that that's a bad thing. It's probably a good thing. But I just think we need to talk about it."

Well, what do you think? Can *you* imagine yourself in either of these two situations? (Remember that in Chapter 5 we talked about how hard it is for executive team members to open up and disclose these private, sensitive feelings to each other.) Because despite the fact that talking about this kind of stuff is difficult (even with a team member who makes you feel "safe"), there are several strong reasons to do it:

Sharing these feelings with the right person can do a lot for your peace of mind. None of us, no matter how good our sense of self-esteem, is immune to occasional feelings of insecurity and inadequacy. If you're not in the habit of sharing these kinds of feelings with someone you trust, it's hard to describe the positive emotional impact this kind of "opening up" can have on you. It's very powerful. It puts things in perspective. It chases the demons away. And it usually makes problems that once seemed forbidding and overwhelming look like you might be able to deal with them and keep your sense of dignity and self-worth intact.

What may seem like a sign of weakness is really a sign of strength. Unfortunately in our society, a lot of men (and some women) grow up with the view that talking about feelings of inadequacy and insecurity is something you never do, at least in any kind of competitive environment. They think this kind of "soul bearing" can too easily be interpreted as a sign of weakness and that it can put them at a severe disadvantage. We can understand that point of view. Talking about these kinds of feelings to someone you don't fully trust is not a good idea. But a team member who does care about you is not going to see your disclosure of these feelings as a sign of weakness. On the contrary, their reaction is likely to be:

> "Art, I know talking about this kind of stuff is not easy for you. I knew you were very nervous about making that presentation to the undersecretary. But I really respect you for being able to tell me about those feelings directly. In fact, I can't ever remember having a boss who would open up to me the way you just did. I'm proud to work for somebody like you."

You open up the possibility of getting help and support when you need it. One of the nice things about letting down your guard and talking about an area where you feel insecure is that you almost always get a genuine offer to help you out. Even if you never accept the offer, it's nice to know that:

— Your boss wants to help you cope with your anxiety about a new job managing people older and more experienced then you.

— One of your partners is ready to come in on weekends to teach you that new computer system that's got you completely confused.

— Your CEO is willing to sit by your side at the board meeting to help you deal with the intimidating questions that a couple of "difficult" board members are likely to ask.

Never underestimate the potential benefits of mastering good talking skills, both at work and at home. Now let's talk about good listening.

9

Learning How
To Really Listen

As far as we're concerned, learning how to be a better listener is probably the single most important thing you can do to improve the quality of your relationships with your team members. Why do we feel so strongly about listening skills? Why did we come on so strong in Chapter 5 when we said that most people—even professional interviewers and counselors and high-level executives—are not anywhere near as good at listening as they could or should be? Well, we could offer a bunch of reasons. We could talk about the powerful effect that good listening has had on our partnership and on our friendship. And we could talk about how good listening has helped scores of our clients out of problems they felt were overwhelming and unresolvable. But, for now, we want to focus on just one reason that learning to be a better listener is so important. *Your team members need it from you.* Consider some examples:

Your daughter needs it from you. You're in your late 50's, and your daughter is in her early 30's. She loves you as much as a daughter could love a father. She's tremendously proud of the business you've built and the fact that you want her to be a part of it and help her carry it on into the next generation. But your daughter has some strong feelings she's never expressed because you've never been a good enough listener to help her get them off her chest. What she'd like to say (but can't right now) goes something like this:

> "Dad, there's no way I could tell you how special and important you are to me. I'm so proud of all you've done with the business. But sometimes you do things—

and I know you don't realize you're doing them—that cause me a lot of pain. And they all have to do with your attitudes toward women. You still refer to me and the other females in the company as the 'girls.' I just get a sick feeling in my stomach every time you do that. But the biggest thing—and it makes me feel angry and frustrated—is the way you've already decided that my two brothers are going to be running the show after you retire. You only see my role as office manager, bookkeeper, and head of personnel all rolled into one. I'm just as smart and capable as my two brothers, and I certainly haven't had all the problems with drugs and alcohol that Jimmy has. It's just not fair."

Your new vice-president needs it from you. You're in your early 50's and the CEO of a wholly owned subsidiary with a work force of about 1,000 people. Less than a year ago you promoted a young fellow you've had your eyes on for quite a while to vice-president of sales and marketing. Within three months you knew you'd made the right choice. All the frustration and lack of confidence you'd felt with his predecessor has just blown away in the wind. You're happy. But your new vice-president is not so happy. If you'd give him the chance, he could really open up:

"Doug, I've enjoyed working for you these past nine months. I think the chemistry between the two of us is good and that we can make a lot of progress together. That's the good part. But I'm having a terrible time with Stacy and Lockdale. They're a couple of old-line operation guys and they haven't accepted me or what I'm trying to do here at all. But I don't think their problem is really me. And this is a little sensitive. I think the problem is you. They're still pissed off that you were made CEO ahead of them. And you haven't been able to lay that problem to rest with either one of them. And it's causing me—and I think a lot of other people in the company—a world of problems."

Your partner needs it from you. You and two other partners run a successful independent insurance brokerage firm. All three of you are in your mid-40's and have been working together about eight years. You get along pretty well with Jack. But you and Tom have always had your problems with each other. If he thought you could handle it, Tom would like to tell you a few things:

> "Sally, I don't know if you realize it or not, but I think you're enormously talented. I've seen a lot of people come and go in this business, but I don't think I've ever seen anyone take to it—especially the face to face selling part—as naturally as you do. But I gotta tell you that there's something really bothering me. And it goes like this. You're always accusing Jack and me—especially me—of not being good 'team players.' And that just frosts me. I think it's bullshit. Whenever you ask for help from me, I'm there. If you want me to meet you somewhere to help close a big deal, I'm there, on time, and I do my very best to help you out. But I don't see that kind of support coming back the other way from you. Half the time when we have partners' meetings you either come late or don't show up. And I've just given up on asking you to look at proposals I've written because you put them in your briefcase and they never come out. I guess what I'm trying to say is you talk a good game when it comes to team play, but you don't act a good game."

Your boss needs it from you. You're in your mid-40's and your boss is about 60. He hired you a little over a year ago to help him straighten out a small company he bought after retiring from the Air Force. When Eric bought the company, it was making money but it was in total disarray from a systems and procedures standpoint. In the last eight months or so you've helped Eric turn the place around. Where there used to be mostly chaos, now there's at least some semblance of order. And you both feel good about the progress you've made together. But your working relationship with Eric is far from perfect. If you could hear him out, there are a few things he'd like to say to you:

> "Martha, you've done an incredible job of turning this place around. I certainly couldn't have done it without

you. But there are some things you do—and I haven't been very good at getting them out on the table with you—that cause me a hell of a lot of frustration. One part of it is that you spend a lot of time pushing me and second-guessing me, and that's probably a good thing. For example, it's really gotten me out there to nail down some customers I don't think we would have gotten otherwise. When you push me, I try to do what you suggest. But what annoys the hell out of me is that the few things I ask you to do I don't get any feedback on. Like the storage situation in our space on Gibbons Avenue. I asked you to check that out and give me some kind of update on it six months ago. I still haven't heard word one from you about that. And when I do ask you about it, you tend to put me off as if it were just a trivial concern. So the message I end up getting is that it's OK for you to push me, but I can't push you. There's something wrong with that."

Your team members need you to be a good listener to them. They need a chance to bring up this touchy, sensitive, painful stuff without your getting defensive, and without your interrupting to jump in and tell them where they frustrate and annoy you. They need you to be a patient and caring listener until they can get these strong feelings out and on the table.

And what about you? Well, you need the same thing from them. You need to talk to your daughter or your new vice-president or to your partner or that retired Air Force guy with the same candor—right from the heart. If you can do that for your team members and they can do that for you, watch out. That kind of high-quality communication leads to good things in any important relationship—whether between business colleagues, husbands and wives, parents and children, or best friends.

A Short Course in Good Listening

There are four basic listening skills we teach to all of our clients. In the next several pages we'll expose you to each of them. Here's how we refer to them:

- Attending

- Asking thought-provoking questions

- Encouraging

- Reading back

Attending

"Attending" means how you use your body, especially your upper torso and face, to send a message to a person or a group that you're really interested in what they have to say. Let's talk about three kinds of attending: good, bad, and god awful.

Good attending. If you want to see an excellent example of good attending, watch Arsenio Hall some evening. (In the highly unlikely event his show has been canceled by the time you read this, it's worth catching a rerun or borrowing a tape of an old broadcast if you can.) Once Arsenio is finished with his monologue and starts interviewing a guest, turn the sound down so you can't hear what they're talking about. Then watch Arsenio. Pay particular attention to how he:

— Leans forward as his guest is talking. Just his posture—forget about his face—seems to be saying, "I'm hanging on your every word."

— Makes eye contact with the guest. His eyes are clear, focused, and steady. He doesn't stare at his guests (notice how he breaks eye contact once in a while), but his eyes show a caring, intense (but not too intense) concentration on the guest.

— Nods his head. He doesn't do this mechanically, but he does it a lot and you can see the encouraging effect it has on his guests. By the way, when he nods his head, it doesn't necessarily mean that Arsenio is agreeing with what his guest is saying. Rather, his nods mean, "I'm right with you. Keep going."

— Uses his facial muscles. According to the anatomy experts, we have more than 100 muscles in our face. Most of us don't use these muscles very much when we listen to another person. But Arsenio seems to use all his when he's interviewing a guest. Watch his forehead for a minute or two. It's constantly crinkling and furrowing into smiles and frowns and grimaces as his guest sends out a stream of differing emotions."

What Arsenio, or any good "attender" does is use body language that says to the person he's listening to:

"I'm intensely interested in what you have to say. All my concentration and attention is on you and whatever you're trying to express. For right now you're the most important person in my world."

Bad attending. Bad attending is really a potpourri of behaviors that include the kinds of things that we talked about in Chapter 5:

— Poor eye contact. This can mean the glazed look that you see in some people's eyes when you talk to them. It can mean eyes that wander off in some other direction to look at that attractive jogger sauntering down the bike path, or that huge airplane floating down onto the runway in the distance. Or it can mean eyes that seem to bounce around in their sockets in a nervous frenzy.

— Poker-faced expressions. These expressions are the exact opposite of what you see on Arsenio Hall's face as he listens to a guest. The head never nods and a facial muscle never twitches. If you've ever seen the painting American Gothic by Grant Wood, you know what it's like to talk to people with this kind of unanimated, inscrutable expression.

— Trying to listen and do something else at the same time. While you're talking about what happened during the day, your husband is looking at you and nodding his head, but he's also trying to keep an eye on what Dan Rather is saying on that little TV on his night stand. Or your boss asks you to update her on your sales trip while she balances her checkbook and neatens up the top of her desk.

— Bad posture. This can mean arms folded across the chest the way baseball umpires do when irate managers question a close call. It can mean slouching back in your chair when an employee is trying to tell you how annoyed and frustrated he or she is about trying to close an important deal. Or it can simply mean keeping your back turned to one of your colleagues who has just joined the small group of people in the hall who are trying to excite you about a new idea.

— Signs of boredom or "I've got more important things to do." These include yawning, stretching, letting your eyes droop, glancing at your watch, drumming your fingers on the desk or table, and squirming or fidgeting in your chair.

Bad attending sends a mixed and confusing message to the person who's trying to talk to you:

> "I guess I'm willing to listen to what you have to say, but could you keep it brief and to the point and as interesting as possible. I don't have a lot of time. I've got other things on my mind. And I'm not willing to sit (or stand) here while you take your sweet time saying whatever it is you have to say."

God awful attending. This is the kind of attending we usually reserve for the people we care most about in our lives: our spouses and our children. Some examples:

— Your son is talking about one of his favorite rock groups. The more animated he gets, the more your lip curls up in disgust and the more you roll your eyes to the ceiling and shake your head.

— Your wife walks into the kitchen while you're eating breakfast. She says, "Tom, I'm still having trouble with the car." Before she can say another word, you throw your head back and your arms up to the ceiling. You don't have to say anything because your body language has already sent the message: *"What the hell is the matter with you?!"*

— Your daughter is sitting next to you as you're driving down the road. Haltingly she says, "Mom, I've got something I need to tell you." Already the look of apprehension on your face says, "Oh, no! What is it this time?"

One of the nice things about attending is that you can improve right away. You can go home tonight or go into work tomorrow morning and immediately start: looking your wife in the eye when she talks to you, put that memo down and lean forward as your new employee comes in to update you on an important project, nod occasionally at your partner (who's not the most dynamic speaker in the world) when he gets up to give his presentation at the staff meeting, and smile (rather than shake your head in disapproval) when your ten-year-old tells a silly story at the dinner table.

If you can make a few small changes like these in the way you listen to your family and team members, the eventual benefits will be well worth the effort. Children who may feel rather distant from you now will start to open up about things they never would have disclosed even a month ago. A wife who's decided you really care much more about your job than you do about her will slowly start to act more like the warm and loving person you married 25 years ago. That vice-president of administration who can be such a problem now may seem more reasonable and accommodating a month or two hence. But don't take our word for it. Give it a try.

Asking Thought-Provoking Questions

One of the things we've noticed about people in general and our selves in particular is that most of us are not good at asking questions that get another person to "think out loud" about a topic. For example, when we talk about listening in our seminars, Peter will often say:

> "Even though I've trained myself to get up and talk in front of large groups of people, I'm still basically a shy person inside. And one of the ways this shyness comes out, I've noticed, is when I'm in social situations with people I've never met before. I have a tendency to ask questions like, 'Do you live here in Seattle?' 'Do you like the food here at the hotel?' 'Did you see that World Series game last night?' 'Do you think the Democrats will win this year?' Even though I'm supposed to be an expert on listening, I ask questions that can be answered with a few words or even a yes or no."

To counteract this tendency to ask questions that don't do a good job of getting people to open up and talk freely, we came up with the idea of a "thought-provoking question." For us, a thought-provoking question has two important characteristics: First, it invites a person or a group to think broadly and freely about some topic, and second, it invites them to think about a topic they'd love to address if they only had confidence in your capacity to listen to their answer.

Here are two rather different examples of thought-provoking questions. For each, try to put yourself into the role of the person being asked the question.

You and your husband. It's a Saturday afternoon and you're sitting in your living room reading a novel. Your two teenage boys have been out all day and you don't expect them back until dark. You look up for a second and there's your husband sitting next to you on the couch with a warm smile on his face. He gives you a lazy wave and says, "Hi." You smile back and say, "Hi." After smiling and looking at you for another 30 seconds or so, he starts to talk:

> "Um, where should I begin here? [slowly nodding his head] Ah, I want to ask you a question. A very important question. And it may take you a while to answer it."

You just smile, nod your head and say, "OK. Sounds good to me." He continues:

> "We've been married a little over 20 years. I think it's been a pretty good marriage. We've got two great kids. We've got a lot to be thankful for. But I've been thinking a lot lately about the kind of husband I've been to you over those 20 years, especially during the last five years. And that's kind of the lead-in to this question I want to ask you."

You just smile and nod your head. He goes on:

"Well, in a second I'll ask the question. But after I do, I'm going to shut up and be the best listener I can possibly be. If you say something that might be a little touchy or sensitive, I'm not going to interrupt and get defensive. I'm just going to listen for as long as you want to talk. OK?"

Inside, you're saying to yourself, "What's going on here? This does not sound like the guy I've known for almost a quarter of a century." But you just smile and say, "Great. What's the question?" And he says: "What can I do to make our marriage a lot more satisfying and enjoyable for you?"

You and your boss. You're a senior civil servant with 25 years of service in the Department of Defense. For the last six months you've been working for a newly appointed undersecretary whom you don't particularly like or respect. You see this fellow as having been given his job only because of the role he played in last year's campaign. As far as you're concerned, he never would have gotten his new job on the basis of technical knowledge and managerial skill. He's asked to meet with you in the conference room for about an hour and a half. In preparation for that meeting he's asked you to think about him very candidly as a boss. He's even asked you to write down some of the things you think he does well as a manager along with some of the things he doesn't do so well. And he's asked you to be prepared to talk about those things when you meet.

As you walk into the conference room, he gets up, walks over to you, shakes your hand saying, "Hey, Brian. How are you? Thanks for coming." After he closes the door and you both sit down, he starts right in:

"Brian, I don't think it's any secret that the two of us didn't get off to the best start when I took this job. I knew right away you weren't overjoyed at my appointment and probably would have preferred somebody with a lot more technical and scientific background than I have. But I'd like to do whatever I can to make our working relationship as positive as possible. And that's the reason I asked to have this meeting with you and asked you to prepare for it the way I did."

You're still pretty skeptical of this guy, but what he says is having a softening effect on you. You just nod. Then he says:

> "Well, Brian, I asked you to think about some of the things that I do well as a manager. And I asked you to think about some things I could do to improve. It looks like you've made some notes and have done some thinking about that. But, in a second, when you start talking, I'd also like you to think about what I could do to make your work here a little more enjoyable. I have to say I think the morale around here is not anywhere near as high as it could be, and there may be some things I could do to change that."

Your skepticism has melted a little more. Then he says:

> "OK. I've given you a lot to think about. But why don't you start with what I could do to make your job at least a little more enjoyable. Don't worry about saying anything critical or negative. I'm always prepared to hear some hard stuff when I ask a question like that. Just take your time. And be as frank and candid with me as you can be."

If your husband or your boss or a team member asked you a question like either of these two, you'd probably have at least a couple of reactions: "I'd really like to answer that question." Since neither your relationship with your husband nor your relationship with your boss is anywhere near as good as it could be, here is a special opportunity to do something about that. Both people have asked what they can do to make your life (in two very different arenas) less frustrating and more satisfying. Well, damn, there are a lot of things they could do differently to make life more enjoyable for you. This is a rare opportunity.

Another reaction may be: "I'm afraid to answer it honestly because that could make things worse." This is the other side of the coin. You'd really like to answer the question, but you know if you're candid and straightforward at least a couple of bad things could happen. One, your husband or your boss—in spite of their guarantees—could easily get defensive about things you would say, and the whole conversation could degenerate into an ugly argument. Two, some of the things you might say could have long-range damaging effects. Maybe your husband or your boss will so resent some of the topics you bring up that things will never be the same between you again. Things aren't great now, but why take the risk of saying stuff that could only make them worse?

So what's happened is your husband and your boss have whetted your appetite to answer their questions, but right now your level of trust in them is not high enough for you to be completely open and candid. Not yet. And that's where the other two listening skills—"encouraging" and "reading back"—come in.

Encouraging
Encouraging is something you do as a listener to help keep the other person talking. It's like a friendly, helpful prod. We'll use the example of your undersecretary boss at the Defense Department to demonstrate this skill, and we'll continue the example into the next section when we talk about "reading back." Let's pick up where we left off with you and your boss:

> **Him:** OK. I've given you a lot to think about. But why don't you start with what I could do to make your job at least a little more enjoyable. Don't worry about saying anything critical or negative. I'm always prepared to hear some pretty hard stuff when I ask a question like that. Take your time. Be as frank and candid with me as you can.
>
> *(Right now you're still skeptical. You're not ready to jump in and talk about the real sensitive and touchy topics.)*
>
> **You:** (With a wisp of a skeptical smile on your face.) Hmm. Well, that's a good question. I guess it's a question any employee would like to have a boss ask.
>
> *(Your boss just smiles faintly and nods. Notice throughout the rest of this example how he uses the good attending skills*

we talked about earlier to show you he's keenly interested in what you have to say and to keep you talking.)

You: (Starting to look thoughtful.) So, what can you do to make my job more enjoyable? Hmm. Well, Tom, one thing you could do is pay more attention to the chain of command around here.

(Your boss continues to make good eye contact, leans forward, and nods occasionally.)

You: I guess what I mean is this. I've noticed that since you arrived here you tend to go down several levels into the organization to assign work to people. And sometimes that causes me a lot of problems.

(You don't say anything, but you turn your palms up to the ceiling and have an expectant, sort of questioning smile on your face. This is an excellent place for your boss to use an encourager. You've gone a little way into a touchy subject, but you've stopped. Both your gesture and the expression on your face seem to be saying something like, "Well, there it is. Now, how are you going to react?")

Him: (Leaning forward and looking you right in the eye.) Brian, I know this is not the easiest stuff to talk about. But it's exactly the kind of thing I need to hear. Please keep going.

That's an encourager. It's something just a little bit more than good attending. It sends the message both verbally and nonverbally that your boss meant what he said about wanting to hear whatever's on your mind—and that he's not going to get defensive or annoyed if you bring up something sensitive.

Reading Back
Of the four skills we're covering in this chapter, reading back is the hardest—for at least a couple of reasons:

— Reading back goes so much against the grain of what we want to do. When somebody is talking to us—especially when they're saying something negative—we don't want to read them back. We don't want to summarize what they've said and then hear even more of what they have to say. No way. We want to respond to what they've said.

— Reading back makes you concentrate on what the other person is saying in a way most of us rarely do. Usually, when we listen to people, we're focusing on how we feel and think about what they're saying. Without even being fully aware of it we're preparing our response. When you have to read someone back, you can't do that. You can't think about your reactions to what the person is saying; you have to hear what they're saying and absorb it. And that takes more concentration than most of us are willing to exert.

So reading back is tough to do. But what is it? Soon we'll return back to the conversation with your boss, and we'll show you. But here's a short definition:

Reading back is an attempt on the part of the listener to capture the essence of what a talker has been saying. It's a summary of what the talker has said that includes both the content and the feelings that have been expressed.

Why is reading back important? Several reasons. First, reading back is proof you're trying to listen. You can fake good attending. You can be at a cocktail party listening to a boring person prattle on while you maintain good eye contact, smile occasionally, and nod your head. And your mind can be 100 miles away on a golf course or a sunny beach. But to read somebody back, you have to listen. You can't fake a good read back. The talker will be able to tell right away.

Reading back allows the talker to correct any misunderstanding you may have regarding what he or she said. Even when you try very hard to listen to someone, you don't always fully understand what is said. Maybe you haven't been paying close enough attention. Or maybe the person hasn't been clear about what he or she is trying to express. At any rate, a read back gives the talker a chance to clear things up for you. After your read back, the talker can say, "Yeah, that's sort of what I'm trying to say, but not quite. Let me take another crack at it."

Most importantly, a read back gets the talker to build on what he or she has already said. As far as we're concerned, this is what a read back is all about. It's a tool a listener uses to help a talker explore thoughts and feelings he or she may never have expressed before and to look at things in a new way. And maybe even to unlock solutions to problems that would otherwise go unsolved.

Now let's pick back up with the conversation you were having with your boss. Let's see how he uses read backs (as well as the other listening skills) to help you think out loud about how he could make your job less stressful and more enjoyable.

> **Him**: (Leaning forward and looking you right in the eye.) Brian, I know this is not the easiest stuff in the world for you to talk about. But it's exactly the kind of thing I need to hear. Please keep going.
>
> **You**: (With a smile that says, "OK, if you really want to hear it!") Well, here's an example of what I'm talking about. At least a couple of times within the last month you've gone to my office directors asking them to respond to questions from Congressmen. And there's nothing wrong with that except, when you don't let me know what you're doing, it causes them problems and me problems, too.
>
> *(Your boss just nods.)*
>
> **You**: See, what happens goes something like this. My people already have a tremendous amount of work to do. And then you, the big boss, come down and tell them to work on some priority item. Well, hell they're not going to say no to you! Right?
>
> *(Your boss nods and smiles a bit.)*
>
> **You**: In the meantime, I don't know you've asked them to do this stuff. I assume they're both working on tasks all three of us have agreed they should work on—like a couple of key reports we're trying to get out the door. So, the next day I go in and ask how they're coming on these reports. And they say, "Oh, gee, we were working on these responses to the Congressmen that the under-secretary wanted us to prepare." And I'm saying to

myself, "What responses to what Congressmen?" See what I mean?

(Here your boss pauses to see if you have anything to add. When it's clear you've stopped for the moment, he'll take a shot at a read back.)

Him: Well, Brian, I think what you're saying is pretty clear. When I go directly to people who work for you and give them assignments, it has a disruptive effect on you and them.

You: Exactly! Disruptive! I didn't say that, but that's definitely what I meant.

(Your words here are a clear sign that, so far, your boss's read back is right on the money.)

Him: (Nodding and pausing to make sure you have nothing to add before he continues.) I think you were pretty specific about what I do that's disruptive. The people I go to already have very full plates of assignments, and then I go and add to their loads with my special requests. In the meantime, you don't even know I've gone to your people. You think they're working on projects you've assigned them. And when you find out what I've done, it sounds like maybe you feel a combination of surprise and confusion and annoyance.

(Here your boss has read back some feelings—surprise, confusion, and annoyance—that you didn't express directly but that were coming across in your gestures and your tone of voice.)

You: Yeah. Yeah. You got me. That's just how I feel.

Him: (Pausing for a few seconds.) Well, Brian, you didn't say it directly, but it sounds like one thing I could do to make your job more enjoyable and less stressful is come to you when I've got one of these little assignments I need done, rather than going around you to somebody on your staff.

(Technically, this isn't a read back. But it's certainly a logical inference your boss could make from what you said a little earlier.)

You: Yep. I'd really appreciate it if you'd do that.

(You smile to indicate that you're finished on this topic.)

Him: OK, Brian. So what else could I do to make your job more enjoyable?

Let's step back a bit and look at what's been going on here. The conversation started off with a thought-provoking question about what he could do to make your job more enjoyable. Since then he's been using good attending, encouragers, and read backs to draw you out— to get you to open up. And you have opened up—a little. But there are still a bunch of more sensitive issues you haven't touched on at all yet. For example, you haven't mentioned how he doesn't know much about the technical aspects of what your office does. In spite of his lack of knowledge, however, he's testified to Congress as if he were an expert. That kind of overconfidence makes you very nervous.

But, all things considered, it's a good start. Slowly, he's getting you to trust him and to tell him things that, from your perspective, are really getting in the way of a solid working relationship between the two of you.

Some Questions You Probably Have about the Use of Listening Skills

We've just given you a short course on how to be a better listener. Whenever we give a course like this to an audience at a seminar or to a small group of clients at a weekend retreat, we get some questions. Here are some of the more typical ones and how we answer them:

**If I Listen Like This, Won't It Seem
Like I'm Agreeing with Everything that's Being Said?**
When we hear this question, we always try to make a couple of points. First, you may think you're conveying an impression of agreeing with the talker, but that's not the dominant impression

the talker has. At least in our experience. The primary reaction the talker has goes something like this:

> "This feels good! I feel heard. I feel understood. It's so unbelievably rare to get listened to like this. What a difference this is from the way most people listen to me. And, I have to admit, from the way I listen to most people."

And you've got to remember that once you've finished drawing out the other person, now you become the talker, and the other person becomes the listener. Take the example we used a little earlier with you and your boss. At some point you'll finish responding to your boss's question. And then it will be your boss's turn to react. Ideally, you would draw him out using the same listening skills he used so effectively with you. Now he has free rein to talk about whatever's on his mind. He'll probably apologize for some of the things he's done that cause you problems. He'll probably explain why he's done some of the things he's done. He'll probably talk about things he wants to do differently on the basis of what you've told him. And he'll probably talk about things you can do to make his job more enjoyable, and to improve the working relationship between the two of you.

That's the way good listening works. And that's exactly what the two of us do whenever we run into a tough problem—whether it's a touchy relationship issue or any other kind of problem we very much want to resolve. One of us starts off as the talker, the other as the listener. When the talker has finished what he wants to say, he says to the listener, "Anyway, you've been doing a real good job of drawing me out. Now I'd like to hear whatever's on your mind." With that, the talker has become the listener. On it goes—switching back and forth between these two roles—until the problem get's resolved, or until we adjourn and pick it up again in the near future.

It's a wonderful method for solving problems. Although it takes time, patience, energy, and tremendous concentration, we've certainly seen it pay huge dividends in our own friendship and partnership. And we've also seen it work small miracles with clients who've paid the price to learn how to do it well.

Doesn't This Listening Stuff Take Too Much Time?

When it comes to listening skills, this is probably the question our audiences and clients most frequently ask us. They say:

> "This kind of listening sounds like it can be a really good thing. But where I work we're all extremely busy. If we take the time to do this kind of listening with everybody, I'm not sure we'd ever get any work done."

We have a couple of reactions. One is that you're right. You don't have the time to listen to everybody about everything in the depth we've been talking about here. That's simply not feasible. But here's our second reaction. In every organization we've ever worked in or consulted to, we've seen gobs of problems that could have been avoided altogether (or at least greatly reduced) if the executive team members in those organizations had known how to listen when it counted. But because these team members were poor (sometimes awful) listeners, thousands and thousands of hours that could have been devoted to more productive ends were wasted on such activities as:

- Fighting off a union's efforts to organize a labor force.

- Mount a legal defense against a wrongful discharge or unfair labor practices suit.

- Deal with a chronic turnover problem in a production unit run by a tyrannical manager who has no business supervising other people.

- Rebuild a burned out plant that all the hourly employees who worked there had been saying for over ten years was a shameful firetrap.

Do I Always Have to Read Back?

We hear this question a lot because reading back not only takes a lot of time, but it also takes a lot of energy and concentration. And the answer, of course, is no. You don't always have to read back what people say when you're doing a good job of listening to them. In fact, the two of us don't use reading back very much with each other. But we do use it when the situation really calls for it. For example, if one of us is clearly upset about something and needs to talk about it, the other will automatically start listening with the intention of reading back what was said. A while back we came up with a definition of levels of communication that may help clarify when reading back is appropriate and when it's not:

Level I: Small talk, casual conversation, and teasing. Even though we've assigned this kind of communication the lowest of the four levels, we think it's very important. Life wouldn't be a whole lot of fun without it. In fact, we think it's a good sign when executive team members stand around in groups of twos or threes and:

- Arguing over the merits of their favorite pro basketball teams.

- Oohing and aahing about a recent play or symphony performance or country music concert.

- Ribbing one member who's made a pretty drastic change in hairstyle.

- Debate the merits of two candidates in a hotly contested presidential campaign.

- Cracking up at one of those rare jokes that won't offend anybody's sensibilities.

Level II: Ineffective discussion. When things move from the level of small talk and banter to more serious matters, this is what we see the vast majority of the time in organizations. Important matters like what new markets to pursue or how to cut costs get talked about in a colossally unproductive way:

— New and potentially good ideas get squashed quickly. New ideas are like infants. If they're not carefully nurtured and allowed to grow and develop, they can die an early death. And that's what happens to a lot of new ideas when they get discussed in organizations. Somebody offers an unusual thought about a new way to solve a problem. As soon as the thought gets expressed, somebody else says, "Come on! That'll never work" or "We tried that years ago. It fell flat on its ass." Over the last 25 years we've sat in on hundreds of meetings where thousands of new ideas were killed just like that. And it's a shame. Because even if most of those ideas weren't worth the powder to blow them to hell, some offered the possibility of doing a tremendous amount of good.

— Too often it's only the extroverted and powerful people who hold forth. This is one of the hallmarks of the discussions we see in organizations. The big shots and the big mouths are the ones who get the air time. Maybe their ideas are better than those of the more shy, introverted, and less powerful folks who sit on the sidelines and hold back their opinions. Maybe. But we don't think so. We think the ideas these folks have to offer—once you give them a chance to speak—are often more solid and better thought out than those of their more powerful and talkative colleagues.

— In most organizational discussions we see, there's not only a lot of lousy listening going on, there's also a lot of pressure for closure which results in lots of bad decisions being made. "We need to act. We need to make a decision now!" And what happens? Well, not only do a lot of good ideas not get off the ground, but a lot of bad ideas do get off the ground. And the consequences can be enormous. Although we can't prove it, we'd bet that at least some of these decisions would never have been made if they'd been discussed effectively: production of the Edsel in the 1950's; the Watergate break-in; the Iran-Contra arms deal; and the continued production of large, gas-guzzling vehicles by Detroit's "big three" well into the 1970's.

Level III: Effective discussion. We don't see very much of this going on in organizations. But if there were more of this kind of interaction among executive team members, we're convinced most companies, most government agencies, and most nonprofit entities would run a lot more smoothly and productively. In order to have effective discussions:

— Someone has to take on the role of facilitator. We feel very strongly about that. The participants in any discussion have to pay attention to the notion that only one person can be the "talker" at a time, and that everyone else has to listen. This is a good rule, but it's tough to put into practice when three or more people are involved in a discussion unless one of the participants takes on the role of facilitator. And the primary responsibility of the facilitator is to make sure that this rule gets followed and that everyone in the discussion has a roughly equal opportunity to participate. If the facilitator is going to be effective, he or she can't participate directly in the discussion. This is a role that should shift from person to person with each new discussion, and maybe even *during* the discussion if it's a long one.

— In an effective discussion people listen to each other respectfully, offer different points of view, and disagree with one another's ideas. When one person "has the floor," everybody else listens attentively to what's being said. Nobody interrupts the talker until he or she is finished. And nobody discourages or puts down what the talker has said. Rather, someone else starts talking and says something like, "Well, I agree and here's why," or "I disagree and here's what I think" or "Let me try to build on what Pat just said."

— Everybody is invited to participate. Earlier we said that it's big shots and the extroverts who get all the air time in ineffective discussions. In an effective discussion, not every one will talk an equal amount. But what will happen is that both the participants, as well as the facilitator, will try to see that everybody gets a chance to contribute. For example, if one of the more shy and reserved participants in the discussion hasn't said anything for a long time, somebody will turn toward the person and say, "Connie, you've been looking very thoughtful over there. What are your thoughts on all of this stuff?"

— The more powerful people should talk less and encourage the less powerful people to talk more. If you're in the one-up position on your executive team, you may have a sense of how difficult this is to pull off. Because you're the boss—or because you hold a lot of sway on the team—people tend to defer to you in discussions. They like to wait and see where "you're coming from" before they offer their thoughts and ideas. This often causes them to tell you what they think you want to hear, rather than what's really on their minds. And what's really on their minds should lead to a much more productive discussion. If you keep relatively quiet and encourage everybody else to talk, in an effective discussion you're going to get a lot more candor and good ideas then if you dominate the conversation the way so many leaders do.

— There's no rush to make decisions. We said that in ineffective discussions there's often a push for premature closure on decisions and that that pressure can cause lots of problems down the road. In effective discussions the participants (especially the more powerful ones) don't put that kind of pressure on each other. They know good decisions take time. They know that sometimes exploring a problem for a while— rather than trying to solve it right away—can lead to better results.

In effective discussions, there doesn't have to be a lot of reading back. Once in a while the discussion facilitator (or a participant) might do what we call a "group read back." That is, he or she might try to summarize a number of inputs various people have been making in the last ten minutes or so just to keep the discussion moving after a pause or a lull. What's important in effective discussions is not a lot of in-depth reading back. What's important is that everybody in the discussion be encouraged to participate and that everybody give everybody else an attentive and respectful ear to their thoughts and ideas.

Level IV: High quality communication. This is the sort of communication that usually goes on between two people in a private setting. The situation we used earlier in the chapter of your boss drawing you out on what he could do to make your job more enjoyable was an example of this level of communication. In these situations the use of read backs is very appropriate because the listener has the time and freedom to draw the talker out in depth. Reading back helps the talker "plumb the depths" of his or her thinking and bring up sensitive issues that would be inappropriate to discuss in a group setting.

So, there you have our short course on how to be a better listener. Once again we'll make the pitch that good listening is a powerful tool for solving problems, and especially for healing troubled relationships. We hope you decide to make the effort to learn to do it well. If you do, what a difference it can make in your life and the lives of others who are important to you.

10

Getting Started

By this point in the book you may be feeling overloaded with all the information we've been sending your way. Of course, that's not necessarily bad. We wanted to stimulate your thinking; we wanted to turn your attention to problems and concepts you probably wouldn't have considered if you hadn't given us the chance to bend your ear.

But now it's time to talk about what you're going to do with all this information. In the long run, we hope you do a lot with it. In Chapter 6, for example, we tried to hold your feet to the fire on a number of tasks you can tackle over the coming months, even years. However, for right now, we're not going to suggest a back-breaking load of activities. In the rest of the chapter, we'll lay out three steps we'd like you to take over the next several weeks. None of these steps will require a great deal of your time, but each should help you get off to a good start:

- Clarify your own thinking.
- Start dealing with the biggest problem on your mind.
- Consider some long range possibilities.

Clarify Your Own Thinking

Very early on we offered the hunch that you probably picked this book up and started reading it because you're a member of an executive team and because you're less than satisfied with the quality of your working relationships with at least some of those team members. If our hunch was accurate and if you've done a fairly careful reading of the book up to this point, the chances are good you've got a lot of thoughts running through your mind. You probably agree with a number of the things we've said. Maybe you're a bit unsure how you feel about other things we've said. And you probably just flat out disagree with a few of the arguments we've advanced and some of the recommendations we've made.

So what should you do? Well, we think it would be helpful for you to get some perspective and clarity on all these thoughts. In the rest of this section we'll lay out some ideas on how you can do that.

Have Someone You Trust, Respect, and Who Knows Your Situation at Work Read the Book

Right now, with all the thinking you've been doing, you could benefit from someone else's perspective on what we've been saying in the book and on the implications it has for you and your executive team. If you possibly can, find someone who will read the book and discuss it with you. If you're open to that idea, let's talk about who might be a good choice:

Someone who knows your situation at work. It's probably better that the person you choose not be a member of your executive team. But he or she should be familiar with your team and the relationships between the various members. This could be someone on your board of directors, a colleague from a neighboring division or department, a spouse, or your secretary.

Someone you trust a great deal. Since what you'll be discussing with this person is highly sensitive stuff, whoever you choose should be someone you know you can talk to in complete confidence. The last thing you need is a person who will talk indiscreetly about any of your thoughts and feelings to another team member —especially someone you don't get along with well.

Someone whose opinions and thinking you respect. For us, this would be someone who will give the book a thoughtful read; someone who will try to be objective, that is, someone who won't automatically take your side and make one or several of your team members the "bad guy;" and someone who can be frank and candid concerning some of the unpleasant truths about you that the book may bring up.

Draw the Person Out

Once the person you've chosen—whether it's your spouse, a member of your board of directors, your secretary, or whoever—has finished reading the book, draw the person out. Find a quiet place and a couple of free hours to sit down with the person. Start off with a good thought-provoking question like:

> "Pat, I really appreciate your taking the time to read the book. And I'm very interested in your reaction to it, especially how you think the book applies to me and my situation at work. I'd like you to talk about whatever's on your mind. I'll try to be the best listener I can. All I ask is that you be frank and candid. Don't worry about hurting my feelings. If you think the book points out things I really need to work on, go ahead and say it. I'm all ears to anything you have to say."

Once you've asked a question like that, use the listening skills we talked about in Chapter 8. If you've picked the right person, you're going to get some interesting and helpful reactions. For example, you'll probably hear what the person thinks about:

The overall helpfulness of the book. You may be rather impressed with the book, but the person you're drawing out may not agree with you. Hearing why he or she feels that way may be enlightening.

Where the book touches on some of the problems on your team. Some parts of the book are bound to get the person talking about relationship "trouble spots" on your team. And that's the time when you want to listen especially well. Don't get defensive. Don't offer your own advice. Just listen. It'll be worth the effort.

The possibility of your getting some outside help. (Getting outside help is the subject of the next chapter.) Maybe your team needs some outside help but you don't feel it would be worth the time and expense to get it. You just might change your mind if the person said, "Jack, you've got a huge problem here on your hands. You can't solve it by yourself. Do what these guys say. Get some outside help."

Once you've done a good job of listening to the person's reactions, ask him or her to draw you out. Of course, you may not get the high quality listening you were doing, but you never know. He or she might even do a better job of listening to you than you did. At any rate, offer your reactions to what the person says. Think out loud, especially about any new ideas that come to mind while you were listening. You'll probably have some interesting insights:

— "It's hard to admit it, but I think I'm a much bigger part of the problem with Tom and Jack than I ever thought I was. Of course, neither one of them is pure as the driven snow, but, then again, neither am I."

— "One thing that's becoming clearer and clearer to me is how my problems at work are affecting Judy and the kids at home. I haven't been the kind of husband and father I should have been over the last six months. That's got to change. That's got to change right now."

— "You said something I can't ignore anymore. You said that Bill has really become a negative and destructive force in the organization. I don't think I ever wanted to see that because I hired the guy early in his career when I thought he was loaded with potential. The thought of firing him tears me up. But not firing him could be a lot worse."

— "As you know, for more than a year now I've been thinking about leaving. But some of the things you had to say have caused me to wonder whether that's really a good idea. You've reminded me of some of the positive things about the company and the people in it that my problems with George had caused me to forget. It was enormously helpful to have you remind me of that."

Let It All Incubate
Scientists, writers, and other creative folks have long talked about the value of letting thoughts and ideas sit for a while. There's something special about how the subconscious mind works on a

problem while our conscious thoughts are focused elsewhere. So, after you have your listening/talking session with your spouse or your secretary or your colleague or your friend, forget about all this stuff for a while. Turn you attention to something else for a few days, even for a week or more. Then come back to it. There's more than a good chance some of your thoughts will have crystallized and some effective course of action will be a bit clearer than it is right now.

Start Dealing with the Biggest Problem on Your Mind

Once you've had a chance to let your thoughts settle for a while, you may be pretty clear about what you want to do next. But before you take any action, we'd like you to consider doing something very similar to what you did in the first step. Only this time we'd like you to do it with a person on your team who is causing you the most concern right now. We'd like you to ask that person to read the book, and we'd like you to draw that person out on his or her reactions.

Before we push this idea any further, let us anticipate some of your objections:

> "Ask my boss to read this book? You got to be kidding me! The guy is an unbelievable tyrant. I'm already on his bad side. Why would I do something to make my stock go down even more in his eyes?"

> "I think I may want to fire this guy, and I don't particularly want to tip my hand. I think he already suspects I may want to let him go. Wouldn't asking him to read the book make him even more suspicious?"

> "I don't know. The two of us hardly speak to each other as it is. I don't know. That's asking a lot . . . of both of us."

> "I'm thinking about leaving this place, and he's the biggest reason. He's an unbelievable sexist. Why would

I want to waste my time trying to get him to talk about this touchy, sensitive stuff?"

Maybe you don't feel quite as strongly about not going to this person as the folks we quoted above. Or maybe you feel even more strongly that it's not such a hot idea. In any case, we understand that doing something like this is not going to be a pleasant proposition for you.

But, we still think you should do it. Here's why:

That person is probably the primary reason you decided to read this book in the first place. We could be wrong, but we doubt it. Most likely, you decided to read this book because of a lousy relationship with one of your team members. Maybe you have more than one not so hot relationship, but our hunch is that there's one that overshadows all the rest. Maybe it's your overbearing father who simply can't understand it's time for him to step down. Maybe it's a colossally insensitive and egocentric partner. Maybe it's your boss who thinks she's a good participative, democratic manager but, in fact, is very authoritarian. And maybe it's an employee who, despite enormous talent and potential, is a constant, buzzing source of frustration for you.

Well, if that person is such a problem for you, maybe—just maybe—you are for him or her, too. If the book has been helpful for you, maybe it will be for your team member. Who knows?

It just might turn things around. Again, who knows? But if there's *any* chance that your gesture could repair things, even a little bit, with your team member, why not give it a shot? As we've said several times throughout the book, we've seen *bad* relationships between our clients improve rapidly because one of them was willing to take a first positive step, sometimes a small one. And asking a team member to read the book is a pretty small step.

No matter what happens, you'll learn something valuable from the experience. It's very hard to predict how your team member will ultimately react to the suggestion that he or she read this book. Maybe you'll get a flat refusal. Maybe you'll get a commitment to read it, but, in spite of several prods from you, the book never gets read. Maybe your team member *will* read the book and end up surprising you by giving you a thoughtful, reflective reaction to what it has to say and to the implications for your relationship. Maybe your team member will even be *touched* by your gesture. You just don't know. But however your team member reacts, you should end up with a little clearer sense of what your next steps should be.

Things to Keep in Mind

If you do decide to ask your team member to read the book and offer you his or her reactions to it, we've got a few suggestions:

Don't make a big deal about asking your team member to read it. Just walk up to your team member with the book in your hand and say something like:

> "Sally, I've been reading this book and thought you might find it interesting. How about taking a look at it? If it grabs you at all, maybe you could go ahead and read the whole thing and we can have a conversation about it."

Don't expect a whole lot. We don't know exactly how your team member is going to respond to your suggestion, but you're probably going to get an, "Humm. Yeah, it does look kind of interesting. OK, I'll take a look at it." And that's fine. But it's fine, too, if your team member says, "Geez, I don't know. I'm pretty busy. Possibly in a few weeks." Maybe your team member will read the book; maybe not. But don't push. Just wait and see what happens.

Just be a good listener when you draw your team member out. If your team member does read the book, try to set up a time when the two of you can meet for at least an hour and a half so you can draw your team member out on his or her reactions. Start off with a good thought-provoking question and then just listen. Whatever your team member says, don't get defensive and don't get sucked into an argument. If your team member shows some real interest in what you thought of the book, go ahead and offer your opinion. But tread lightly. This isn't the time to get into a lot of heavy issues. This is just a first step. If you say something that "sets your team member off," go right back to being a good listener. If it seems like it makes sense to set up another meeting between the two of you, go ahead and try to set one up. Again, your primary goal in this meeting is simply to get your team member's reaction to the book. Trying to do much more than that could hurt more than help a relationship that needs a lot of long-term work.

Check in with yourself afterward. Once you've asked your team member to read the book and have had a chance to draw him or her out, it's a good idea to ask yourself a number of questions. For example:

— "How am I feeling about the future of this relationship right now?"

— "Am I more optimistic than I was before or am I more pessimistic?"

— "If I'm more optimistic is it because my team member actually read the book? Found it thought-provoking? Talked about some of the ineffective things she does that the book identified? Talked about how the book might help the two of us? Talked about how the book might help our whole team? Talked about other ideas for improving things that the book may have stimulated for him?"

— "If I'm feeling more pessimistic is it because my team member never read the book? Had sort of a ho-hum reaction to it? Thought the book was a bunch of baloney? Was confused about why I even asked him to read it in the first place?"

Your answers to these questions will help give you a better sense of what the future probably holds for the relationship between you and this team member. In essence, is this a relationship you want to spend some time and effort trying to improve? Or is this a relationship that you might be better off trying to disengage yourself from?

Consider Some Long-Range Possibilities

Let's say you've been able to clarify your thinking with the help of somebody you trust and respect. And let's say you've at least asked the team member you're having problems with to read the book. What's next? Where do you go from here?

In the rest of the chapter we'll outline three other courses of action for you to think about. None of them is mutually exclusive. In fact, it's even possible you could be in the process of doing all of them at the same time.

It might be wise to consider approaching each member of your team to have a relationship improvement session. What's a relationship improvement session? It's just a meeting between you and a team member where the two of you talk about what you both can do to make your mutual relationship less frustrating and more satisfying. Why take the time and why make the effort to do these sessions? Here's a brief recap of some reasons we've already offered:

These relationships are important and they deserve it. As we said in Chapter 2, whether you like it or not, when you're a member of an executive team, you're automatically involved in a very important set of relationships. And the personal and professional price you can pay for not working on these relationships—for not keeping them as vibrant and healthy as they can be—can be enormous.

If you're the head of your team, the potential value of these sessions is hard to imagine. We can't stress this point enough: your role as boss of your executive team is pivotal in the worth and success of any activity designed to improve the quality of working relationships in your organization. If you make a sincere effort to have these sessions with the people who work with you, you'll end up doing a lot of good. People who might have been unmotivated, stressed out, and even on the verge of leaving the organization will begin to feel a sense of hope. Trust us on that one.

These sessions *do* take time, but the time they can save in the long run is enormous. We're a little biased, of course, but the vast majority of big problems we see when we walk into organizations can usually be traced back to at least one lousy relationship between a couple of people at the top of the organization. If these two people had taken a couple of hours every several months to work on their relationship, thousands and thousands of employee-hours devoted to cleaning up messes and undoing crises could have been avoided.

For an in-depth discussion of how to do one of these relationship improvement sessions, you should read the book we mentioned earlier: *Problem Employees: How To Improve Their Performance.* But the basic things to keep in mind are pretty simple:

You should talk to each team member about doing it ahead of time. The big point here is not to take any of your team members by surprise. Tell each one you've been reading this book. Suggest that they read it too, and even if they don't have the time, say you'd still like to have one of these sessions with them. Tell them you're going to be thinking about some of the things you particularly like and admire and respect about them. And that you're also going to be thinking about some ways they could make your job a little easier and a little more enjoyable. Say you'd like them to do the same thing. You'd like them to think about some of the things you do well, but especially some of the things you could do to make their jobs less frustrating and more satisfying.

Always set up a comfortable time and place to meet. This may seem too obvious to mention, but it's very important that you find a place to meet where you won't be interrupted, or overheard. The session should be scheduled at a time that allows you to go for at least an hour and a half. Remember to pay attention to the rules of good talking and good listening. Before each session, it would be a good idea to review Chapters 7 and 8. When your team member is talking, be the absolute best listener you can possibly be. When it's your turn to talk, pay particular attention to the guidelines we offer for giving feedback in Chapter 7.

Look at each session as part of an ongoing process, not a single event. If you take a stab at doing these sessions with your team members, the first few you do may not go so smoothly. That's to be expected. And that's not a problem unless you look at these sessions as a "onetime deal." On the other hand, if you look at these sessions as part of an ongoing process to improve the quality of the relationships between you and your team members, no one session—no matter how badly it goes—will end up being that important. You'll just see that session as part of a process that sometimes goes smoothly and sometimes doesn't.

Organizing a Team Retreat

In the last five years or so, we've noticed a lot of professional partnerships have started doing what they call "partner retreats." These are usually two or three-day meetings where the senior partners in a firm get away to some pleasant environment—maybe a conference center or a university campus—to talk about important matters having to do with their firms and where they're headed. It probably won't surprise you that we're in favor of these kinds of experiences for any executive team, especially when the focus of these meetings is on how the team members can get along better and also make their organizations more satisfying places to work.

At some point soon, doing a retreat with your executive team may be a good idea:

There's a lot of value to stepping back and taking a look at the big picture. Once in a while the two of us sit down, kick back, and ask each other a question like this:

> "We haven't had one of these conversations for a while. So, how are things going? How's life in general? What's going really well for you? What, if anything, is getting in the way of your personal and professional enjoyment? Any touchy subjects in our relationship that you think need to get talked about? And anything else you think we should be talking about?"

And then the other guy talks. Sometimes for over an hour without stopping. In the meantime, the first guy listens attentively. Maybe he'll do a read back here or there. Maybe he won't. After a while, we reverse the roles. The guy who was the talker becomes the listener and the listener becomes the talker. And another hour or so sails by.

We don't have these conversations very often. Two or three times a year at most. But when we do have them, they always turn out to be special experiences. They give us both a chance to think out loud about our lives, about our friendship, and about our work together in ways we just couldn't if we didn't make time to do this sort of thing. For us, these conversations are like a "mini-retreat." Of course, the situation with your team members may be very different from our partnership. You may have some very serious relationship problems, and the "comfort level" may be far lower than what it is between the two of us. Still, it's probably a good idea for you to consider having a retreat if only because of the tremendously reinforcing value of asking each other questions like the one above. When a team member—even a person you're not getting along with at all—asks you questions like that, it's pretty nice. Your emotional reaction (whether or not you express it openly) is, "Well, thanks. That's a good question. Nobody ever asks me questions like that. I'd like to answer that question."

Retreats are a chance to clean out the chimney. In any important relationship—ours included—problems crop up. Issues unfold that don't get talked about and don't get dealt with. Retreats are an opportunity to get that kind of stuff out on the table. Stuff like:

— The argument you and your boss had over the marketing consultant he eventually hired for the membership campaign. As far as you're concerned, the guy has turned out to be worse than useless, and your boss still hasn't given you the satisfaction of saying, "Yeah, you were right."

— You're still annoyed at your partner over some of the last-minute changes he wanted to make in the presentation for your most recent board meeting. As far as you're concerned, you gave him every opportunity to make adjustments well in advance. He didn't. And then he got all bent out of shape when you weren't enthusiastic about making his last minute changes.

— You and your deputy, a GS-15, had a significant misunderstanding about how long she was going to be out on maternity leave. You had a heated discussion about it when she finally did come back. But it's clear both of you are still feeling some resentment that needs to get talked about and cleared away.

Retreats can be landmark events in the history of an organization. In some respects, retreats are just one more step in what should be an ongoing process to improve the quality of relationships on your executive team. But retreats are important *events*, too. We like to think of them as the organizational equivalent of a summit conference. It's a chance for the top leaders in an organization to get together and talk about issues they don't talk about on a day-to-day basis. Sometimes not a whole lot emerges from these retreats. But sometimes, like the 1978 meeting Jimmy Carter engineered between Anwar Sadat and Menachem Begin, important progress gets made that has an enduring effect on the organization. And even years later, people will talk about what happened at "Annapolis" or the "Green Briar" or "Lake Arrowhead" or whatever the venue for that memorable retreat.

If you and your team decide to have a retreat, give some serious thought to hiring a facilitator. A good facilitator can help make sure you stay focused on important issues and don't get bogged down in squabbles and side arguments that keep you from talking about the important stuff. (We've got some suggestions in the next chapter for where to look for this kind of outside help.)

Getting Some Outside Help
We realize that seeking outside help is usually a tough step for an executive team to take. It's tough because deciding to get outside help for the relationships on your executive teams is a little like deciding to get into marriage counseling. Couples don't get into marriage counseling when their attitude is, "Well, things are pretty good, but they're not terrific. Why don't we get some counseling so we can make a good thing better." It doesn't work that way. Husbands and wives decide to get marriage counseling when things are pretty bad, or even downright awful. Executive teams are the same way.

You'll have a much better idea if getting outside help is something to consider after you read the next chapter.

11

Getting Outside Help

There may come a time when the interpersonal problems on your team are beyond your ability to solve effectively without some outside help. By "outside help" we mean professional consultants like ourselves who help executive teams, partner groups, and owners of family businesses sit down and discuss sensitive, "difficult" topics. In this chapter, we'll try to answer three questions centered around the issue of getting outside help:

- Why you probably won't get outside help (even if you really need it).

- What kind of help should you be looking for?

- Where can you find outside help?

We'll start by making one assumption: you and your group are at least candidates for outside help. That is, you're having some problems that affect not only the happiness and satisfaction of individuals on the team, but also the effectiveness of the entire group (and, probably, the entire organization).

Why You Probably Won't Get Outside Help(Even if You Really Need It)

Even though we don't know your exact situation, we predict you and your group will not bring in outside consultants to help you—no matter how much you need it. That's what we said in the very beginning of the book; that's what our experience has taught us. On the other hand, you may change your mind after reading this chapter. One way to get you to consider changing your mind is to offer a number of reasons why people in your situation typically don't bring in outsiders. Here they are:

The Whole Issue of Getting Outside Help is a Complicated One
In general, people say they're willing to seek outside help when a) they've tried some things on their own to resolve a problem and it hasn't worked or b) they're reluctant to try to solve a problem on their own because they don't want to risk making things worse. That seems very clean and simple but it is not. Even when only one person is involved, the issue of getting help is a tricky question. For example, take two individuals of the same age and gender who've just begun to suspect they might have a potentially serious physical problem like a heart condition. Depending on their prior medical experience, their family and cultural backgrounds, and, most of all, their different personalities, these two people could make totally different decisions about seeking medical help.

When two people—say, a married couple having problems—try to decide whether to get help, it becomes much more complicated. All of the individual factors are at work (family and cultural background, personality, etc.), but now these factors may clash as the couple tries to make some kind of joint decision. Sometimes, they'll agree to get into counseling or not. More often they'll disagree—with one person promoting the idea and the other person balking or refusing to consider it.

With business partners, owners of family businesses, and people on executive teams, it gets even more complicated. Often, as many as a dozen people are involved in the decision. But it's not just a question of numbers. How people feel about the idea of seeking help is affected by all the individual variables we mentioned above plus their power position in the group, the amount of "hurt" they feel, and a host of other factors.

You've Got the Power, but You're not Hurting
As we've already said, it's extremely common for people in the one-up position to be among the biggest problems—if not the biggest problem—on an executive team. Despite that, it's extremely rare for people in the one up position to think something like this:

"You know, I'm really a big problem for the people on this team. Everybody seems to be in agreement on that. Maybe I'll bring in some outside consultants to help me learn how to manage this group more effectively. I know it means I'll have to face up to some things about myself I'd just as soon ignore, but it's the right thing to do—for the firm, for the team, and for myself."

Have you *ever* heard a boss say something like that? If you did, you'd probably say, "Pinch me! I must be dreaming," or, "Are we on 'Candid Camera'?"

It's quite possible that you're a huge problem for the people that report to you. But since they're the ones who are hurting—not you—and since you're the only one who can decide to bring in help, no help is coming in. At least not right now. Who knows what might happen a year from now when an important member of the team threatens to resign and take the best employees along with him? Or a family member walks out of a board meeting in disgust and isn't seen for two weeks? Or a disgruntled junior partner walks in and demands full-partner status, otherwise she takes all her clients with her? Then, *maybe*, you go get some help.

You've Got the Power, but not the Fortitude

Sometimes, bosses have the power and authority to bring in outside help but they don't have the courage to do it, even when they know the problem is serious. Here's how it usually works. The Big Boss is a "nice" person, but has a number-two person who's talented but obnoxious or abrasive. Everybody else on the team is upset by Number Two's behavior and they frequently go to the Big Boss complaining about the situation. Big Boss knows something should be done. But does Big Boss bring in help to deal with a problem affecting the morale and productivity of other key players in the firm? No. Big Boss justifies the decision to do nothing:

"I know Number-Two is a huge problem. But the contribution he's making is essential to the success of the firm. We could probably get along fine if anyone else left. But if Number-Two decides to leave, we'd be in deep trouble. I can't risk doing anything that will up the chances of his taking a hike."

Here's an example of a big boss who overcame his lack of fortitude with the help of an employee who gave him a little "encouragement":

For the last decade Denny McAllister has been working for a manufacturing company in South Carolina, where he's risen to the level of vice-president in charge of sales. Bill Tabor, the current president of the company, is in his mid-60's now and would like to retire. The problem is, Bill has picked a successor that Denny (and several others on the executive team) don't like. His name is Carl Roskin. Carl is in his late 50's and has been with the company for over 30 years. He's very intelligent, but he's definitely from the "old school" when it comes to managing people. According to Denny, "He's rigid, he's authoritarian, and he has no idea what participative management means." For about two months Denny pleaded with Bill to "do something" about this problem. This is what he'd been saying:

> "Bill, if you want to make Carl the next president of this place, that's your business. You have every right to do it. But you've got to realize the rest of us in the management group are going to have trouble rallying around Carl. This is the 90's. Carl has got to understand that he can't treat people the way they did 30 years ago. Mark my words, if he doesn't make some changes, some of us are going to leave."

About a month later Bill attended the annual convention of his trade association and, by chance, sat in on our seminar. Within a short time, because of Denny's pushing, we started a round of individual interviews in preparation for a team-building session. Carl wasn't wild about the idea, but he went along with the idea after meeting us in person. Carl got a lot of tough feedback at the team-building session, but he took it well. He ended up making a number of small but important changes in his operating style as a result. When we came back a month later for a follow-up session,

Denny made a dramatic statement in front of the whole group. He said:

> "You know, Carl hasn't changed his personality this past month, but he has changed some of his old-line ways. He's trying and that's all I expect from someone. If he keeps this up, there's no question I can stay here and rally behind his leadership."

Carl responded by getting out of his chair, walking over to Denny, and shaking his hand warmly. Bill Tabor then confessed he never would have considered a team building session if it hadn't been for the persistent pressure he got from Denny.

The Thought of Bringing in Outsiders is Threatening to You
Maybe you're the "problem person" that everyone on your team is concerned about. And maybe you know that. Maybe you don't want any outsiders coming in and threatening to expose you. On the contrary, you want to block attempts to discuss things openly and candidly. We've seen it happen enough times over the years. Or maybe you're so concerned about preserving and protecting your position in the group that you'll try to thwart any change in the status quo. If this is true, we can understand why you don't want to bring in outside help. After all, you don't see it as *help*. You only see it as something that can hurt you.

Getting a Consensus to Bring in Help Can Be very Difficult
If you have about the same amount of power as your other team members, you can influence the decision to get outside help, but you can't make it unilaterally. For example, in most equal partnerships, every single partner has to agree to the decision about outside help if it's going to happen. It's a little bit like the United Nations Security Council—one "no" vote can successfully veto any course of action. Sometimes, the decision can take forever. That's what happened with some accountants we worked with a few years ago.

Gerry Marsden and Sally Clark were two of the three founding partners of an accounting firm that had been up and running for five years. Gerry and Sally were very concerned about their third partner, Jim Tucker, who was not working out as well as they had hoped. Both partners felt that Jim would probably be effective supervising a team of associates in a larger firm. But in their small firm things were different. Each of them had to do a lot more of the detail work than is normally true with partners in a large firm. And Jim was not good at details. According to Gerry and Sally, he had lost the firm several clients simply because he failed to keep track of important filing deadlines. Several other clients had come to them and said they'd go to another firm rather than work with Jim again. Gerry and Sally weren't sure what to do. They knew that if a breakup occurred, it'd be messy. Jim wasn't the kind of guy who would like the idea of being pushed out. He also had a reputation for being "litigious." Their biggest fear was that a protracted and expensive legal battle would bring them all down.

It took over 18 months between our first conversation with Gerry and Sally and the date we scheduled our first meeting with the three partners. In between, we had countless telephone conversations with all three partners; they met many times to discuss us, and all three called some of our previous clients to "check us out." We'd almost given up on working with them when a seminar in a nearby city allowed us to get the three of them in a room together for the first time. We talked about how we might work with them and what the "downside" was if they didn't get help. We said if they didn't want to use us, that was fine; we'd help them find someone else. That did it. Happily, they were able to "work through" their problems with a little help from us and a lot of effort on their part.

By the way, trying to get partnerships to agree to work with us has been one of the most frustrating aspects of our work over the past dozen years. This is what happens. We meet Partner A at a convention and he tells us about the problems he's having with his three other partners. A week or so later, we send Partner A a letter explaining a little bit more about us and how we might help the group. (We also include a few "press clippings" to enhance our credibility.) We suggest that Partner A share the letter and accompanying material with his three partners at their next meeting. We also invite any of them to call us if they have questions or concerns. Within the next week or so, Partners B and C call us and we go over some of their attractions and reservations about a doing a partners' retreat. At some point, they agree that it'd be a good idea to go ahead, but they tell us that Partner D "might be a problem."

We leave message after message on Partner D's voice mail, but he doesn't return our calls. After a few weeks, Partner A calls and tells us the group has decided not to do a session at this time. It's clear that Partner D has successfully blocked the idea. Whenever this happens, we're reminded of a principle we learned in graduate school: The people who need help the most are often the least receptive to getting it.

You Have Opinions and Attitudes
that Run Counter to the Idea of Getting Help
Maybe you're a person for whom the whole idea of bringing in "relationship counselors" to help your executive team just doesn't cut it. If we asked you why, you could come up with a number of plausible answers:

"It's too expensive." Bringing in outside help *can* be expensive. Depending upon who you hire, outside helpers can cost hundreds of dollars an hour or thousands per day. If you're part of a successful, cash-rich company, this kind of money is not a problem (especially when you consider what you're currently doing with some of that money). On the other hand, if you're part of a small business struggling to make ends meet, any unanticipated expense can be a burden.

"We don't need shrinks to help us solve our problems." In spite of massive attitudinal changes in the last 30 years, there is still a stigma in our society attached to the idea of going to a "shrink." We run into people almost every week who could benefit enormously from seeing a psychologist or becoming part of some kind of therapeutic or self-help program. But they never seriously consider it for fear of being considered "weak" or "crazy" or both. The same holds true for married couples. In our opinion, lots of unhappy spouses ought to be in marriage counseling. But they won't go because one or both partners consider it an admission of weakness or a sign of personal failure. And how about the people who are running the show in organizations all across the country? If anything, there the stigma is worse:

"Bring in psychologists to help us with management problems we should be able to solve on our own? We may have a few problems, but we're not nuts!"

"What if other people find out?" This is related to the previous point, but different enough to make it a reservation in its own right. Sometimes organizations in deep trouble decide not to seek outside help because they fear their competitors or customers would find out about it, jeopardizing their "image" or reputation. We've even worked with some family teams and partner groups who didn't want employees in their own companies to know they were working with us.

"It'll make things worse." This is a big fear, and one of the most commonly expressed reservations we hear. The essence of it goes like this:

"Yeah, we may be unhappy, but we're not miserable. What if we start leveling with each other and all hell breaks loose! Right now at least we're making money and we have our careers intact. We don't want to open up Pandora's Box and jeopardize it all."

"This touchy-feely psychological stuff has no place in the business world." Over the years, we've noticed that people vary markedly on the dimension of receptivity to using an "open-communication" approach to solving their problems. Some people are unreceptive, if not antagonistic, to the idea. With some exceptions, the folks in this camp tend to be older males with an authoritarian, "my-way-or-the-highway" approach to management. A group with one or two people like this is not likely to call in helpers like us, no matter how badly they're struggling. Groups like this don't get help. They either get rid of the "troublemakers" or make them so miserable they leave on their own.

We've been frank and pessimistic in this section. We've offered a number of reasons why you and your team probably won't bring in outside help—no matter how severe your relationship problems have gotten.

Now we'll change our tune just a bit and offer some optimism. We sense a change in the air. We don't have any hard data to back it up, but it seems like there's an increasing number of high-level business and professional people who are receptive to a "let's-talk-this-thing-out" approach to solving relationship problems. Part of it may be due to the baby boomers rising to positions of power and more women in the work place. But it goes beyond that. We think authoritarian, top-down, command-and-control management is a flawed system that may be on its last legs. And gradually it will be replaced by a more egalitarian, participative approach to management that stresses group involvement over one-man rule and open communication over unquestioning obedience. Executive teams that adopt this new style of management will still have problems. They may even seem to have more problems than more traditional teams where issues aren't debated openly and ideas aren't expressed forthrightly. But they'll be healthier teams. And they'll be more likely to seek some kind of outside help when they need it.

What Kind of Outside Help Should You Be Looking For?

Let's say you agree with or are at least open to the idea of seeking some kind of help. What kind of help should you be looking for? In this section we'll talk about six things we think those helpers should be able to do.

They Should Be Able to Help You (and Your Team Members) "Open Up" to Them About Sensitive, Hard-to-Discuss Issues

If the people you bring in are going to help, they've got to be able to make you—and every other member of your team—feel comfortable talking to them about some very sensitive matters. They'll probably want to sit down with everyone individually for at least an hour to get each person's perspective on the various problems confronting the team. (If they don't plan to do this sort of individual interviewing in advance, that should raise some "red flags" about the effectiveness of their approach.) In these individual interviews, you should feel comfortable talking about:

- How thoroughly intimidated you feel by your boss's aggressiveness or anger whenever you advance a contrary or counter point of view.

- How hurt and resentful you are that your children have never acknowledged what it took for you to build the successful business they stand to inherit.

- How angry and upset you are that your father thinks he can get away with having an affair with the office manager of the business your family owns.

- How embarrassed you feel when one of your partners has had a few drinks and starts blabbering about his political and social philosophy to prospective clients.

- How disappointed and disgusted you felt when the outgoing president of your firm didn't choose you as the "heir apparent," but chose a colleague who sucks up to people in positions of power. You cringe at the thought of having to report to this "brown-noser."

Confidentiality
As we said earlier, when the helpers you bring in do individual interviews with you and your team members, they'll be hearing very sensitive stuff, which should be kept strictly confidential—both inside and outside the firm. For example, let's say your boss—an overbearing, tyrannical sort—has brought in two consultants to do some team building work. You're seated in the conference room with the consultants and the door is closed. They ask you to give them a frank, "no-holds-barred" assessment of your boss as a leader. You're a little reluctant to open up at first, but they convince you that everything you say is confidential. So you start in:

> "Well, I do think Art has some real strengths as a leader, but he's got some unbelievable weaknesses, too. And right now those weaknesses are having a really bad effect on morale in this place. You asked me to be frank. OK, I'll be frank. At times, Art can be a real bully. And, every now and then, he shows a nasty side that can be pretty scary. Now, let me tell you what I mean by that."

"Keeping things strictly confidential" means that what you've just said will never get back to anybody. Not your boss. Not your boss's boss. Not any of your team members. Absolutely nobody. If you can't be very sure the helpers you bring in can keep remarks like these confidential, don't bring them in. Unfortunately, too many so-called helpers pass this kind of information on (usually unwittingly, but sometimes intentionally). The negative effects can be enormous.

This principle of confidentiality also applies to talking with people outside the company, especially competitors and customers (and anyone else who may be curious about your business). For us, this has never been a problem. As psychologists the principle of confidentiality is at the very heart of our work. But that's not true for everyone. We were appalled several years ago to find one of our colleagues blabbing to the press about his work with a famous family business whose problems had just made the national news. Not only did he talk about his work with the firm, he made some uncomplimentary remarks about several members of the family. It was inappropriate and unethical. So, if you have any doubts about the capacity of your prospective helpers to keep their mouths shut, don't hire them.

Taking Sides

If consultants come into your organization to help the people in your group improve your relationships with each other, don't expect them to be welcomed with open arms by everyone on the team. In fact, it's likely that several people will be suspicious of these "outsiders" (including some who were originally opposed to bringing them in). For example, they may be thinking:

"Are they here to shape us up?" Let's say you're in your early 30's and the boss of your executive team is well over 50. For the last six months your boss has shown increasing frustration over what he considers "major communications problems" among his key staff. Last week you found out that two consultants will be coming in the day after tomorrow to do some interviewing in preparation for a two-day team-building session to be held next month. Since your boss is an opinionated and domineering fellow, we wouldn't blame you if you suspected he'd hired these consultants to "fix" you and the rest of the staff when it comes to communicating

effectively. That's not a particularly comforting feeling when you know your boss is a huge part of the communication problems he's so concerned about.

"Are they in here to see if I should be fired?" It's not at all unusual for us to hear this concern when we first go into an organization. One of the team members who was definitely not part of the decision to bring us in realizes her "stock" with the powers that be is not so good. Maybe they haven't come right out and said it, but it's clear they're not happy with her performance and she better shape up— fast! Then she finds out the two of us are coming in to do something called "team building." Then she finds out the first thing we're going to do is interview a bunch of people individually, including her. Her anxiety about her future in the organization skyrockets and she thinks:

> "These guys aren't in here to do team building. They're in here to do an assessment of all of us and they're going to make recommendations about who should stay and who should go."

Neurotic? Paranoid? Not at all. We know of consultants who do exactly that kind of work, even though it borders on the unethical.

"Are they in here to help ease me out the door?" This is a concern we hear from people who think the decision to get rid of them has already been made. When they see us coming into their organization, they simply don't believe we're there to help the team talk about and resolve important issues in their relationships with each other. They believe we're really there to help the boss or the "other partners" get them out of the organization as painlessly as possible. They think:

> "Well, I guess this is the beginning of the end. They don't want me around anymore, but they don't quite know how to break it to me. So they've brought in the shrinks to do their dirty work for them."

These are realistic and powerful concerns. We know from hard experience that anyone you bring in to work with your team can't be effective unless they're able to dispel these kinds of concerns. They'll have to be able to convince people they're there to help the entire team, not just the person who's paying the bill. They'll also have to convince people they're looking for "win-win" solutions to problems the team is experiencing. They should be sending a powerful message: "We want everybody to be better off as a result of our involvement, not just some people."

But how can your helpers do this? How can they convince people they won't take sides and they're not there to perform some unpleasant task, like getting rid of somebody or easing somebody out the door? Well, they won't be able to wipe away these concerns immediately. But if the people you hire really don't want to take sides, it will eventually show in how they work with your team:

They'll put extra pressure on people in the "one-up" position to do the most changing. We feel very strongly about this. The most successful work we've done with executive teams is when the people at the top—the most powerful people on the team—are willing to try to make important changes in their behavior. Whoever you bring in needs to make it clear to people in the "one-up" position that they need to be committed to an "open-discussion" process and willing to change some of their behavior. They should even tell the rest of the group they intend to put extra pressure on the top people. They don't have to do this in a heavy-handed, overly serious way. They can even do it with good-natured teasing. But they have to be clear to the whole team that they're expecting the top people to take the lead in making changes.

They won't compromise their values or principles to extend their stay or keep from being fired. If your helpers are really going to do their job, they have to be willing to put their money where their mouths are. They have to be willing to stand up to the most powerful people on the team—the ones who made the financial decision to bring them in—and challenge these folks if they're not "getting with the program." We've been thrown out of a few companies when we confronted the most powerful people about their lack of commitment or for not being honest and straightforward. We lost some money when that happened, but we didn't lose our self-respect (or the respect of the others in the group who saw the same lack of effort or sincerity we did).

They'll make a special effort to see that "problem" team members don't get beat up on and scapegoated. Think for a moment about your own executive team. There's probably at least one person in the group who's difficult, frustrating, or irascible. When outside consultants come into an organization, it's easy (even tempting) to gang up on these "problem" people. But if these kinds of difficult team members are ever going to be open to changing their ways—and to become better "team players"— the folks you bring in will have to win them over. They'll have to convey a message like this:

> "We respect your point of view as much as we respect anyone else's on this team. We care about your feelings as much as we care about anyone else's. Just because you're not the most popular or well-regarded member of the team doesn't mean we won't look out for your interests as much as we will anyone else's."

Focusing on Issues

Anyone you bring in should be able to help you all sit down together and talk about the most important issues you're wrestling with. Given the approach we take, maybe this seems obvious. Unfortunately, it's not obvious to a lot of consultants who claim to help executive teams. They don't see the importance of helping people "talk out" the difficult, sensitive issues we've referred to throughout the book. Still others don't have the training or skills to help executive teams this way. In particular, we see three kinds of consultants you may consider but who probably won't help you all that much with your most important problems:

Consultants who gather information and then deliver a report. This has been the standard operating procedure for management consultants ever since the field started to blossom after the end of World War II. The consultants come in and collect a lot of "data" and then write a report describing what they think the problems are and how those problems should be solved. Now there's nothing wrong with that approach to a lot of problems in the business world. But it simply will not work as an approach to resolving the tough relationship and performance issues that occur so frequently in businesses large and small.

Consultants who do long-range or strategic-planning. As valuable as this kind of thing is—and as much as many companies need to improve in this area—long-range or strategic-planning sessions won't work for the same reasons we mentioned above with report-writing consultants. Yes, the strategic-planning consultants may interview all the key participants. And, yes, the long-range planning consultants may take you all off for a few days to plan for the future. But you'll end up talking about things that—while very important—are not central to the reason you're struggling in the first place. It's a great treatment, but not for the particular malady you're suffering from.

Consultants who get you together to do a lot of team-building "exercises." There are lots of consultants these days who take executive teams "away from the ranch" for a weekend (or a week!) to do a number of exercises designed to build a better sense of teamwork among the group. Maybe they'll take you off to a nice conference center and put you through a number of role-playing exercises or get you to take some personality tests and have you all discuss the results with each other. Or maybe they'll take you off to a rustic, "Outward Bound" type setting where you and your colleagues will spend an exhilarating weekend climbing ropes, scaling rock faces, and then discussing the implications for your work back at the office.

We want to be very clear about this. There's absolutely nothing wrong with these kinds of experiences. They can be very enjoyable. They can be a pleasant break from your normal routine. They're almost always an opportunity to learn something worthwhile about yourselves—as individuals and as a team. And strategic planning is essential. But, we don't think these kinds of exercises help very much in resolving the tough relationship issues that got you to consider bringing in outside help in the first place. The only way to resolve these kinds of problems is to sit down face to face and talk about them effectively. As enjoyable as taking personality tests and climbing ropes can be, there simply is no replacement for talking candidly and caringly about these issues, with or without the help of a competent facilitator.

Ability to Teach Communication Skills

The people you bring in should be good facilitators. That is, they should be skilled at getting you and your team members to talk with each other effectively about important topics, "touchy" subjects, and other difficult-to-discuss issues. But they should be able to do more than just facilitate good communication. They should also be able to teach you how to communicate more effectively with each other.

We subscribe to the old adage: "Give a man a fish, he'll eat for a day; teach a man to fish, he'll eat for a lifetime." If the helpers you bring in can teach all of you to do a better job of talking and listening to each other—whether or not they use the same techniques we've described in this book—the long-term effects on your team will be far greater than if they just come in and facilitate a series of effective discussions.

Commitment

Even if you get some effective outside help, it's unlikely all the problems that lead you to seek outside help originally will get fully resolved the first time around. They should be able to make a long-term commitment to helping you. Even if the consultants you hire can help you put a big dent in these problems, there's always a good chance some of them may resurface later on (or new ones will crop up). For example:

— The strained relationship between two of your vice-presidents that seemed to have gotten "fixed" during the weekend team-building session has shown signs of becoming "unglued" during the last several weeks.

— That division director in your agency who you thought had really started to commit himself to the organization's goals now seems to have slid back into "active retirement."

— Your son, who is also your business partner, seemed to have faced up to his alcohol problem after a series of weekly sessions with you and a psychologist you brought in to help. But, all of a sudden, everything seems to have come unraveled. You got a tearful call from your daughter-in-law late last night saying he's started drinking again.

— Three months ago you and the other senior partners in your firm had a week long retreat where all kinds of sensitive issues got discussed openly. After that session the younger partners on your team stopped making noises about leaving the firm to go off on their own. However, yesterday one of them came in and said:

"Frank, I'm not sure you and the senior partners got the message we were trying to send at our retreat last spring. You haven't lived up to a lot of the commitments you made. I don't know. You're not leaving us a whole lot of options."

Hopefully, these kinds of problems won't crop up later on. But, again, our experience says they will. So you need helpers who are willing to go the distance with you. Specifically, you need consultants who will:

Make you feel comfortable about calling them anytime. This is very important. The kinds of problems we're talking about can be distracting. If you don't get a chance to talk about them quickly, they can eat away at you. When you call your helpers at times like these, you need several things: a quick return of your call if they're not in; a patient and understanding response to whatever concerns you have at that time; and confidence they won't automatically start the meter running every time you ask for advice.

Check in with you periodically. We know how much our clients appreciate an occasional phone call or leisurely lunch where we simply ask them how things are going and give them a chance to think out loud about their situation (rarely does anyone in the office do this for them). If you use consultants who care about the long-term effects of their work with you, they'll do the same thing. And if you tell them you don't want to hear from them for a while, they'll respect your wishes without getting pushy or defensive.

Be able to come in quickly if a crisis erupts. When and if an unforeseen problem occurs, you may need some help right away. When you call your consultants, you can expect them to be busy. If they're any good, they should be. On the other hand, they should be willing to fit you in as soon as they can, even if it means scheduling a weekend session. If helping you deal with your crisis means some inconvenience to them, so be it. That's part of what they're getting paid for. And a good test of how committed they are to helping you.

Where to Find Good Outside Help

Part of the problem of finding people who can help you has to do with something we mentioned in the very beginning of the book. There aren't a lot of professionals out there doing this sort of thing, whether it's called "organizational marriage counseling," "business therapy," "executive coaching," or plain old management consulting.

Whatever you call this kind of work, we have some thoughts on how to find somebody who can help. We'll start by talking about their probable background and training, and then we'll suggest some places to look for them.

Background and Training

Ideally, you should bring in someone who's spent a lot of time helping executive teams like yours sit down face to face to talk out tough interpersonal problems. To be honest, though, that's easier said than done. So, if you can't find someone who's experienced with this kind of thing, look for someone who's done something similar with other groups. It might be someone with a wealth of experience working with church groups or community agencies (like the YWCA, the Boy's Club, or a community counseling center). It might be somebody with many years of experience as a marriage counselor or family therapist, even though that person's work in the corporate or business arena is limited (or even nonexistent). It might be a psychologist or other professional who specializes in working with personal growth or self-help groups. What matters most is finding someone who's had solid experience helping people who want to grow individually as well as improve their relationships with the people around them.

What kind of professional training should your helpers have? There are no hard and fast rules on this, but probably they'll be people with advanced training in the "helping professions," like psychologists, marriage and family counselors, or social workers.

Even though they may not have had a lot of "business" experience, their training in conflict resolution and their emphasis on effective communication may be exactly what you need. However, just because someone is trained in the helping professions doesn't mean they're good helpers. We know a few psychologists and psychiatrists who are not only not helpful, they're pretty much useless when it comes to helping other people solve difficult problems. And there's a small percentage, to be frank, who actually do some damage. So, be careful.

You should also be wary of any consultants who claim to do this kind of work if their only educational credentials are an MBA or a degree in engineering, law, or accounting. While some of these folks are mature and very helpful, some of them have no business "helping" other people. We know of one guy who says he does this kind of work and the very thought of it is sobering to us. He's despised by his former business partners, reviled by a couple of ex-wives, and hardly speaks at all to members of his own family. Call it a hunch, but we're not sure a guy like this is going to be too good at helping you and your group learn how to resolve your problems with each other.

If you're resourceful, you may find excellent help in unexpected places. A few years ago, we got a call from the owner of a small family business in the Pacific Northwest. He was struggling mightily in his relationship with his eldest son, who also worked in the business. There was no way we could help them ourselves, but we referred them to a most unusual "management" consultant—the pastor of their church! With a little coaching from us, he turned out to be far more effective (and far less expensive) than almost anyone else they could've found.

As we're writing this chapter, we're consulting long-distance to a marriage counselor on the West Coast who's working with a group of physicians in a small practice. Several years ago, this counselor had worked with one of the physicians and her husband in marriage counseling. Recently, that same physician called us and described some of the knotty problems she was having with her three other partners. Because of the distance and prohibitive costs, we couldn't help the group ourselves. However, when we asked if she could think of anyone locally that had the kind of skills and qualities we talked about earlier in this chapter, she immediately thought of the marriage counselor. One thing lead to another and we ended up "coaching" the marriage counselor. He read our two previous books and is now in the process of adding a new dimension to his marriage and family counseling practice.

Additional Thoughts about Finding Outside Help

Even though there aren't lots of professionals who specialize in this emerging line of work, we're convinced you can find someone good if you're willing to be a little persistent and resourceful. One way to start is by:

Asking people you know who may already have gotten help. Because of the sensitive nature of our work, some organizations (especially family businesses and business partnerships) don't want the outside world to know they're getting this kind of help. Other organizations are quite willing to talk about it and tout its benefits, especially if it's worked well for them. If you know somebody who's had some success with this kind of help, ask them about it. Find out why they did it in the first place, what the consultant did to help them, and what the results were. You'll learn a lot, and you may find exactly the kind of help you're looking for.

Try to find someone in your own time zone. This may not be possible, but if you can find someone close by, we think there are several advantages. The obvious one, of course, is that if they are geographically close to you, they can get there quickly. And sometimes that's important. Another advantage of physical proximity is "emotional" proximity. As the years have gone by and we've gained more and more experience, we've sensed that clients who were close by seemed more connected to us then the ones who had to worry about a time zone difference before they picked up the phone to call. A third advantage to being really close to your helpers is that they can schedule two or three-hour meetings as opposed to full-day sessions. When it comes to the follow-up work we do with our clients, we know we can help them much more in four two-hour sessions spread out over a month then we can in one full-day session.

Talk to staff at the trade associations or professional societies you belong to. The paid staff of trade associations and professional societies get to know lots of consultants because consultants see these organizations as a way to reach potential clients. If a particular consultant has had some success in helping the members of an association solve a certain kind of problem (whether it's long-range strategic planning or the kind of thing we're talking about here), chances are someone on the staff will know about it. The only caveat we'd offer is discretion. Bringing in outside help for the kinds of problems discussed in this book is not necessarily something you want your fellow association members knowing about. So choose a staff person you trust and one who can keep things confidential.

Check with the departments of psychology or counseling at local colleges and universities. Lots of college and university professors spend more time (and make more money) at consulting than they do at their teaching jobs. Do some checking. You might find somebody right in your own back yard who'll be able to help you. Or they may know of someone you can call.

Feel free to contact us. We debated whether to say this because it might sound like crass self-promotion. But then we thought, "What the hell? Why not?" Maybe we can help. Or maybe we can suggest somebody else. So if you'd like to talk about getting help—or anything else—get in touch with us through the publisher. We're also listed in the phone book (Peter in Washington, D.C. and Mardy in Bedford, Massachusetts). We'd love to hear from you.

12

Making a Hard Decision

Well, here we are. The last chapter. And maybe the toughest, too. Because, before we leave you, we want to talk about three different hard decisions you may have to make someday. The decision to: fire somebody on your team, get rid of a partner on your team, or leave your team. If you've been out there in the world of work for at least a couple of decades, you've probably already had to make one of these decisions. You know decisions like these aren't easy. If you haven't had to make one yet, you will soon enough. And you'll discover how demanding it can be.

Even though there's no way you can completely avoid the hardships that go along with making these decisions, we do think there are some ways you can keep them to a minimum. And that's the purpose of this last chapter. Specifically, we'll try to answer three basic questions for you:

- What does each decision mean?

- Why is each decision so hard?

- What's important to keep in mind about these decisions?

What Does Each Decision Mean?

Clearly, each of these three decisions is different from the other two. Firing someone who works for you is not the same thing as getting rid of a partner who shares ownership of your firm. And leaving your team or partnership, of course, is just the opposite of getting someone else to leave. But these three decisions do share a common characteristic: You make them. They're not being made about you. You're deciding to fire someone; you're deciding to get rid of a partner; and you're deciding to leave. (It's quite another matter to be on the receiving end of these decisions—to get fired or to be asked to leave your partnership or to have a valued team member leave you.) Now let's talk in some detail about what each of these decisions means:

Firing Someone

For us, there are at least two important characteristics about a decision to fire someone on your team: 1) You're removing the person from his or her job; and 2) you are clearly in the one-up position, and the person you're firing is clearly in the one-down position. Let's start with the first characteristic. Firing someone doesn't always mean the person has to leave your organization and find another job somewhere else. All firing means is that you're unequivocally deciding to remove the person from whatever position he or she is in right now. This "removal" can take a number of forms:

Classic firing. Marty Coleman and Jessie Ranter are a good example of a classic firing. Both Marty and Jessie were in their early 40's, and both were energetic and strong-willed. When we started working with the company (a rapidly expanding retail operation in the northern Midwest), Marty had been at the helm just about six months. Jessie, the company's advertising head, had come on board only about a month before Marty. Right from the start (according to all the team members we talked to) it was clear that Marty and Jessie weren't going to get along. The fellow in charge of their shipping and warehousing department told us:

> "Oil and water. That's what those two are. Marty is a very opinionated guy, and Jessie is a very domineering woman. The two of them get into pissing contests all the time. The fact that they can't seem to get along is becoming a drag on the organization. Something's got to be done."

Well, not too long after that interview, something was done. Marty fired Jessie. She's now working for another company in a similar position where she seems very happy. But the best news about Marty's painful decision to let her go came when she called us a couple of months ago:

> "At first I was very angry at Marty for firing me. But, oddly enough, he and I have become good friends. We realized we actually liked and respected each other a great deal and that, finally, we didn't have to compete with each other anymore. It's kind of amazing."

A demotion. If you've been a boss for a number of years, you've probably had more than one person working for you who had some valuable skills but was hopelessly in over his or her head. (Laurence Peters devoted an entire book to this phenomenon when he wrote *The Peter Principle* (by Lauerence Peters, NY: Wm. Morrow, 1969) in the late '60s.) In this kind of situation you remove the person from the job you think he can't handle and move him into one that takes better advantage of what he does well and minimizes what he doesn't do well. Whether this kind of move is truly a demotion, that's almost always the way the employee sees it. Managers of struggling baseball teams who get "promoted" to the front office know full well they're being demoted because they couldn't produce a winner. In the late 80's we worked with a large construction company where Doug Grant, the CEO, did the same sort of thing with Craig Belinski, his chief financial officer. More than once Craig had embarrassed Doug by not being prepared to answer tough questions at quarterly board meetings. Doug eventually moved Craig to the position of Senior Vice-President of Human Resources. On paper this looked like a step up for Craig. But everybody in the company, especially Craig, knew otherwise. Doug saw the Human Resources Department as a low-level staff function that just ate up precious overhead dollars.

Telling the person to find something else in the organization. Some organizations, like *Fortune 500* companies or the federal government, are so large that people who aren't working out in one job can often find another job somewhere else in the organization. As the boss of an executive team who wants to fire somebody but who doesn't want to put that person "out in the street," this gives you an option you wouldn't have in a smaller organization. This is the kind of option Laura Hamden chose to use with Paul Scarborough. Laura was a center director in the Department of Commerce and Paul was one of her deputies. When Laura recruited Paul from another agency, he looked like a real star to her. But within three months, Laura knew she'd missed the boat in picking Paul. If firing someone in the federal government weren't such an overwhelming task, that's exactly what Laura would have done. She decided on a more realistic alternative. One day she simply called Paul into her office and said:

> "Let's face it, Paul, this isn't working out. I think you should start looking for another job somewhere else. There are all kinds of opportunities throughout the government. I'm not going to set a deadline for you, but if you haven't found something within six months, we're going to have to talk much more concretely about what your options are. I'll help you in any way I can, but I see it as your responsibility to take the initiative here."

Now let's talk about the second characteristic of firing someone: the fact that you're clearly in the one-up position and the person you're firing is clearly in the one-down position. When you fire someone, that employee pretty much has to accept your decision. He or she try can try to fight your decision, but the chances are very good that you, not your employee, will prevail. For a moment, let's go back to the three examples we just talked about. Jessie Ranter could decide to fight Marty Coleman's decision to fire her by filing a wrongful discharge suit against him or lodging a sex discrimination complaint with the EEOC. She might even succeed in getting a favorable judgment, but she's not going to get her job back. Craig Belinski could try to go over Doug Grant's head to someone on the board of directors to protest his demotion, but a move like that would probably only make a bad situation worse for him. The same holds true for Paul Scarborough. He can file a grievance against Laura Hamden for trying to move him out of her center, but that's only going to increase the stress and dissatisfaction he's already experiencing in his job. He'd be better off to follow Laura's advice.

Getting Rid of a Partner

Getting rid of a partner is a different matter from firing someone on your executive team. Unlike an employee, a partner has "ownership" in your organization, and that ownership gives your partner power to resist your decision in a way that an employee can't. Sometimes this ownership is clearly spelled out in legal, contractual terms. At other times this ownership is less concrete than the legal type, but it's no less powerful. A couple of examples:

A legal partner. Pat Colter, Cal Humphries, and Chuck Scaglia—three associates in an accounting firm just northwest of Chicago. For the last 18 months Pat and Cal have been talking seriously about getting rid of Chuck. They've lost confidence in Chuck's ability to attract new clients to the firm and keep his current ones (especially the"biggies") happy. But getting rid of Chuck is not going to be an easy matter. The agreement each of them signed over five years ago clearly spells out procedures for the removal of a partner. And that agreement is particularly clear about how financial remuneration of a partner will be considerably more favorable if his departure from the partnership is involuntary rather than voluntary. In addition, Pat and Cal are quite sure Chuck won't be at all happy about being asked to leave. They expect he'll fight for everything he has coming to him according to the agreement, and probably a lot more than that.

A family member. Given all of our experience over the last decade and a half, we can say this with a lot of confidence: If you're the CEO of a family business, you probably have at least one family member working for you who deserves to be fired. Maybe it's a son who takes advantage of his family status by coming and going whenever he pleases while he draws a salary way out of proportion to his contribution to the organization. Maybe it's a brother-in-law who tries very hard to do a good job but whose personality and temperament aren't suited to your business. Family members like these may not be partners (own stock in your company) in the technical sense of the word, but it doesn't matter. Since they're family members, you can't just fire them the way you can nonfamily employees. Not if you don't want to encounter more than a little trouble and strife.

Jack Barrow was painfully aware of this kind of problem with his brother George. Jack ran a multi-state beer and wine distributorship in the Southeast that he had worked hard to build up since the late 50's. About ten years ago his aging parents talked him into taking George (ten years his junior) into the business as a minor partner. Jack didn't think this was a particularly good idea at the time, and now he knows it was a terrible idea. George likes being part of the business, but he doesn't like hard work. His glib, "all-talk-and-no-action" style has worn thin with other employees and key customers. Jack desperately wants George out of the business. But he knows that won't be easy. Technically, of course, he could fire George. But the bad blood and ill will that would cause in his closely knit family doesn't seem worth it to Jack. He needs to find a way to get George out without causing family divisiveness that could last for years and years.

Leaving

We're familiar with at least three kinds of leaving:

Leaving a partnership. This is a big step. You aren't only leaving a job and an organization, you're leaving something that belongs to you—something you have legal ownership in. You may get paid for your stock, but there's no way to truly "take it all with you." Dave Paxton found himself in this kind of situation. Dave was 35 and had worked in his dad's construction company since he was a teenager. When his father died, primary ownership of the company passed to Jim Whitely, Dave's uncle. With our help, Dave made a valiant effort to get along with Jim, but according to Dave:

> "I just don't think it was meant to work out with Jim and me. I was able to accept him as a boss when I was a teenager, but I can't do that anymore. And I don't think he can accept me as an equal, either. It's time for me to move on. It'll be tough, but it's the right thing to do. I'd really love to run this place some day, but the pain and frustration I'd have to go through to make that happen aren't worth it."

Leaving a job and an organization. This is almost as tough as leaving a partnership. Sometimes it's even tougher. Tom Finley was the executive director of an association we consulted with on and off for almost seven years. Tom had taken over the association in the late '70s when it was still a "small potatoes" kind of operation. With a hell of a lot of hard work and savvy, Tom rapidly built the association into a first-class organization with a national reputation. Because of his controversial style of management, Tom had a lot of supporters on his board of directors, but he had a few detractors too. One of the most outspoken of these detractors finally got elected president of the association. When that happened, Tom told us:

> "I love this place. I love what we do here. But, I gotta go. And it'll break my heart to leave. But if Art (the newly elected president) and I have to work together, this place could go up in smoke. And I won't be a party to that. So I'm outa here."

Leaving a team. A little earlier we said that some organizations are so large that employees who aren't working out (or who are unhappy) in one job can sometimes find a more satisfying position in another part of the organization. We see this happen quite a bit in the work we do with the federal government. Carla Frampson is a good example. She's a member of the Senior Executive Service in the Department of Health and Human Services. When Carla inherited Gabe Harkness as the head of her office two years ago, she knew it was just a matter of time until she had to find another job. Gabe hadn't been in his new position more than a month and a half when Carla told us she was having trouble sleeping and an old ulcer was starting to act up. Three months after that she'd found another job in the agency with a lot more responsibility and pressure. But she told us:

> "Yeah, it's a tougher job and the hours are a lot longer. But I love it. Besides, I've got a boss I like and respect; I don't feel my ulcer anymore; and I sleep like a baby. I'm happy."

Why Is Each Decision So Hard?

These decisions are hard. If they weren't, people wouldn't avoid making them so often—especially when they need to be made. But why? Why do all of us find these decisions so hard? We think the answer is pretty straightforward; these decisions are emotional. They conjure up powerful feelings. In this section, we'll be talking about three sets of feelings that you're very likely to have whenever you consider firing someone, or getting rid of a partner, or leaving:

- Your caring and concern for another person's well-being

- Your sadness over a loss

- Your fear of how the other person might react

Your Caring and Concern for Another Person's Well-Being
Most of us have a strong sense of caring and concern for a lot of the people in our lives. And whenever you think about firing someone, or getting rid of a partner, or leaving, that kind of caring and concern usually comes to the surface. The focus of your concern can vary:

The person's livelihood. Remember Jack Barrow, the fellow who owns the beer and wine distributorship and who'd like to get his brother, George, out of the business? Jack's reservations about getting rid of George don't only have to do with his concerns about the furor that firing his brother would cause in the family. Jack is also concerned about George's capacity to earn a reasonable living if he were pushed out of the business. Jack is very aware there's no way George could pull down his current salary in another organization where he wasn't a "protected" member of the family. Jack is also very fond of George's wife and two children. Jack doesn't even like to think about the financial hardship that getting rid of George would cause the three of them.

The person's sense of self-esteem. Let's go back to the example of Marty Coleman and Jessie Ranter. Even though Marty didn't drag his feet a long time in making his decision to fire Jessie, he did have one big reservation:

"Jessie has a very tough exterior. She'd like you to believe she's hard as nails and can handle anything that gets thrown at her. But, as insensitive as I can be at times, I knew that was a facade. Right under the surface I saw a person who had a lot of doubts about herself. And I was really worried that getting canned would devastate her. I mean, she was a big source of irritation to me back then. But the last thing I wanted to do was hurt her."

Somebody else's growth and development once you're gone. When Carla Frampson was looking around the federal government for another job, she wasn't only concerned about escaping from Gabe Harkness. She was concerned about Ray Donovan. Ray was a young fellow Carla had just hired out of graduate school. She liked Ray a great deal and thought he had tremendous potential to grow both as a technical expert and manager. She was very concerned that once she left Ray's career might founder because of Gabe's incompetence as a leader and developer of people.

Your Sadness Over a Loss

Whenever you fire someone or get rid of a partner or leave a job, you're losing something or someone. Sometimes, not always, that loss can have a deep sense of sadness attached to it:

The loss of a "home." When Dave Paxton decided to leave the business his father had founded because he couldn't get along with his uncle, he went through a very rough six month period:

> "It was almost like I was in mourning. Here was this business I had literally grown up in. I took a few years off for junior college, but even then I was working on a part-time basis, and full-time on vacations and during the summer. I know I made the right decision, but I still miss the place terribly. That business will always have a little part of me in it."

The loss of something you've created. Just a month after he left the trade association he had built up over a decade, Tom Finley talked to us over a drink in a watering hole not five blocks from his old building:

> "When I get up in the morning, sometimes I have to remind myself that I don't work there any more. There's no question that I did the right thing. Staying there and trying to work with Art would have been impossible. But, damn, I feel an emptiness at times. It just sort of sneaks up on me when I least expect it. It's not the same thing, of course, but I think I have a little better sense of what parents must feel like when they've been abruptly separated from their kids."

The loss of a friend. Remember the accounting firm in Chicago where Pat Colter and Cal Humphries wanted to get rid of their partner, Chuck Scaglia? Pat and Chuck (like lots of business partners we've run into over the years) had known each other for almost 20 years. They'd even roomed together in college. For Cal, who'd only known Chuck about three years, the decision to get Chuck out of the partnership seemed like a wise business move. For Pat, the decision was much more personal and emotional. Pat knew the chances were very slim that he and Chuck could maintain any semblance of a friendship once Chuck was out of the firm. Pat agreed with Cal that this was clearly the smart thing to do from a business standpoint. But the thought of losing Chuck as a friend ate away at him in a way that Cal would never understand. Cal just hadn't been there all those years when Pat and Chuck were buddies.

Your Fear of How the Other Person Might React

Whenever there's a breakup of a relationship between two people, it's rarely a mutual decision. Almost always one person is the "rejector" and the other person is the "rejectee." If you decide to fire someone or get rid of a partner or leave a job, you are definitely the rejector, not the rejectee.

Well, we've noticed a few things about rejectees, whether they're wives being left by husbands, boyfriends being dumped by girlfriends, employees being fired, or partners being forced out of a firm. They feel hurt and anger toward their rejectors, and they can find unpleasant ways to take their feelings out on them.

So if you're thinking about "rejecting" someone, it's natural for you to be at least a little fearful of how that person might react. For example:

— Marty Coleman knew that Jessie Ranter was an emotional person. He knew she was going to be upset about being fired. Would she do something irrational to get back at him? Like filing a wrongful discharge suit? Or making a stink with some of the venture capitalists and other investors who had hired him? Probably not. But you never know.

— Carla Frampson was more than a little concerned about how Gabe would react if he found out she was looking for another job in the government because she had such little regard for him. She knew Gabe was quite capable of being vindictive. She also knew he had a lot of friends in "high places" who could disrupt her career if they wanted to.

— Pat Colter and Cal Humphries were definitely worried about how Chuck Scaglia would react to being ousted from the partnership. Chuck was a "street fighter." And they'd seen Chuck when he was bent on revenge toward someone. They didn't look forward to being the target of that vengeance.

What's Important to Keep in Mind about These Decisions?

We'd like to leave you with a couple of thoughts about these tough decisions—decisions that you may be making right now or may be making pretty soon:

• Nothing is worth being miserable for.

• Try to treat the other person the way you'd want to be treated.

Nothing is Worth Being Miserable For

Over the years we've seen an awful lot of people make themselves unhappy because they wouldn't make one of these three decisions, even though they knew it was the right thing to do. They wouldn't fire someone who needed to be fired. They wouldn't get rid of a partner or a family member in their businesses who shouldn't have been there in the first place. They wouldn't exit from a partnership, even though they were completely miserable. Or they wouldn't leave a job where a boss (or some other person in the one-up position) was stifling any real satisfaction they might have gotten from their work.

If you're one of these folks, if you're making yourself unhappy because you can't bring yourself to fire someone or get rid of a partner or leave a job, we want to try to convince you of one thing. It ain't worth it. We feel very strongly about this. Every working day of the year millions and millions of people in this country get up in the morning and dread going to work. That's not good. If you can't make one of these decisions, you're cheating yourself out of the satisfaction and enjoyment we think everyone is entitled to. And you're also cheating the important people in your life— your close family members, your good friends, and the people you work with—out of someone who could be a lot more enjoyable to be around if he or she weren't so distracted by the failure to make one of these decisions.

Treat the Other Person the Way You Would Want to Be Treated

If you end up making one of the three decisions we've been talking about in this chapter, you're going to be dealing with at least one of three people: an employee, a partner, or a boss (or some other powerful person in your organization). All the concepts and skills and techniques we've talked about so far in the book (especially the chapters on "talking" and "listening") should stand you in good stead. But we think the most important thing to remember in dealing with these folks is this: Follow the Golden Rule. Treat them the way you'd like to be treated if you were in their shoes and they were in yours. A few specifics:

An employee you're thinking about firing. If you haven't already done it, give the employee a fair chance to improve. This means having the kind of meetings we've talked about throughout this book—meetings where you make it clear what you expect of the employee and where you listen carefully to what the employee needs from you. If these sessions don't lead to improved performance and you have to let the person go, do it with compassion and sensitivity. Let the person resign and explain the resignation publicly the way he or she wants. Give the person as generous a severance package as you can. If you can offer the person "outplacement" counseling, do it. If you can provide an office and a telephone and a copying machine the person can use while he or she looks for another job, do it. In short, do what you'd want your boss to do for you if you got canned.

A partner who's not working out. Again, meet regularly with your partner to talk about the problem—whatever it is—and what the two of you can do to solve it. Recognize that you are part of the problem. Be willing to make some changes. If at all possible, bring in some some competent outsiders to help you work things out. Use attorneys if you have to, but don't let them drag you into a senseless legal battle that only lines their pockets and turns you and your partners into enemies.

A boss or partner who causes you to decide to leave. Even though you may feel a tremendous amount of resentment toward a boss or some other powerful person who's made you decide to leave your job, try to put yourself in that person's shoes. Paint a positive picture of why you're leaving. You don't have to be bluntly frank and honest. And above all, don't tell anyone you don't trust completely why you're really leaving. That will only lead to rumors and gossip that won't do anybody any good.

Well, you've been a patient and attentive reader. We appreciate that. We've thoroughly enjoyed talking to you, and we hope what we've said has been interesting and thought-provoking. But, most importantly, we hope it can help you and the people you work with get a little more fun and enjoyment out of your work.

We'd enjoy hearing from you, even if you want to argue or disagree with us. Just contact the publisher. They'll put you in touch with us. We wish you the very best.